The Politics of Language in Puerto Rico

UNIVERSITY PRESS OF FLORIDA

Florida A&M University, Tallahassee
Florida Atlantic University, Boca Raton
Florida Gulf Coast University, Ft. Myers
Florida International University, Miami
Florida State University, Tallahassee
New College of Florida, Sarasota
University of Central Florida, Orlando
University of Florida, Gainesville
University of North Florida, Jacksonville
University of South Florida, Tampa
University of West Florida, Pensacola

The Politics of Language in Puerto Rico

Amílcar Antonio Barreto

University Press of Florida

Gainesville · Tallahassee · Tampa · Boca Raton

Pensacola · Orlando · Miami · Jacksonville · Ft. Myers · Sarasota

First cloth printing, 2001
First paperback printing, 2018

23 22 21 20 19 18   6 5 4 3 2 1

Library of Congress Cataloging-in-Publication Data
Barreto, Amílcar Antonio.
The politics of language in Puerto Rico / Amílcar Antonio Barreto.
p. cm.
Includes bibliographical references and index.
ISBN 978-0-8130-2077-8 (cloth : alk. paper)
ISBN 978-0-8130-6407-9 (pbk.)
1. Language policy—Puerto Rico. 2. Bilingualism—Puerto Rico.
3. Language and culture—Puerto Rico. I. Title.
P119.32.P84 B37 2001
306.44'9795—dc21 00-053660

The University Press of Florida is the scholarly publishing agency
for the State University System of Florida, comprising Florida A&M
University, Florida Atlantic University, Florida Gulf Coast University,
Florida International University, Florida State University, New College of
Florida, University of Central Florida, University of Florida, University
of North Florida, University of South Florida, and University of West
Florida.

University Press of Florida
15 Northwest 15th Street
Gainesville, FL 32611-2079
http://upress.ufl.edu

To my aunt,

Olga Iris Barreto Castro

Contents

Tables

Figures

Acknowledgments

The term *guagua aérea*, or "air bus," refers to that familiar conduit linking Puerto Ricans on the island to those on the U.S. mainland. That constant back-and-forth is symptomatic of a people who in the twentieth and early twenty-first centuries epitomize a kind of nomadic lifestyle stereotypically associated with the Romany. In the late 1980s, I joined that caravan and returned to the United States to pursue my graduate and legal studies. It was while living in Buffalo, New York, that I heard that a political Vesuvius in Puerto Rico had arisen from its slumber. Culture and politics had long been one of my passions. However, schoolwork, my dissertation, and later on my teaching responsibilities prevented me from returning to this story for almost a decade.

After almost nine decades of official bilingualism, Puerto Rico's government adopted Spanish as the island's only official language. This legislation alarmed some in the U.S. Congress and triggered a series of countermeasures by a subsequent Puerto Rican administration. Traditional premises in the discipline suggested that these were integral parts of an electoral strategy. However, the facts in this case did not seem to fit this standard supposition. It could be that Puerto Rico was simply too unique to fit inside the parameters of standard social science. In terms of politics, Puerto Rico's atypical status as a colony in the twenty-first century feeds such assumptions. Perhaps this is why some scholars fall into the predictable pattern of resorting to Puerto Rican exceptionalism to explain away a broad array of sociopolitical phenomena.

Intuitively I felt that I was seeing part of a larger pattern also witnessed in other societies. If this were the case, Puerto Rico's language anomalies could be explained in terms of recognized theoretical approaches. Conducting the research for this project helped me to understand the extent to which politics is gripped with more than just winning elections. In societies where culture and policy questions are inseparable, political actors constantly wage war on multiple fronts. Nationalism and ethnic politics speak to cultural policy making not as a mere afterthought but as a strategy in a larger (yet veiled) contest.

In the course of this project I was reintroduced to a theoretical approach that was first presented to me in graduate school. To be honest, as a graduate student I loathed game theory. I considered it a callous line of reasoning that inadequately addressed matters of cultural identity that are critical to the study of nationalism. To the shock of friends and colleagues the infidel became a messenger, of sorts. Two great friends, Vesna Danilovic and D. Munroe Eagles, had the courage and the patience to open my mind to new theoretical possibilities. At the same time three special people in my life helped me to see Puerto Rico in a whole new light. My special thanks go to my dear friends Félix Matos-Rodríguez and Ana Yolanda Ramos-Zayas, and to my uncle Rubén Márquez Quiles.

Beyond ideas there are also the practical problems associated with research. I am grateful for a research grant from the Office of the Provost at Northeastern University. In particular I want to thank Vice Provost Coleen Pantalone for her continued support. Several friends and family members provided me with practical assistance in numerous ways. My research in Puerto Rico could not have come to fruition without the love and assistance of Ana Delia Castro, Luis Tulier Miranda, and María de los Angeles Soto Balbás. The New York City leg of this venture would not have been possible without the kindness and support of Joan and Robert Brand.

Researching this book took me from Boston, to New York City, to Puerto Rico. I am grateful for the assistance provided by the staff and librarians at Northeastern University, Boston University, the New York City Public Library, Puerto Rico's Senate Archives, and José Sánchez at the archives of *El Nuevo Día*. I am deeply indebted to two stupendous librarians at the Universidad del Sagrado Corazón in San Juan, Yoshira Castro Tomassini and María de los Angeles Morales de Garín.

In the course of exploring Puerto Rico's language dilemma, I was fortunate enough to speak with several former and current officeholders and hear their views on the nexus between language and Puerto Rican politics. I appreciate the fact that these individuals generously took time out of their busy schedules in order to accommodate my research needs. First of all, I want to thank Governor Michael Dukakis of Massachusetts—*gracias, Don Miguel*. I am grateful to Governor Rafael Hernández Colón for granting me an interview in his Ponce office despite his very hectic schedule. Two Puerto Rico Senate presidents were generous enough to grant me interviews: Miguel Hernández Agosto and Roberto Rexach Benítez. I also thank former house speaker José "Rony" Jarabo Alvarez, who was exceedingly generous with his time. Several current and former legislators kindly granted me interviews: Angel Cintrón

García, Víctor García San Inocencio, Fernando Martín, David Noriega Rodríguez, Sergio Peña Clos, Alba "Albita" Rivera Ramírez, and Enrique Rodríguez Negrón. I want to call attention to one lawmaker who, much to my surprise, quizzed me before I interviewed him. I am indebted to Professor Héctor López Galarza, for his one-of-a-kind outlook on Puerto Rican language policy.

Outside Puerto Rico's legislative assembly, I sought the viewpoints of local political actors and Education Department administrators. Two local political leaders, Rafael "Rafo" Alicea Vázquez and Félix Méndez Soto, were kind enough to share with me their perspectives. I thank former education secretaries Celeste Benítez and Carlos Chardón for sharing their viewpoints on the role of language in Puerto Rican society and policy making. Notwithstanding an extremely busy schedule on the heels of the new school year, Juan Rodríguez González at the Education Department generously granted me the opportunity to speak with him about the government's new language initiatives.

Lining up these interviews was a rather daunting task, given my limited time on the island. Onerous burdens were lifted from my shoulders thanks to the help of: Enrique "Kiko" Alverio, Nilsa Beltrán, Marsha and Walter Bustelo, Maritza Ramos Calvo, Carmen Díaz, Ramón Carlos Díaz, Luis Hidalgo, María Teresa Quintana, Aida and Ferdinand Quiñones, and Johanny and Héctor Torres.

Once the research was completed I turned to the manuscript. I am grateful for the support I received from the staff at the Political Science Department at Northeastern University, especially Barbara Chin, Janet-Louise Joseph, and my research assistant, Kar-Yen Leong. Throughout this process I was the beneficiary of a great deal of moral support. I am grateful to the faculty of the Political Science Department, especially Christopher Bosso, Robert Gilbert, William Kay, David Schmitt, and Bruce Wallin. My task was also made easier with the *good vibes* from our Latino Student Cultural Center and the program in Latino, Latin American, and Caribbean studies. I thank Linda Delgado, Ada Medina, Terry Mena, Sara Rivera, and Gloria Wojtaszek. Outside my university I thank one of my greatest supporters, Michael Foss. My acknowledgments would not be complete without thanking Arlene Dávila for her highly constructive comments on earlier drafts of this manuscript.

Finally, I want to highlight the invaluable assistance and support I received from my aunt, Olga Iris Barreto Castro. Throughout this research project she became a secretary, liaison officer, travel agent, translator, research assistant, and in the tradition of Hyacinth Bucket ("Bouquet") an unrivaled social activities coordinator. Without her assistance, truly beyond the call of familial duty, this project would not have been possible. She is a woman who is always *a la vanguardia* and it is to her that I dedicate this book.

List of Abbreviations

AEPPR   Asociación de Escuelas Privadas de Puerto Rico (Puerto Rico Association of Private Schools)

AMPR   Asociación de Maestros de Puerto Rico (Puerto Rico Teachers Association)

ICP   Instituto de Cultura Puertorriqueña (Puerto Rican Institute of Culture)

PAC   Partido Acción Cristiana (Christian Action Party)

PER   Partido Estadista Republicano (Republican Statehood Party)

PIP   Partido Independentista Puertorriqueño (Puerto Rican Independence Party)

PNP   Partido Nuevo Progresista (New Progressive Party)

PPD   Partido Popular Democrático (Popular Democratic Party)

PSP   Partido Socialista Puertorriqueño (Puerto Rican Socialist Party)

Preface

Buried in the cliché *the more things change, the more they stay the same* is a tacit acknowledgment, or perhaps only a grudging resignation, that dramatic and profound ruptures in some fields of life have remarkably little impact on others. Regardless of our best efforts to yoke together disparate phenomena they remain staunchly independent of one another and proceed along distinct paths. In the spirit of discussing change versus continuity, or change alongside continuity, I would like to reflect on some of the most dramatic transformations that have transpired since *The Politics of Language in Puerto Rico* was published in 2001.

For over a century, the U.S. territory of Puerto Rico has remained economically orphaned in the liminal spaces between the industrial and post-industrial North and the developing South. This imperial ward has at times been showered with attention; at others it has been a casualty of malign neglect. Federal indifference during the first few decades of U.S. rule maintained the island's inhabitants in bitter poverty. Such conditions seemed indefensible under a sovereign promising liberty and equality under a common citizenship. Suffering fueled resentment and cast doubt on the veracity of the country's civic creed. While Puerto Rico's economic plight did not produce nationalist sentiments, protracted misery has a way of shoveling fuel onto its already simmering coals. And so the 1930s witnessed the rapid ascent of both moderate and militant nationalist movements whose demands ranged from greater autonomy to all-out independence from the United States. While differing significantly in their tactics and their outlook on federal-territorial relations, the two movements joined forces in their opposition to Americanization—a federal policy implemented in the first half of the twentieth century designed to induce language shift from Spanish to English.

From the late-1930s until the end of the Cold War, the federal government did promote Puerto Rico's economic development, but it did so as a way of maintaining a semblance of peace and order. In time, I suspect, historians will refer to this period as Puerto Rico's economic golden age. For federal policy makers, industrialization was a sure way to pull Puerto Rico deeper into the U.S. mainland economy and, in so doing, deflate support for independence. The political persecution of independence supporters aided Washington considerably in that mission. And the

Cold War years added another interesting dimension to U.S. economic initiatives in Puerto Rico: brandishing the capitalist Commonwealth as a *showcase for democracy* vis-à-vis any socialist alternatives. During that era, which includes the New Dealers, Washington saw improving Puerto Rico's economy as something in its own self-interest.

These motivations to bolster the island's economy withered as the Berlin Wall crumbled, however. In 1996, Congress eliminated the federal tax incentives sustaining the industrial pillars of the island's manufacturing sector. Phased out over ten years, the last of these incentives expired in 2006, inaugurating the downward slide in the Puerto Rican economy. In better times the Commonwealth government and its agencies borrowed billions of dollars from banks and investors to build and maintain infrastructure and sustain a large payroll. As manufacturing plants pulled out of Puerto Rico, the island's tax base deteriorated and, in 2016, the territorial government defaulted on its debts. Washington responded to this crisis by creating a new entity over and above Puerto Rico's elected government: the appointed Financial Oversight and Management Board. In the spirit of the French philosopher Michel Foucault, the Board was created to economically *discipline and punish* Puerto Rico's government and its inhabitants. In the years following its establishment, this body would force the Commonwealth government to lacerate administrative budgets, close schools, and begin laying off hundreds, later thousands, of public sector employees. If ever anyone needed a clearer sign that the Commonwealth's claims of grand autonomy were a sham—that it remains, in the words of former Puerto Rico Supreme Court Chief Justice José Trías Monge, the *Oldest Colony in the World*—look no further than the Board's creation.

Under these dire circumstances, shall we stay or shall we leave? These are the questions Puerto Rican families have been asking themselves on a daily basis. Unfortunately, Mother Nature took no pity on those who were already down. In September 2017, Puerto Rico suffered two devastating back-to-back hurricanes: Irma and Maria. Washington's lethargic post-hurricane response to Puerto Rico and the U.S. Virgin Islands contrasted starkly with the quick response to the devastation wrought on Houston-area residents following Hurricane Harvey one month prior. Irma and Maria eviscerated Puerto Rico's electrical power grid, leaving millions in the dark for months. Many businesses decided they had had enough and relocated to the fifty states. These storms and their aftermath forced additional islanders to consider whether they would join the mainland-bound exodus. Over the past decade, hundreds of thou-

sands of islanders have booked passage on the *guagua aérea*, the prover-
bial "air bus," to reunite with their families on the U.S. mainland. About
half have relocated to one state: Florida. In the twentieth century, Latin
Florida was Cuban. Its twenty-first century counterpart is much more
heterogeneous, and Puerto Ricans may outnumber Cubans in Florida in
the not too distant future. This demographic influx has become a major
concern in Tallahassee, but, notably, Washington has given Puerto Rico's
economic plight along with its migratory consequences the cold shoulder.

White House and congressional responses to this crisis are indicative
of economics' and demography's diminished importance to federal-territorial relations. What has remained the same is the federal government's concern with culture and obedience. The matter of subservience
abruptly erupted on the political stage in the course of the Vieques
peace campaign two decades ago. In their vigorous and continuous protests over the U.S. Navy's bombing range on the island-municipality of
Vieques, Puerto Ricans in the thousands borrowed a page from the civil
rights movements of the 1960s and took to the streets demanding that
the bombing range be closed. While Puerto Ricans viewed their actions
as affirming their rights as citizens, the same deeds were reinterpreted in
many quarters as ingratitude and disloyalty.

Regarding how the status question is discussed in Congress, we have
come to the point where we expect the debates to follow a well-worn, almost ritualistic, trajectory. As the deliberations begin, members of Congress express their profound gratitude for the millions of Puerto Ricans
who have served in the U.S. armed forces. This glowing praise in phase
one is followed by an expression of concern during phase two. Federal
lawmakers, particularly those in the GOP, sidestep discussions of two
status options—independence or Commonwealth—and narrowly focus
on statehood. These naysayers begin resurrecting old concerns—after
more than a century of U.S. rule, not enough Puerto Rican islanders
speak English. The status question, to the chagrin of statehood supporters, is repeated, tethered directly to cultural identity and language use.
The diplomatic concerns expressed during phase two are followed by
phase three. Here, the most openly nativist members of Congress uncer-
emoniously assert that cultural and linguistic incompatibility rules out
statehood—Puerto Ricans represent a different *people* whose identity is
discordant with full membership in the Union. Effectively, the Spanish
language is racialized as *other*, as are its Puerto Rican speakers.

The academic study of the Puerto Rico language controversy has, logically, focused on what transpires on the island. However, if we tear away the intellectual blinders we see a broader panorama with larger implications. This issue has clearly resonated in the halls of Congress and in the White House for over a century. Rarely discussed in an open forum the Puerto Rico language issue speaks volumes about *American* identity and its connection to the English language. A weak nexus would fortify the official civic creed—a national identity devoid of racial, confessional, and cultural characteristics—while a strong link would bolster the alternative—one that situates white, Christian, English-speakers as *bona fide* Americans vis-à-vis others, regardless of formal citizenship status. The interconnected issues of culture, language, and political status will remain an integral part of the federal-territorial equation as the United States experiences angsts associated with the *browning* of its population.

At this juncture it is difficult to say where Puerto Rican islanders will be, and under what conditions. What has not changed is the dual tactics—the *Nested Games*—employed by politicians in San Juan and Washington to manage federal-territorial relations. While Puerto Rican *politicos* keep one eye on the next elections they focus the other on Washington. The latter endeavors to anticipate whether Congress is willing to debate the status question and its willingness to entertain changes in the status quo. Federal lawmakers are also playing their own two-sided game. Congress and the White House lavish praise on the country's sacrosanct civic creed and its promise of equality under a common citizenship. But when they debate the Puerto Rico status quandary and are forced to lay out the conditions for statehood, numerous stateside political operates stomp on the civic creed and display an adherence to a multitiered American national identity—one dispensing privileges based on race, language, religion, and other cultural characteristics. Additionally, federal lawmakers expect Puerto Rican islanders to display their obedience regardless of whether their U.S. citizenship is truly equal or second-class in nature. Culture and obedience remain at the core of U.S.-Puerto Rico relations.

Amílcar Antonio Barreto
Boston, Massachusetts
May 2018

Culture, Identity, and Policy

The eleventh chapter of Genesis narrates the mythical nascence of languages. According to the saga, the Creator imposed linguistic diversity in order to deliberately partition humanity into unintelligible collectivities as a form of punishment. A common medium of communication facilitated collaboration; linguistic incongruity obstructed it. Beyond interaction, languages also denoted group affiliation. In the thirteenth chapter of Nehemiah we are informed that non-Hebrew speakers were regarded as foreigners and marriage with them was a sin. To employ another idiom as a mother tongue was a sign of exclusion determining the degree of acceptable social interaction. These biblical narratives illustrate that for long ages communicative media delineated social barriers. Next to observable phenotypic characteristics, linguistic peculiarities are among the most frequently employed traits used to single out "them" from "us."

Cultural traits not only differentiate but also reinforce socioeconomic hierarchies. In a given community, commercial transactions take place in a common form of speech. However, in a multilingual society the question remains, which one? Scholars agree that the language affiliated with the wealthier social group usually has the upper hand. Yes, languages are communicative instruments, but they also serve as group labels drenched with social baggage. The words spoken by the dominant group acquire greater prestige than those uttered by the subordinate status groups. This badge of inferiority may apply to dialects as well as languages. Grammar is not at issue; it is a matter of social prestige and economic prowess.

This association between language and socioeconomic status is further reinforced when society's dominant group controls the state and bureaucratic apparatus. Over the past couple of centuries, the public sector has expanded remarkably. Services previously provided by other institutions—whether charitable organizations or houses of worship—are currently administered by the state. Public education, health programs, and social welfare are among many examples. Using a common medium of communication facilitates the administration of large bureaucracies. Naturally, economic and social mobility will depend on fluency in the state's language. At the same time, those who do not speak the consecrated language are marginalized and shoulder the burden of learning another language. When one understands that most states are culturally and linguistically heterogeneous, it becomes abundantly clear that tensions over language, socioeconomic status, and public policy are exceedingly common.

When contemplating cases of linguistic conflict, societies in the developing world frequently come to mind. Out of the hundreds of languages spoken within their borders, rulers of postindependence Nigeria and Papua New Guinea were forced to determine how many would be accorded an official status. India's independence marked a new era, whereby this former British colony was administratively redivided roughly along linguistic boundaries. Yet in the course of the past few decades the emergence or resurgence of public debate over language status has redirected the spotlight onto various industrialized western democracies such as Belgium, Canada, and Spain. Undeniably, the renewed interest in proclaiming English the official language of the United States shows that not even this presumably unilingual country is free from linguistic anxieties.

The United States has always been a multilingual society. However, rather than being embraced, linguistic diversity was all too often seen as a problem needing a solution. Proficiency in English became a litmus test for determining one's loyalty to the United States. Immigrants, whether they were German speakers in the eighteenth century or Spanish-speaking Latin Americans in the twentieth century, were slated for linguistic assimilation. Government policy and social attitudes are reflected in the country's motto, *E Pluribus Unum*—out of many comes one.

Throughout the eighteenth and nineteenth centuries, English took root wherever the Stars and Stripes flew. This linguistic juggernaut hit a snag as the country expanded beyond the North American continent. During the Spanish-American War of 1898 the United States invaded several Spanish colonies in the Pacific and Caribbean. These colonies were densely populated and far from the mainland, and linguistic assimilation proved a challenge. Not long after the war Cuba was granted its independence, and the Philippines was freed in the 1940s. Over a century later the United States still controls both Guam and Puerto Rico. At present Puerto Rico represents the most populous U.S. territory and one of the few American jurisdictions where English is not the vernacular.

To this day, the continued existence of Spanish as the mother tongue of most Puerto Ricans remains a fundamental issue in the island's relationship with the United States. Cultural identity and language policy in Puerto Rico are inextricably tied to the debate over the island's fate. Rarely does it come up when discussing the prospects for independence. It occasionally surfaces when assessing Puerto Rico's current status as a semiautonomous American commonwealth. These issues are most volatile, however, when the question of statehood comes to the foreground. Statehood is the one status option that asks how Puerto Ricans view themselves and also how American society assesses the compatibility of a culturally distinct state in its otherwise Anglophone union.

On the one hand, these Caribbean islanders are proud of their cultural distinctiveness vis-à-vis Americans. Ironically, this pride was fueled by a half-century mêlée against the federal government's policy of cultural assimilation. Instead of this policy reshaping the island's cultural milieu to reflect Anglo–North American norms and traits, a struggle ensued. It successfully elevated the Spanish language to the zenith of Puerto Rican cultural icons. Notwithstanding more than a century of U.S. rule, only a small portion of the population is fluent in the American vernacular.

On the other hand, Puerto Ricans associate the English language with socioeconomic mobility. It is the dominant medium of communication in international commercial transactions. Most trade between Puerto Rico and the United States is conducted in English. American multinational corporations dominating large segments of the insular economy employ English, especially in a company's upper echelons. Additionally, English is the unofficial language of the federal government—the regime subsidizing a significant portion of the local administration. Thus, Spanish speaks to Puerto Rico's heart, while English speaks to its wallet. Puerto Ricans live in purgatory, trapped between Anglo North America and Latin America. And this no-man's-land is epitomized by the perennial debate over the island's political status.

Language policy, an issue usually discussed among pundits and intellectuals, suddenly took center stage in the 1990s. The focus was the symbolic status of English. Unlike the U.S. mainland, the dispute here was not over the merits of "English Only" but rather official bilingualism versus the codification of Spanish as the sole official language. For decades, few dared to question the status of English as one of Puerto Rico's official languages. Something changed in the early 1990s, and traditionally timid lawmakers suddenly took up the banner of the Spanish language and fought to institute official unilingualism. In the final analysis, the debate over unilingualism versus official bilingualism may have as much to say about linguistic attitudes and cultural identity in the United States as it does about Puerto Rico. To those interested in the study of language, culture, and ethnicity, Puerto Rico provides a fascinating case study.

Beyond historic peculiarities, this book explores a fundamental question in the social science literature. Puerto Rico presents a serious problem for the universal applicability of one of the most respected and frequently employed theoretical approaches in the study of legislative action. Standard political science premises boldly assert that politicians are rational actors who focus on one thing—winning elections. According to some of the classic works in the field, these politicians do not care about issues but about augmenting their electoral base. In order to wield power, one must win public office, and this means pleasing the electorate. Scholars employing this approach say that rational actors will logically modify their public stance on the major issues in order to appeal to the median voter.

If this hypothesis is true, Puerto Rico represents an anomaly. Through interviews with key political figures and archival research, it becomes abundantly clear that the 1991 law establishing Spanish as the lone official language was enacted despite the fact that its proponents were conscious of its electoral pitfalls.[1] Well-publicized surveys clearly showed that, while relatively few islanders could speak English, most wanted to retain it as an official language. The pro-commonwealth government that promoted the unilingual law in 1991 was swept out of office the following year, and a new pro-statehood administration lived up to its promise to restore official bilingualism.

Subsequently, this pro-statehood administration drafted a proposal to fortify the teaching of English in the public school system. True, most Puerto Ricans wanted to maintain English as an official language, but they were also proud of their own language. The government was proposing to employ English as a medium of instruction. Additionally, the local Education Department was planning to contract teachers from the mainland in its drive to augment the number of Puerto Rican bilinguals. The last time that these policies converged was when the federal government actively pursued its program of cultural assimilation. At that time, teachers rallied against the directive and responded by promoting a cultural nationalism that resonates to this day.

Both in the early 1990s and the later part of the decade, rival Puerto Rican administrations promoted particular language policies that could risk their standing with the electorate. Are Puerto Rican politicians fundamentally irrational? Are these examples of suicidal tendencies in Caribbean politics? Perhaps standard political motivation theory is inapplicable to this island because of its uniqueness. Furthermore, we might even consider heeding the advice of some who suggest that the search for universal explanations of social phenomena should be abandoned in favor of local or particular explanations.

Instead of throwing out the baby with the bathwater, this book uses this case to test a novel approach to the study of political behavior. Conceivably, Puerto Rico's unique setting involving the intersection of language, politics, and cultural identity can shed light on sociopolitical phenomena beyond the confines of the Caribbean. It is possible that we see in Puerto Rico a pattern frequently found in societies engaged in ethnic mobilization and the politics of nationalism. What superficially appears to be a case of electoral politics is in fact facets of a much larger and more complex calculus that downplays the role of holding office in favor of a more significant prize. Students of ethnic conflict are often quick to point out that the politics of nationalism go beyond holding office. In this context, symbols and gestures can take on a life of their own. Like a *matryoshka* doll, the figure we see masks another one underneath. Politicians here may be engaged in what some call a "Nested Game." Thus, the Puerto Rican language controversy may represent a manifestation of a common rule rather than an irrational exception.

Before embarking on a study of universal phenomena, we begin with the particulars of Puerto Rico and examine under what conditions the links between language and identity were forged.

2

Spanish and Puertorriqueñidad

Although a distinctive Puerto Rican identity predated the arrival of American troops in 1898, its evolution throughout the twentieth century was profoundly influenced by the federal government's policy of cultural assimilation. For generations, a policy of *Americanization* was applied to European immigrants to the United States, who learned the English language and American customs mainly by means of public education. Proponents assumed the superiority of all things American. Toward this end, the federal government created a large and publicly financed school system. Teachers were designated as the street-level bureaucrats primarily responsible for implementing these directives. This process of Americanization was carried out in Puerto Rico as well. Ironically, pedagogues, rather than obeying the policy blindly, resisted Americanization and helped to forge a new ethnic identity that elevated the cultural significance of the Spanish language. These cultural elites spearheaded the drive to eliminate some policies but not others. One such policy, untouched for nearly ninety years, was the establishment of official bilingualism in 1902. This chapter describes these processes and places Puerto Rican nationalism in the context of other cases of elite-driven social movements.

Puertorriqueñidad and Americanization

While the word is difficult to render into another language, Morris (1995: 3) translated *puertorriqueñidad* as "Puerto Ricanness." This word embraces those sociocultural attributes that are typical of Puerto Rico and its inhabitants. One could even argue that it should also include the thought processes of Puerto Ricans—how they see themselves, their surroundings, and their world. This secondary attribute of *puertorriqueñidad* falls in line with a Pedreirist (1978: 44) analysis of Puerto Rican identity as one founded on an "insular" outlook. As with other examples of ethnic autoclassification, designees use *puertorriqueñidad* as a badge of pride and a symbol of honor. It differentiates the familiar from the foreign. The Atlantic Ocean and Caribbean Sea carved out the island's physical parameters; a different process forged Puerto Rico's ethnocultural parameters. The creation of a new identity was the result of a long process whereby islanders responded to five centuries of the social attitudes and repressive policies of two historic metropolitan sovereignties—the Kingdom of Spain and the United States of America.

Scholars have debated the precise birth of Puerto Rican ethnogenesis. Some argue that it came as early as the late eighteenth century; others suggest that it did not develop until the following century (Barreto 1998: 77–78). Regardless, there is no question that a distinctive Puerto Rican identity emerged while this island was under Spanish rule—a period when the regime favored Spanish subjects born in Europe over their Caribbean-born counterparts (Maldonado-Denis 1972: 22).[1] Politically this manifested itself in the form of autonomist and separatist movements. This development paralleled an analogous process in Spain's other colonies in the Americas.

Most of the island's Creole elites endorsed an autonomist political agenda. Autonomy's apogee was reached at the end of the nineteenth century under the short-lived Autonomy Charter of 1897 (Trías Monge 1980: 131–32). Creole elites embarked on a process of ethnogenesis whereby their cultural traits became the anointed elements of *puertorriqueñidad* (Ferrao 1993; Guerra 1998; Janer 1998; Scarano 1996). Their hopes of exercising local autonomy were dashed as a result of the Spanish-American War of 1898. With a new American sovereign, Creole elites initiated a new process of ethnic boundary articulation, one that defined the parameters of cultural and political discourse in the twentieth century.

Under the terms of the 1898 Treaty of Paris, the Spanish Crown yielded its authority in Puerto Rico to the United States. A few local interests, such as private property rights, were safeguarded (Ramírez 1988: 42). However, this accord made no mention of any cultural rights nor guaranteed any minimal level of political autonomy (García Martínez 1976: 67–68). Puerto Ricans, along with their fellow Spanish subjects in Guam and the Philippines, were left to Washington's mercy and whims.

In the first couple of years of American rule, two government studies were commissioned. Regarding Puerto Ricans the Carroll Commission reported that: "They will learn our customs and usages, in so far as they are better than their own, as they learn our language" (Carroll 1975: 59). The proposal was based on the presumably innate superiority of American social norms (Barreto 1998: 88–90). Indeed, among the proponents of Anglo-Saxon racial superiority were some of the first Protestant missionaries to arrive in Puerto Rico following the Spanish-American War (Agosto Cintrón 1996: 56–59). Federal policy makers regarded Puerto Rican culture as a problem demanding a solution.

> Throughout this century, the predominant object of Puerto Rican public policy, reinforced by social science research, has been to figure out what is wrong with Puerto Rico and Puerto Ricans and what needs to be done to bring them up to American expectations. U.S. attention remained so focused on what was "wrong" with Puerto Rico that administrators and policy makers rarely acknowledged what actually existed, or how much economic damage had been done by incorporating Puerto Rico into the U.S. political economy after centuries of neglect by the Spanish. Education and language policies became an integral part of that political economy and eventually came to stand for it. (Urciuoli 1998: 42)

Language acquisition was a prime element of Americanization (Urciuoli 1994). Consistent with federal policy toward European immigrants on the U.S. mainland, Puerto Ricans were encouraged to forego their vernacular. Mastery of English was considered evidence of one's loyalty to the new country (Baron 1990; Steinberg 1981). Federal policy makers understood that promoting language shift among adults is an extremely difficult undertaking. On the other hand, children are far more malleable. Compulsory school attendance provided the state with the opportunity to promote cultural defection. Experience showed that Americanization on the U.S. mainland was an effective mechanism for implementing language shift. Officials presumed that the same model could be transferred to the Caribbean. Thus, English was imposed as the medium of instruction in Puerto Rican schools (Carroll 1975: 65).

Rulers, we understand, have a dominant strategy of governing their culturally distinct peripheries in the center's language—a process referred to as "State-Rationalization" (Laitin 1988: 291). Where dominant and subaltern groups speak different vernaculars, bilingual intermediaries will be necessary. Efficient governance of the periphery does not require the subaltern masses to learn the central language (Laitin 1989: 309). A small coterie of bilingual peripheral elites suffices. Yet, elites from the country's core attempt to coerce their peripheral subjects into forsaking their mother tongue. Cases of central-elite promotion of language shift among all peripheral social strata are examples of "Nation-Building" strategies (Laitin 1988). If a critical mass of defectors is reached, the remaining peripheral inhabitants find linguistic defection their only logical course of action (Laitin 1993).[2] Contrary to Laitin's "Nation Building" scenario, language shift in Puerto Rico was never fully implemented. Unlike European immigrants, these Caribbean islanders were racially heterogeneous and thus consigned to a permanent outsider status (Oboler 1995: 43; Steinberg 1981: 42).

While Americanization was officially in force from 1899 until 1949, it was most vigorously promoted in the first three decades of the twentieth century (Osuna 1975: 282). Early on, American policy makers determined that the only way to achieve their goal was to employ American schoolteachers in Puerto Rican schools (Negrón de Montilla 1975: 10). When available, Americans were hired and they were paid higher wages than were Puerto Ricans (55). This created resentment among Puerto Rican educators. However, this island's distance from the U.S. mainland made staffing an all-American school system an impractical proposition.

In response, public schoolteachers lobbied the territorial government to institute reforms. Spearheading their action was the Asociación de Maestros de Puerto Rico (AMPR—Puerto Rican Teachers Association), the largest teachers' union (García Martínez 1976: 100–101; Negrón de Montilla 1975: 160). At first this organization asked authorities to modify the policy and allow a few classes to be taught in Spanish, particularly in elementary schools. Government indifference and occasional hostility to their demands fed the teachers' frustrations. The AMPR broadened its protest to include the entire policy and demanded that the local vernacular become the medium of instruction in all public schools (Negrón de Montilla 1975: 135–37). Joining their struggle was José de Diego, the speaker of the House of Delegates (García Martínez 1976: 86; Ferrao 1993: 49). Insular politicians advocating greater autonomy used the language dispute as an important tool in their rhetorical repertoire against the American colonial system (Algren 1987: 34).

Responses to teachers' demands varied considerably among the appointed education commissioners.[3] Some went as far as threatening the careers of teachers and the diplomas of students who patently opposed Americanization (Negrón de Montilla 1975: chap. 9). Threats and persecution linked the fates of teachers and students. Their status as grassroots intellectuals put pedagogues in a strategic position to instill in children a strong sense of collective solidarity (Barreto 1998: 91).

One of the preeminent studies of elite political attitudes demonstrates the powerful legacy of the first few decades of American rule. Notwithstanding the endeavor to patronize culturo-linguistic displacement, most Puerto Ricans do not identify themselves as Americans (Morris 1995: 7). The strong connection between language and Puerto Ricanness stands, regardless of partisan preferences (71). Perhaps more surprising than finding separatists and autonomists rebuffing any identification with the United States was the revelation that some supporters of Puerto Rican statehood failed to identify themselves as Americans at all (107–8, 125). Of all the elements of *puertorriqueñidad*, the Spanish language holds a preeminent position (82). Contemporary Puerto Rico has a "clear linguistic consciousness" that exalts the Spanish language (Alvar 1982: 37). When asked about the origin of this identity, respondents to Morris's (1995: 144) study pointed to the half-century of government-sponsored assimilation.

These Caribbean islanders incorporated the defense of the Spanish language as an integral part of safeguarding *puertorriqueñidad*—a subject of perennial debate among intellectuals and in pedagogical circles (Morales 1983: 335). The Americanization policy gave the Spanish language a function that it would not have had otherwise (Meyn 1983: 52). Local indignities resulting from a colonial political relationship, combined with the social, political, and economic inferiority of Puerto Ricans vis-à-vis Americans, made conflict inevitable. Puerto Rican nationalism during this period obeyed Steinberg's Iron Law of Ethnicity that states: "when ethnic groups are found in a hierarchy of power, wealth, and status, then conflict is inescapable" (Steinberg 1981: 170).

Clearly, cultural nationalists and those who advocate the island's independence from the United States celebrate the connection between language and *puertorriqueñidad*. On the other hand, those favoring stronger ties with the United States prefer to diminish the political significance of language. Statehood advocates chastise separatists and autonomists for their symbolic struggles to protect certain cultural institutions, such as promoting the island's separate Olympic team or the establishment of official unilingualism in 1991.[4] They point out that today millions of ethnic Puerto Ricans live in the United States and many of them are English dominant. Supporters of stronger ties between Puerto Rico and the United States charge that classical *puertorriqueñidad* peripheralizes these Anglophone Puerto Ricans (Negrón-Portillo 1997: 53). In the same vein, elites on the island of Puerto Rico are reproached for emphasizing "good Spanish." This course of action allegedly attempts to outcast mainland Puerto Ricans (Negrón Muntaner 1997: 271).

Among those who advocate the island's annexation into the American union, there is no inherent contradiction between *puertorriqueñi-dad* and the American culture. They see Puerto Rico's future tied to the

American experience. Two members of the Puerto Rican legislature accentuated this point. One was Alba Rivera, a member of the Puerto Rican House of Representatives for the pro-statehood Partido Nuevo Progresista (PNP—New Progressive Party). "Albita," as she is better known, argued that American rule has not harmed the Spanish language. "We Puerto Ricans speak Spanish at all times, in all places, and in all spaces. And we think in Spanish. And I think that despite having had such a great North American influence we managed to prevail, in terms of language, more than any state in South America" (Rivera Ramírez 1998).[5]

Going beyond Rivera, some of her PNP colleagues would tout that American influences are beneficial and indivisible components of the island's history. A fellow pro-statehood member of the House of Representatives, Angel Cintrón García (1998), stated: "So, for example, to speak of Puerto Rico without talking about the United States, without talking about American citizenship, without talking about all the other elements that have globally affected the United States—and in effect Puerto Rico—is to practically dislocate the true history of Puerto Rico."[6]

Intellectuals as Nation Builders

Local intellectuals led the movement against Americanization. Island intellectuals had a stronger sense of nationalist fervor, particularly in the 1930s, than other strata of society (Ferrao 1993: 39–40). "The tremendous expansion of literacy and the need to couch symbolism in the language of critical discourse, puts a premium on the activity of intellectuals and their professional followers and rivals" (Smith 1986: 160). This group forged a new Puerto Rican identity that highlighted the Spanish language as a culturally defining trait. Intellectuals are the architects and engineers in the nation-building process.

In the words of a noted scholar, nations are "imagined communities" (Anderson, B. 1983). Group members believe they belong to an extended family; they are linked by a myth of common ancestry (Connor 1994: xi; Smith 1989: 344). Nationalist and ethnic identities do not eliminate other important differences such as class; instead, they attempt to assign them a lower priority (Eriksen 1993: 102). Frequently, these identities are responses to modernization rather than the result of primordial sentiments (Eriksen 1993: 9).

A critical component of nation building is "objectification" (Handler 1988: 13–15). Influenced by the respect accorded the natural sciences, ethnic leaders seek to "prove" their group's distinctiveness. One of the most convincing ways to do this is to point to readily observable cultural elements. While ethnic groups have a potentially limitless supply of traits to choose from, they customarily define themselves on the basis of a finite number of features (Barth 1969: 38; Roosens 1989: 12). "Like ethnic ideologies, nationalism stresses the cultural similarity of its adherents and, by implication, it draws boundaries vis-à-vis others, who thereby become outsiders" (Eriksen 1993: 6).

Language, a readily discernable characteristic, remains one of the most convenient nation-defining traits (Anderson, B. 1983: 44–49; Urciuoli 1998: 4). Scholars such as Hobsbawm (1983: 14) pointed out that standardized national languages, like national identities, are artificial constructs. The basis of officially sanctioned national languages are dialects spoken by the society's elite stratum. Elites select their particular speech pattern as the one to be used in authoritative publications and official elite mass communication (Smith 1986: 137–38). State bureaucracies add to the greater prestige of the elite-sanctioned idiom, which facilitates its propagation (Weber 1976: chap. 18).

From intellectual to illiterate, elite to subaltern, virtually everyone is capable of discerning the difference between languages A and B. Even if outsiders learn the local language, their accents reveal their foreign origin and hence their outsider status. Of course, not only do accents divide insider from outsider, but they also distinguish in-group members on the basis of class or regional identification (Barreto 1998: 32–35). Mastery of Spanish is a marker of cultural authenticity among insular and mainland Puerto Ricans (Ramos-Zayas 1997: 24). Similarly, learning English is a necessary, but insufficient, condition for acceptance as an American. Full recognition requires a command of "good English"—a dialect modeled on a written and elite variant of the American vernacular (Urciuoli 1998: 127).

Nonetheless, a nationalist consciousness can survive without language (Edwards 1985: 37). Irish nationalism, with the loss of Gaelic as the lingua franca, is a case in point. Likewise, the decline of Scottish Gaelic did not impede the growth of a Scottish nationalist movement in the twentieth century (Urwin 1982: 28). One could also use as an example nationalistic sentiments among English-dominant Puerto Ricans living in the U.S. mainland. Linguistic assimilation has not meant the detriment of ethnic consciousness in either of these cases.

If only a few cultural traits are used to define ethnic parameters, which ones would be utilized in the construction of *puertorriqueñidad* and who would employ them? As Weinstein (1983: 12) noted: "It is the cultural elites and political leaders working together who choose which linguistic, cultural, racial, or class characteristic to emphasize or to discount, depending on their interests." Hobsbawm said:

> The classes which stood or fell by the official use of the written vernacular were the socially modest but educated middle strata, which included those who acquired lower middle-class status precisely by virtue of occupying non-manual jobs that required schooling. The socialists of the period who rarely used the world "nationalism" without the prefix "petty-bourgeoisie," knew what they were talking about. The battle-lines of linguistic nationalism were manned by provincial journalists, schoolteachers and aspiring subaltern officials. (Hobsbawm 1990: 117)

This statement points to the pivotal role of intellectuals in natio-genesis. Those commanding the means of production may control vast material resources, but alone they are poor conveyers of a national myth. In traditional societies formal education was often the cleric's area of expertise. Aristocrats suppressed the masses while the clerics kept them humble. Clerics preached loyalty to the state and in return regimes assured ecclesiastics a spiritual monopoly within their borders.

With the advent of the industrial age and the expanded role of the state, rulers found it necessary to educate larger segments of their populace. Despite their origins in the lower classes the newly educated became the backbone of the state bureaucracy and the middle classes (Anderson, B. 1983). Regime needs necessitated the creation of a state-run public education system. The respect accorded to pedagogues as instructors extended to their role as ethnic mythmakers. "In the ethnic community . . . the intelligentsia are welcome because only by means of their skills and specialist knowledge can a 'true' education arise, which will bring self-understanding and self-fulfillment for the whole community" (Smith 1981: 127–28). As a system of secular education spread, so did the influence of these grassroots bureaucrats.

> In the villages, local intellectuals were those who labored to reproduce and rearticulate local history and memory, to connect community discourses about local identity to constantly shifting patterns of power, solidarity, and consensus. Political officials, teachers, elders, and healers—these were the ones who "knew," the ones to whom the community would turn in times of crisis, the ones who provided mediation with the outside. They supervised communal hegemonic processes,

organizing and molding the different levels of communal dialogue and conflict into a credible consensus. (Mallon 1995: 12)

A significant portion of the intellectual and professional sectors that spearheaded the populist and nationalist movements in twentieth-century Puerto Rico descended from hacienda-owning highland families who were on the economic decline even before the American conquest. This class later formed the backbone of the autonomist movement and the Partido Popular Democrático under the leadership of Luis Muñoz Marín in the late 1930s (Quintero 1993: 127–28). Naturally, they would emphasize those traits that promoted their class interests.[7]

Beyond topography, the highland-lowland dichotomy also divides the island racially. Spanish and other European peasant farmers largely populated the highlands. In contrast, Puerto Rico's heavily populated coasts represented a "melting pot" of Europeans and Africans. After centuries of miscegenation, few Puerto Ricans are "pure" African or European in ancestry. Nonetheless, among those with "light" skin color there is a frequent denial of African ancestry. When something cannot be identified as European it is often described as *Taíno*—pertaining to Puerto Rico's pre-Columbian indigenous people (Dávila, A. 1997: 71–72). Rejection of non-European ancestry is reflected in the saying: *¿Y tu abuela, dónde está?*—And your grandmother, where is she?

The intellectuals who sprang from the ranks of the frustrated hacienda-owning families adopted the *jíbaro*, the island's white mountain peasant, as the archetypal Puerto Rican (Scarano 1996: 1401). By embracing the *jíbaro*, local intellectuals differentiated the "us" (Puerto Ricans) from the "them" (Spaniards, and later on Americans), setting up Creoles as the bedrock of Puerto Rican nationhood and thus marginalizing nonwhites (Janer 1998: 31–33). As Gellner (1983: 57) noted, "nationalism is, essentially, the general imposition of a high culture on society, where previously low cultures had taken up the lives of the majority, and in some cases the totality, of the population."

The *jíbaro* was romanticized despite the fact that Creole elites were city dwellers.[8] "If the nationalism prospers it eliminates the alien high culture, but it does not then replace it by the old local low culture; it revives, or invents, a local high (literate, specialist-transmitted) culture of its own, though admittedly one which will have some links with the earlier local folk styles and dialects" (Gellner 1983: 57). Logically, under American rule, the local intelligentsia found it in their best interests to highlight their Spanish heritage (Ferrao 1993: 40–46). The "Spanish" element, or the more-Spanish aspects, remain the focus of the Puerto Rican government's Institute of Culture (Dávila, A. 1997: 62). With the arrival of American troops in 1898, Puerto Rican elites redefined "us" to fit a new reality.

> Originally, the distinguishing features of a view of national identity—the jíbaro's white skin, Spanish culture, materially impoverished lifestyle, preference for political autonomy if not neutrality, and patriarchal masculinity—were defined, legitimized, and romanticized by discrete members of the elite for their own class purposes. Eventually, broad acceptance of the jíbaro by all classes came to represent not only a legitimation of a sense of Puerto Rican-ness, which all Puerto Ricans discursively shared, but also a form for contestation of the legitimacy of the North American colonial project and the corresponding colonial identity it assigned to Puerto Ricans. (Guerra 1998: 14–15)

Intellectuals carried the *jíbaro* paradigm into the twentieth century (Guerra 1998: 52). For Pedreira (1978: 26), Puerto Ricans "culturally continue being an Hispanic colony." While his Hispanocentric view of Puerto Rican culture was later chastised by subsequent mythmakers who celebrated the African and indigenous elements of Puerto Rican culture (González, J. 1980; Flores 1993), the Spanish features of Puerto Rican culture, including its language, are considered an indisputable part of *puertorriqueñidad*.[9] Support for a Hispanofile cultural interpretation was not unanimously espoused by all sectors of Puerto Rican society (Ferrao 1993: 49). Nonetheless, the Spanish elements corresponded to the cultural lowest common denominator. The virtually unquestioned acceptance of language as a distinguishing group characteristic was a clear signal that Puerto Rican elites succeeded at entrenching a hegemonic belief in civil society.

Some critics referred to this elite-sponsored *puertorriqueñidad* as a largely conservative movement (Negrón-Portillo 1997: 47). Frequently, statehood supporters accuse Puerto Rican intellectuals of thriving on linguistic conflict (Negrón Muntaner 1997: 270). To a large degree one could objectively describe this as a conservative movement. Scholars concur that traditional Puerto Rican nationalism exalted the Spanish elements of *puertorriqueñidad* above other cultural traits, especially African ones (Dávila, A. 1999; Duany 1999; Jiménez Román 1999). Yet, Puerto Rican nationalism was no more conservative than the Americanist ideology sponsored by the U.S. federal government. To the contrary, one could maintain that the social movement espoused by Puerto Rican elites was far more progressive than flagrantly racist theories of cultural supremacy found in the United States. Puerto Rican elites may be accused of offering the masses an inferior or second-class status whereby the insular elites would continue to enjoy the benefits of a ruling class; but compare this to what Anglo-American society was offering at this time.

Their Spanish language combined with their darker skin color relegated subaltern Puerto Ricans to a third- or fourth-class status within the American empire (Oboler 1995: 32–43). As Connor (1994: 50) noted, the primary source of ethnic conflict in the United States has been the unwillingness to accept minorities—particularly nonwhites—as equals. If the Puerto Rican ethnic ideology was conservative, the American group myth was downright reactionary! So, for the Puerto Rican masses, their decision to espouse a strong sense of Puerto Rican identity was a very rational choice given the North American alternative.

When it comes to the formation and articulation of a nationalist ideology, the masses are dependent on intellectuals for their mythmaking skills. Nonetheless, subalterns possess beliefs and ideologies of their own. History teems with examples of peasant rebellions and riots employing these beliefs to justify peasants' collective activities. However, in order to succeed, "the native or traditional ideology of the common people requires to be wedded to and merge with an ideology or a 'theory' (to repeat Marx's term) of a more sophisticated and more 'forward-looking' kind coming from 'within'—that is, from a higher social group" (Rudé 1995: 4). Elites seek the creation of a new ideology that will be embraced unquestionably by all social strata—a hegemonic belief. The complexities and nuances of such an ideology, the rhetorical skills necessary to spread this ideal from peasant to patrician, and the resources to carry this out are most frequently found among those with a formal education.

In the final analysis, the lower classes ultimately decide whether or not to accept the elites' call to action. Those who criticize Puerto Rico's "conservative" ethnic identity either fail to comprehend or simply ignore the fact that subaltern Puerto Ricans voluntarily joined the Creole elites in their endeavor (De Granda 1972: 122). When they did so, subaltern islanders joined elites for their own benefits and attributed different meanings to nationalist symbols (Guerra 1998: 9). Without mass support a nationalist movement perishes at an embryonic stage.

In return for their support the masses expect a new social status. Their class status does not change. Nationalist elites offer the lower classes a new social status, membership in a newly defined "high-status" group (Barreto

1998: 41). Elites argued that it was better for the island's masses to be low-class members of a newly defined Puerto Rican group than what American policy makers were offering the insular masses: low-class membership in a low-status group. Peripheral elites redefined their subaltern status as a new "center." The former periphery now becomes the focus of social and spiritual discourse.

The Official Languages Act of 1902

Americanization helped to cement the bond between Puerto Rican identity and the local vernacular. Concurrent with this cultural and educational policy was the enactment of the Official Languages Act of 1902—a territorial law stating that both English and Spanish could be employed in the Puerto Rican territorial government, although it excepted the island's municipalities (see appendix 1). In order to facilitate communication the law provided for the use of interpreters and translations in government procedures. This territorial law did not affect the federal government's operations in Puerto Rico. To this day the federal administration on the island operates only in English.

This territorial statute was passed early in the twentieth century when local elites still hoped to develop a cooperative relationship with the United States. After two years of military rule, and without consulting its Caribbean subjects, Congress drafted an organic law known as the Foraker Act, which functioned as Puerto Rico's constitution from 1900 until 1917.[10] Congress ignored the autonomy charter Spain gave Puerto Rico in 1897. In theory the bilingual law passed under the Foraker Act gave the local vernacular and the metropolitan language equal footing. The practical effect of this law was to facilitate government activities for Anglophone administrators from the U.S. mainland rather than to create true parity between the two languages. Former senator Fernando Martín noted:

> Well, the original law that made Spanish and English official languages at the beginning of the [twentieth] century evidently responded to a very clear reality. That is, the key figures in the Puerto Rican government under the Foraker Act were Americans and they did not know how to speak Spanish. And therefore it was evident, at the time, that English had to be one of the official languages of Puerto Rico. If not the North American colonial administration would not have been able to function. (Martín 1998)[11]

Until the enactment of the commonwealth constitution in 1952, the justices on the island's highest court were also appointed directly by the American president, with the advice and consent of the federal Senate (Ramírez 1988: 68–69; 97). Justice Wolf, writing for the Puerto Rican Supreme Court in 1905, held that where a dispute arose between the Spanish and English versions of a particular statute, the English redaction would be considered the authoritative one.[12] If on paper the two were co-equal, the court made clear that English was *more equal* than Spanish.

This bilingual law from 1902 remained on the books with relatively little debate or discussion until the 1990s. Language policy making generated a new legislative fervor and laid the groundwork for future political maneuvering in San Juan and Washington. Cultural nationalists saw the 1902 law as an anachronism and an affront to Puerto Rican cultural identity. Summing up the historic processes of language policy and legislation, David Noriega, a former member of the House of Representatives and a longtime advocate of Puerto Rican independence, stated: "I believe that there is no nation in the world that has survived such a systematic and massive attempt at transculturation, to rip up the people from their roots. Therefore, I saw the '91 law as a relief for the heroic struggles of a people that managed to overcome that stage" (Noriega Rodríguez 1998).[13]

The old bilingual law was abolished in 1991 by a symbolic and controversial law that declared Spanish the only official idiom. By the spring of 1993 a new administration in San Juan restored official bilingualism and began calling for a new emphasis on English-language instruction in the island's school system. Although short-lived, the establishment of Spanish as the island's sole official language in 1991 entered the Puerto Rican nationalist pantheon and reinforced the identification of a people with their language. Beyond its contribution to the debate over identity and the politics of status discussions over language policy in the 1990s, it also highlighted the complex political strategies used when assessing the benefits and risks of cultural policies.

3

The Power of English

Intellectuals responded to Americanization by incorporating language-as-identity into their nation-building project. Following the island's first gubernatorial elections in 1948, debates over language policy subsided dramatically. Federal officials originally saw assimilation as a means to secure their hold on the island. Conversely, the rise of nationalism changed this assumption. In order to appease local calls for autonomy, Congress amended the 1917 Jones Act, thus allowing islanders to elect their governor (Ramírez 1988: 103–6).

Luis Muñoz Marín, founder of the Partido Popular Democrático (PPD—Popular Democratic Party), became Puerto Rico's first elected governor in 1948 and led the movement to create the commonwealth status.[1] While the 1952 constitution granted a limited degree of self-rule, it failed to remove the island from the federal constitution's territorial clause, which gives Congress final say over the territory's final status. Fundamentally, Puerto Rico's condition as an American colony has not changed (Meléndez and Meléndez 1993: 1). Early in his administration, Muñoz Marín contended with a new public school language policy. Mariano Villaronga, Muñoz's first education secretary, was a contentious figure in federal circles. Appointed by President Truman in 1946 to head Puerto Rico's Education Department, Villaronga's nomination was rejected by the U.S. Senate (Muntaner 1990: 149). During his confirmation hearings Villaronga clearly stated that if he was confirmed, Spanish would become the primary medium of instruction. While the AMPR and island intellectuals praised him, federal legislators and supporters of Puerto Rican statehood interpreted such statements as anti-American (149–50). Once appointed, Secretary Villaronga fulfilled his stated goal (García Martínez 1976: 109).

Studies find that Puerto Rico's teachers still culturally resist the United States (Nieves and Cintrón 1975: chap. 4) and much of that resistance targets the English language (López Laguerre 1997: chap. 8). Teachers of English as a Second Language are often viewed as agents of cultural defection

(Pousada 1996: 500). Antagonism toward the English language within the school system has hampered the creation of a bilingual citizenry (Resnick 1993). "The language issue in Puerto Rico has been ideologically coded in such a way that statements made by linguists are often ignored in the discussion on language" (Vélez 1986: 10). Yet the public does not always share teachers' views.

With an end to government-sponsored assimilationist policies, popular attitudes toward the English language changed. Indeed, mastering English is often a requirement for socioeconomic advancement in the insular private and the federal public sectors. Additionally, English benefits from its stature as the preeminent channel of international commerce. Moreover, many mainland-based ethnic Puerto Ricans are English dominant. All of these factors add to the power of English in Puerto Rico.

The Bilingual Status of Puerto Rico

According to Celeste Benítez, a secretary of education under the PPD in the early 1990s, "Puerto Rico is not bilingual and census data proves it. . . . Here a small portion of the population handles English with agility and ease. The majority of Puerto Ricans are unilingual; we are Spanish speakers. But certainly one of Puerto Rico's greatest educational aspirations is to teach English well" (Benítez 1998b).[2] Census data reveal that 98.22 percent of island residents speak Spanish (U.S. Dept. of Commerce 1993b: 70). Yet, not all of these Spanish speakers are Puerto Rican.

In the twentieth century Puerto Rico was unquestionably a net exporter of people. Holding American citizenship, Puerto Ricans traveled freely to and from the U.S. mainland in search of opportunities. Yet high unemployment and economic deprivation are relative terms. Political and economic turmoil led many Cubans in the 1960s and Dominicans in the 1980s to immigrate to Puerto Rico (Duany 1992).[3] Currently, Dominicans represent the largest immigrant group, followed by Cubans (Rivera-Batiz and Santiago 1996: 113–14).[4] Cubans and Dominicans may impact local politics[5] and economics[6] but they have not weakened the status of Spanish in Puerto Rico. To the contrary, they refortified Puerto Rico's linguistic status as a Spanish-speaking Caribbean enclave.

Even without a large influx of English speakers, Puerto Ricans have increasingly learned English (see table 3.1). Early in the twentieth century less than 4 percent could speak English. By the end of that century, almost 48 percent claimed the ability to speak both languages. However, the 1990 data reveal that among Spanish speakers only 23.63 percent spoke English

Table 3.1
Speaking English in Puerto Rico

	Percentage Able to Speak English		
Year	Total	With Difficulty	With Ease
1990	47.7	24.1	23.6
1980	42.2	22.9	19.3
1970	42.7		
1960	37.7		
1950	26.1		
1940	27.8		
1930	19.4		
1920	9.9		
1910	3.6		

Source: U.S. Dept. of Commerce 1993b: 87; 1984: 11; 1973: 625–26; 1963: 121.

with ease, while 24.1 percent could communicate in English with difficulty. Thus, less than a quarter of the population is truly bilingual. A majority of the island's Spanish-speaking residents—52.27 percent—reported that they could not speak English (U.S. Dept. of Commerce 1993b: 70). How should these data be interpreted?

In congressional hearings on the status of Puerto Rico, the aforementioned figures are frequently cited as evidence that efforts to promote English have failed. Now, the manipulation of data is not only a science but can develop into a grand art form, especially when outliers come into the picture. Assessing data on bilingualism at the municipal level reveals how homogeneous Puerto Rico is and also reveals the geographic niches occupied by bilingual Hispanophones and the island's resident Anglophones.

The Commonwealth, which includes the main island of Puerto Rico and the offshore islands of Culebra and Vieques, is divided into seventy-eight municipalities. There are no county governments sandwiched between the Estado Libre Asociado (ELA, Free Associated State)—the Commonwealth's name in Spanish—and the individual municipalities. The largest is San Juan with 440,000 inhabitants; the smallest is Culebra with 1,500 residents (U.S. Dept. of Commerce 1992: 2). The federal government uses these municipal boundaries and their subdivisions, the *barrios,* as data-collecting boundaries for the census.

We find that the municipality with the highest percentage of Spanish speakers is Maricao. In this *municipio* in the western highlands, 99.48 percent of the inhabitants speak Spanish (U.S. Dept. of Commerce 1993b: 70). San Juan, the largest city and the island's seat of government, is ranked number forty-four in terms of the number of Spanish speakers. Over 98 percent of the capital's inhabitants speak Spanish. Based on the percentage who speak the local vernacular, the seventy-seventh ranked town is the island municipality of Vieques, located off the southeastern corner of the main island of Puerto Rico. Slightly more than 96 percent of all *Viequenses*, 96.05 percent, are Spanish speakers. Puerto Rico's linguistic anomaly is the town of Ceiba on the eastern coast of Puerto Rico. It is only 80.71 percent Spanish speaking. Interestingly, on an island where most of the non-Spanish speakers do not speak English we find that 96.15 percent of Ceiba's non-Spanish speakers happen to be fluent in English (U.S. Dept. of Commerce 1993b: 70).[7] Explaining its linguistic peculiarity is Ceiba's proximity to Roosevelt Roads Naval Base. American military installations tend to bring together English speakers in large numbers.

From the percentages of different language speakers we turn to the levels of bilingualism. As stated above, less than a quarter of the population can speak English easily. At the municipal level the picture is quite varied. In eight municipalities we find that over 30 percent speak English with ease. Guaynabo has the highest percentage of bilingual Hispanophones—39.4 percent (U.S. Dept. of Commerce 1993b: 70). As the most affluent municipality in Puerto Rico, this San Juan suburb has a per capita income of over $8,000 (208). San Juan's per capita income, the second highest on the island, is just under $6,400, while the islandwide per capita income remains below $4,200 (208). In Puerto Rico one cannot ignore the connection between fluency in English and socioeconomic status.

There are nineteen *municipios* where between 20 and 30 percent of residents are fluent in English. For the majority of the municipal governments—forty-seven out of the seventy-eight—between 10 and 20 percent of their inhabitants are fluent in English. In four towns, under 10 percent of the local populace is bilingual (U.S. Dept. of Commerce 1993b: 70). The municipality with the lowest percentage of bilinguals is the town of Las Marías in the western highlands. Only 7.85 percent of its inhabitants speak English with ease (70). Las Marías is also the fifth poorest town in Puerto Rico, with a per capita income of only $2,500 (208). Areas with low levels of bilingualism tend also to be among the poorest areas in Puerto Rico.

In terms of the municipalities with the highest percentages of bilinguals, we find two clear patterns. Four out of the eight most bilingual *municip-*

ios in Puerto Rico—Bayamón, Carolina, Guaynabo, and San Juan—are core segments of the San Juan metropolitan area (U.S. Dept. of Commerce 1993b: 70). With so many bilingual Puerto Ricans here monolingual Anglophones can live in the *zona metropolitana* without having to learn Spanish. Among the most bilingual *municipios* are four eastern towns that are somewhat removed from metro San Juan; these are Ceiba and Fajardo on the main island of Puerto Rico, and the island municipalities of Culebra and Vieques. Geographically these small islands lie between the main island of Puerto Rico and the English-speaking U.S. Virgin Islands. However, propinquity to the Virgin Islands is not the prime factor here. The common bond among these four municipalities is their proximity to a large American military installation, the Roosevelt Roads naval complex. With the noted exception of American military bases or their environs, residing in Puerto Rico consists of swimming in a sea of functionally unilingual Spanish speakers.

The Economics of Bilingualism

Language diffusion is intimately connected to its social prestige (Aitchison 1991: 75) and its potential for economic mobility (Edwards 1985: 50). English is the preeminent global medium of commerce and links Puerto Rico to the colonial metropole. For example, an attorney conducting business in the federal court in San Juan must do so in English—a language not spoken by a majority of Puerto Ricans (Delgado Cintrón 1990: 20). It is also the language of all official federal interactions.

Exceptions to this norm, rare at the highest government levels, occur with street-level bureaucrats. Walking up to the counter of a U.S. Post Office, a local patron will likely be greeted by postal employees in Spanish. At this level mail becomes *correo,* stamps are referred to as *sellos,* and patrons do not talk about postage but *franqueo.* Nonetheless, most of the signs around them are in English, as is the paperwork a postal employee must file.

Linguistically speaking, federal offices in Puerto Rico operate in much the same way as do American embassies overseas. Interactions with the local populace take place in their vernacular, but administrative matters are conducted in English. Thus, when Puerto Rican government officials want or need to correspond with federal agencies they do so in what amounts to a foreign language. This phenomenon is not unusual in linguistically heterogeneous societies such as India, Nigeria, or Papua New Guinea, and it led many postcolonial leaders to adopt their old colonial languages.

While it is not the official language, English prevails as the de facto federal language, which adds to the language's prestige and the prominence of those who speak it.

Outside of the federal public sector, many American-owned businesses on the island conduct their affairs in English (Muntaner 1990: 233–34). For firms in the tourism sector, using your customer's language is imperative. In much the same manner, American companies in Puerto Rico need employees who can interact with their local Spanish-speaking customers.[8] Such a practice does not change the language of the boardroom nor the language skills needed to climb the corporate ladder. In addition, this sends a clear message that English is not only a necessary language but is superior to Spanish (Muntaner 1990: 243). Trade with the United States dominates the island's economy.

At the time of the U.S. conquest, the island's principal export-oriented economic sectors were in crisis. "The United States in 1898 had come into possession of a colony in disarray from Spanish mercantilism, and its transition into the American economic sphere accelerated the crises in its traditional sectors" (Weisskoff 1985: 118). Early in the twentieth century the coffee industry began its decline while the sugar industry was taken over by American corporations (Wells 1979: 94–95). From that point on American firms dominated the insular economy in a "dependent development" relationship (Evans 1979). Local entrepreneurs enjoyed relative prosperity from their role as intermediaries between local and outside corporations. As a group they became a "stepchild of imperialism" (Evans 1979: 39).

Puerto Rico's shift from an agricultural to an industrial economy occurred toward the middle of the twentieth century under a program known as *Operation Bootstrap*. American industries were lured by low corporate taxes, cheap labor (relative to the U.S. mainland), and open access to American markets in the 1940s and 1950s. These incentives proved insufficient by the late twentieth century, and American firms found it more profitable to relocate their plants, particularly after the extension of federal minimum wage laws to Puerto Rico, to countries with lower labor costs. Instead, Puerto Rico was left with capital intensive firms interested in exploiting the Commonwealth's tax exemptions (Weisskoff 1985: 54). "Puerto Rico by 1980 had become little more than a way station economy, a transfer for business activity, with a Caribbean flair" (58). These companies are in greater need of a well-educated and trained workforce than are labor-intensive firms.

Competition for these jobs is dependent on proficiency in English. Thus, most affluent families send their children to private schools, especially those that employ English as the medium of instruction (Muntaner 1990: 259). Former education secretary Celeste Benítez noted that there "prevails the mistaken idea that private schools are better simply because they are private" (Benítez 1998b).[9] As a general rule, private-school students learn English better than their public-school peers. Yet Benítez suggests that fluency in English is not connected to the type of school one attends, per se, but to one's parents' socioeconomic background.

> The highest incomes are usually linked to a higher level of learning such that the student has—[simply] by coming from this kind of home—a stimulus to learn English well, to excel in school, etc. Sadly many public school students, because they come from another kind of home, do not have the household stimuli that helps them to do better work at school than those who come from homes in other circumstances. (Benítez 1998b)[10]

That their children learn English is a key goal for most parents, but it takes on added importance for upwardly mobile families. Many private schools teach some of their courses, if not all, in English; this is particularly true of parochial schools. As a result, religious schools in Puerto Rico have been accused of engaging in an ecclesiastical version of Americanization (García Martínez 1976: 135–39). Church officials counter that the use of English as the medium of instruction results from the inability of American clerics, who teach much of the curriculum, to communicate effectively in Spanish (Beirne 1976: 71).

Language skills affect the university one attends. Decades ago, leading families wanted their children to study at the University of Puerto Rico. Nowadays families having the means increasingly tend to send their children to American universities. Degrees from stateside institutions serve as status symbols. The underlying assumption here is that anything American is superior to its Puerto Rican counterpart. Degrees from the mainland open doors to careers and this is especially true for U.S. multinational corporations. Naturally, college admittance is based in large measure on standardized tests in English.

The connection between language and socioeconomic mobility is frequently underscored by statehood advocates (Fernández 1997a: 49). If privileged families have the means to teach their children the English language well enough to study abroad, the Puerto Rican government should not deny the same benefit to those of lesser means (Romero-Barceló 1997: 37). Former education secretary Carlos Chardón (1998) felt strongly that parents should have the right to choose what language to educate their children in. Some in the pro-statehood camp go much further and accuse their separatist and autonomist opponents of hypocrisy. Many opposed to English-language instruction in public schools send their own children to private schools where English is the medium of instruction. Along the same lines, many statehood advocates accuse their opponents of demagoguery and elitism. Senator Enrique Rodríguez Negrón said:

> Because the most incredible thing is that there have always been politicians here who do not want this country's poor to learn English. They no longer want to give incentives to teach English in Puerto Rico fearing that this will bring Puerto Rico closer to annexation by the United States. Nonetheless, almost all the politicians here first send their children to study in private schools in Puerto Rico where elementary education is conducted in English. (Rodríguez Negrón 1998)[11]

Regardless of the partisan orientation the message is loud and clear. Choice jobs in Puerto Rico require not only mastery of the substantive area but also a thorough understanding of English. Once employed, promotions within the workplace may depend, again, upon one's language skills in English. This is particularly the case if one is transferred to one of the firm's mainland branches. For some of these positions a stateside diploma may be imperative. Performing well in a North American college is easier if one attended a primary or secondary school where English was the medium of instruction. Puerto Ricans identify with Spanish but the job market requires mastery of English.

Welfare with a Caribbean Twist

Another dimension to the language-economy nexus is often dismissed or ignored since it is not always obvious. One cannot ignore the impact of Puerto Rico's dependency on welfare, food stamps, and other federal subsidies. Federal programs and grants to the Commonwealth or its municipal subdivisions provide a fiscal bond between Puerto Ricans and the United States. Dependency on federal dollars foments the political loyalties of politicians and ordinary citizens whose livelihoods depend directly on monetary transfers from Washington.[12]

Federal transfers to the island are symptomatic of a contradictory federal policy toward Puerto Rico. On the one hand the United States supports a policy of exclusion by maintaining a colonial regime. On the other hand granting U.S. citizenship and expanding federal programs of financial support represent a measure of inclusion (Meléndez 1991: 117–18). Thanks to the island's importance to the military and certain sectors of the U.S. economy, Washington has been willing, until recently, to bear this burden (Cabán 1993: 32).

Puerto Rico's population density, over 1,000 inhabitants per square mile in the early 1990s, is a higher population density than that of any state of the American union (Rivera-Batiz and Santiago 1996: 22). The island's relatively small size and dependent economy has left it incapable of economically absorbing its population. As a result, over 800,000 Puerto Ricans emigrated to the U.S. mainland between 1940 and 1970. This number represents about half of the natural increase in the island's population during this thirty-year period (43). Even large-scale emigration was insufficient to entirely alleviate the economic stresses of a growing populace. The island's official unemployment rate remains in the double digits (12–13). Whereas around 13 percent of the U.S. population lives below the poverty line, in 1990 the majority of Puerto Ricans—just under 60 percent—lived below the official poverty line (75).

In order to ameliorate the economic predicament and to dissuade another mass exodus, the federal government included this Caribbean territory in its food stamp program (Weisskoff 1985: 65). Federal transfers and emigration became staples of the territorial government's economic planning.

> Locked politically into fruitless haranguing about political status and with no economic alternatives forthcoming, Puerto Rico has, in the last analysis, pursued a two-fold strategy: one, encouraging mass emigration, a form of economic exile, for a large part of its population rendered surplus by the decline of agriculture; and two, for those who remain at home, providing a life dependent on federal subsidies. (Weisskoff 1985: 72)

During its first year Puerto Rico received $388 million from the food stamp program; by 1993 the annual intake from this program had more than doubled to around $1 billion (Rivera-Batiz and Santiago 1996: 15). Looking at federal transfers, Puerto Rican individuals received $500 million in 1970; this sum increased to $6 billion by 1990 (14). Hence, American dollars buy Puerto Rican loyalty (Weisskoff 1985: 121). This is a new kind of "lite colonialism" (Flores 2000: 37).

Largely bypassing local political elites, the federal government has created its own basis of material support. If we add those who work for the federal government and those employed by the island government in federal programs or with federal funds, we have a clearer idea of the material and ideological support basis of the North American state in Puerto Rico. Those advocating close relations with the United States, the status quo or statehood, benefit from this support (Meléndez 1998: 10).

Puerto Rico has the highest standard of living, measured in terms of per capita income, in Latin America and the Caribbean. Just as many immigrants around the world endeavor to enter the United States either legally or without legal documentation, the same applies to many Caribbean islanders who try to enter Puerto Rico. During the Commonwealth's first decade, the most intensive period of industrial development, the island was showcased. Yet this relative prosperity is not the sign of a healthy or vibrant economy. Weisskoff's analysis described a contorted economy in the tropics founded on the twin pillars of federal handouts and corporate tax exemptions. Individual American taxpayers pick up the bill for maintaining a colonial economy in the Caribbean that benefits a few corporations and their stockholders.

In short, the U.S public underwrites the Puerto Rican people, while U.S. corporations shift profits through their Puerto Rican plants and back to the United States, tax free. The Puerto Rico family then buys its consumption needs, which consists for the most part of imported goods, shifting its public money back to the U.S. private sector. As its own economy decomposes, Puerto Rico becomes the revolving door for funds flowing from the American public back to the American corporations and from the multinational company back to itself to avoid taxes. Puerto Rico has become a geographical laundry for corporate profits to avoid federal taxes. Meanwhile, these corporations employ only a token Puerto Rican work force. The rest of the island's people live peaceably on welfare or not so peaceably in the ghettoes of America's industrial cities. (Weisskoff 1985: 59)

By the late 1990s several federal policies were fundamentally modified. Congress eliminated many of the federal tax benefits to American-based companies investing in Puerto Rico under Section 936. As a result of these tax reforms many question whether these U.S. firms will remain on the island in the long term. Additionally, Washington initiated various welfare reforms. The decline in these transfers may contribute to a further downturn in the local economy. Without the economic infrastructure to absorb the unemployed, let alone the growth in the numbers of unemployed as a result of federal tax policies and the closure of 936 plants, Puerto Ricans could face another exodus to the U.S. mainland early in the twenty-first century. Changes to the federal tax code and social welfare policies will significantly impact Puerto Rican loyalty to the United States.

Leaving speculation to one side for a moment, we return to the connection between language and economics under welfare. To restate an important point, receiving federal benefits is not dependent on knowledge of English or any formal linguistic test. Welfare benefits do, however, add to the *power of the English language* in Puerto Rico. This language is directly associated with the United States. Welfare, food stamps, social security, and other federally funded programs reinforce the notion that money is associated with all things English and that the affluence Puerto Ricans have come to expect is tied directly to their continued relationship with the United States. Puerto Rico's heart and soul may speak in Spanish, but the Puerto Rican wallet is filled with greenbacks emblazoned with English. As far as many Puerto Ricans are concerned, rejecting the English language is seen as an affront to the United States, which may respond by reducing or eliminating financial aid to Puerto Rico.

Nuyoricans in the Family

The *English factor* in Puerto Rico has important repercussions that travel beyond discussions of financial dependency. Hundreds of thousands of Puerto Ricans have left the island for the U.S. mainland. In search of jobs, principally in the industrial sector, these migrants primarily settled in working-class neighborhoods and the ghettoes of the northeastern states and parts of the Midwest. New York City became, in a manner of speaking, the largest Puerto Rican city. As the American economy expanded following the Second World War, Puerto Rican migrants were welcomed as a needed source of unskilled labor. Mobility was not an issue since Congress collectively made Puerto Ricans U.S. citizens in 1917. The ability to travel freely back and forth between the United States and the country of origin made Puerto Rican migration a unique element in the American immigration experience.

Some migrants intended to remain in the United States; others planned on returning to Puerto Rico some time in the future. Most who left the island during the great exodus of the 1940s and 1950s, and their descendants, remained in North America. Today over two million ethnic Puerto Ricans reside in the continental United States. Over 80 percent of the respondents to a public opinion survey said they had relatives living in the states ("Goza" 1993: 6). From the most militant nationalist to the most passionate pro-American, few Puerto Ricans escape the social and cultural consequences of having family members living outside the country.

Ethnic Puerto Ricans are increasingly moving outside of their conventional northeastern urban enclaves (Rivera-Batiz and Santiago 1996: 131–35). Mobility is not limited to migration across the United States. Over 100,000 Puerto Ricans traveled between the island and the U.S. mainland in the 1980s (59). Almost half of the Puerto Rican migrants who lived in the U.S. mainland during the 1980s did so for less than two years (59).

The Puerto Rican migration story stands in stark contrast to traditional European immigration patterns. Previously, immigrants came in large waves. Their descendants were culturally and linguistically assimilated into the American milieu via direct and daily contact with American society in schools and the workplace. The distinctiveness of their individual cultures would theoretically blend into the American *melting pot*. Yet Puerto Ricans, as is the case with indigenous peoples and Chicanos, find their ethnic homeland or place of origin falling under American jurisdiction. "[E]ven when many Puerto Ricans in the United States imagine themselves pragmatically as an 'ethnic group' with no territorial (state) claim in the United States, Puerto Rico is at least claimed symbolically as the territorial site where ethnics become nationals through the magical operation of the air bridge" (Grosfoguel et al. 1997: 18). Freedom of mobility means that the assimilation of Puerto Ricans residing in the United States is *incomplete*, based on the prototypical immigrant paradigm.[13] Puerto Rican migration questions the historical pattern of immigrant becoming American by way of assimilation (Zentella 1990: 82).

While their immigration pattern is different from other historical immigrant groups, some experiences are common. Among families that remained in the United States for a generation or more the Spanish language, while still holding great symbolic importance, is used with declining frequency (Urciuoli 1991: 298–301). Ethnic Puerto Ricans in the United States share an "inner sphere of interaction" with other Latinos, and in this realm language mixing is rarely a problem. Additionally, their lives include an "outer sphere"—the workplace, business, school, and government—that is monopolized by a standard American English that frowns upon language mixing (Urciuoli 1998: 77).

Ethnic Puerto Ricans in the United States increasingly are becoming English-dominant. The English language, once the undisputed cultural attribute of the American, is spoken by members of the stateside Puerto Rican family as a vernacular. While there is no official term for these mainland ethnic Puerto Ricans, one of the most frequently used labels is *Nuyorican*—New York Puerto Rican. The Nuyorican straddles a linguistic, cultural, and geographic border that combines elements of Puerto Rico and the American immigrant and minority experiences. In the long run a question remains as to whether Nuyoricans will view themselves as primarily Puerto Rican, American, both, or their own unique entity, or whether they will blend into the category of "Latino" or "Hispanic."

An Ecological Model of Bilingualism in Puerto Rico

So far, we have painted a multifaceted portrait of language in Puerto Rico. Islanders overwhelmingly speak Spanish and they culturally identify themselves with this language. Yet Puerto Ricans value the many benefits, most of them economic, associated with speaking English. Mastery of English has been attributed to several factors: long-term residency in the United States by ethnic Puerto Ricans, education, and income. For ethnic Puerto Ricans in North America, daily contact facilitates developing fluency in English. Additionally, the greater one's level of educational attainment, the more likely one is to know English. With regard to income we understand that, again, English is the language of socioeconomic mobility, and the higher one's income the more likely one can afford the opportunity to learn English.

All three of the aforementioned elements were incorporated as independent variables in an ecological model (see table 3.2). Turning to the 1990 census, one can obtain data from the seventy-eight *municipios* or municipal governments. The dependent variable in this model—English Proficiency—is defined as the percentage of Spanish speakers in each *municipio* that can speak English with ease. The first independent variable (USA-Res) assesses the impact of ethnic Puerto Ricans, in particular those who have resided on the U.S. mainland for at least ten years. The second variable (Affluence), also taken from the 1990 census, is the level of affluence as measured by the percentage of families in each *municipio* whose income is above the poverty line. Lastly, the model explores the impact of education on bilingualism. Education is measured in terms of the percentage of local residents with at least a bachelor's degree (College). As with any ecological model we can talk about these variables' impact on bilingualism at the municipal level, but we cannot automatically assume that the results will apply to individuals without risking an "ecological fallacy" (Langbein and Lichtman 1978: 9–10).

The regression results in table 3.2 tell an interesting story. This model, with an adjusted R^2 of 0.77, explains 77 percent of the variance across

Table 3.2

Ecological Model of English Proficiency in Puerto Rico, 1990 (Unstandardized O.L.S. Coefficients)

Variable	b	t-score	significance
Constant	−4.768	−3.018	.003
USA-Res	0.885	3.820	.000
Affluence	0.318	5.633	.000
Education	0.777	5.598	.000

N = 78, Adjusted R^2 = .770, F = 86.982, Sig. = .000
Source: U.S. Dept. of Commerce 1993a: 243–50; 1993b: 52, 87, 208.

Puerto Rico's *municipios*. Not only is the model statistically significant (Sig. = .000) but so are each of the independent variables. Alone, these three independent variables explain the vast majority of our story. The variable with the largest impact on bilingualism is prolonged residency in the United States (USA-Res). With an unstandardized coefficient of 0.885, we can say that for each one-percent increase in the municipal population that lived for an extended period in the United States, the percentage of bilinguals goes up by 0.885 percent. Education's impact was almost as strong as long-term U.S. residency. Although statistically significant, the weakest of the three variables was income (b = .318). These statistics do not bode well for the island's educational system.

Still, this picture is slightly blurred. When it comes to language usage in Puerto Rico the eastern municipality of Ceiba stands out. Due to its proximity to the Roosevelt Roads naval complex, Ceiba maintains, proportionally, the largest enclave of non-Spanish speakers of any municipality. Above we mention that almost 20 percent of this town's population is made up of Anglophones. Such a large expatriate American community constitutes a noteworthy statistical exception. In order to expunge the model of any undue influences from this one outlier, the same regression was run omitting data from Ceiba (see table 3.3).

By excluding Ceiba our picture of Puerto Rican bilingualism becomes much clearer. The adjusted R^2 in this modified model increases to 0.83. Thus, we have increased our explanation of variance in the remaining municipalities from 77 percent, in the first model, to 83 percent. Not only does the model do a better job of explaining bilingualism, but it also reveals the veiled impact of returning ethnic Puerto Ricans on levels of bilingualism. In this modified model the unstandardized coefficient increased to 2.257. Thus,

Table 3.3
Ecological Model of English Proficiency in Puerto Rico Excluding Ceiba, 1990
(Unstandardized O.L.S. Coefficients)

Variable	b	t-score	significance
Constant	−10.035	−5.963	.000
USA-Res	2.257	6.894	.000
Affluence	0.316	6.520	.000
Education	0.865	7.207	.000

N = 77, Adjusted R^2 = .830, F = 124.680, Sig. = .000
Sources: U.S. Dept. of Commerce 1993a: 243–50; 1993b: 52, 87, 208.

for every one-percent increase in the municipal population that lived in the United States for a prolonged period, the percentage of bilinguals goes up over two percent. The impact of education and affluence changed little with the new model.

These statistics point to the remarkable impact that returning ethnics have on bilingualism. Ethnic Puerto Ricans living on the U.S. mainland are obliged to pick up at least rudimentary English. Outside the confines of their barrio, speaking the dominant society's language is an imperative. We should restate that many second-, third-, or fourth-generation Puerto Ricans are English dominant. English has been transformed into a vital aspect of inter-boricua communication (boricua is a slang term for Puerto Rican).

Recognizing the impact of Nuyoricans on levels of bilingualism in Puerto Rico should not move us to ignore the role of education. The percentage of municipal residents holding at least a bachelor's degree had a clear and statistically significant association with the percentage of municipio residents able to speak English with ease. Still, those holding college degrees often learn to read in English but few learn to speak it. Except those working in tourism or directly with the U.S. federal government, few have either the need or the opportunity to use what English they know. It appears that to appreciably augment the number of bilinguals the Puerto Rican government would either have to encourage large-scale Anglophone immigration or radically alter school curricula. As we see in subsequent chapters, the ability of ordinary Puerto Ricans to communicate in the American vernacular dramatically impacted congressional debates over the island's political status.

4

The Politics of Status

Columbus arrived on the island of Boriquén during his second voyage to the Americas in 1493 (Brau 1978: 5–10). With Spanish colonization came the enslavement of the island's inhabitants—the Taíno. Authorities responded to a Taíno rebellion in the sixteenth century with the virtual annihilation of the island's aboriginals. Various other European powers attempted to conquer it (Morales 1983: 14–22), but Puerto Rico's colonial history has been dominated by two powers—the Kingdom of Spain until 1898 and the United States of America after that date.

Puerto Rican politics are obsessed with "status"—the island's politico-juridical relationship with the central power. Public opinion surveys show that the electorate is interested in other issues (Meléndez 1995: 71). However, wrangling over links with the United States lies at the heart of local politics (Anderson, R. 1965: 12). Some favor stronger ties to the "center," or metropolitan power; others seek to align themselves with the "periphery," the island itself. This political obsession persists since the current Commonwealth is essentially a continuation of centuries of colonial rule (Meléndez 1995: 72). Indeed, with the transfer of Hong Kong from the United Kingdom to China in 1997, Puerto Rico acquired a dubious distinction—it is now the world's most populous colony.

Attempts to forcibly liberate the island, such as the 1868 Grito de Lares uprising against Spain or the 1950 Gesta de Jayuya insurrection against the United States, failed. Rebellion leaders Ramón Emeterio Betances and Pedro Albizu Campos, respectively, accrued insufficient arms to eject a well-entrenched power and they failed to amass adequate popular support. Culturally, Puerto Ricans are very nationalistic. But cultural nationalism and separatism, although related, are distinct phenomena.

This chapter explores the political consequences of the tug of war over U.S.–Puerto Rican relations. Each of the island's three major parties overtly stakes a position on the status question: independence, limited autonomy, or statehood. Absent government-led assimilationist initiatives, the average voter weighs economic concerns above cultural matters. To capture this dynamic we created a model that illustrates that the electorate definitely imposes restrictions on both the cultural and economic policies of the island's main political parties.[1]

Commonwealth—The Status Quo

In response to a growing nationalist movement in the 1930s and 1940s, Congress authorized the territorial government to convoke a constitutional convention whose end product was approved by a comfortable majority in an islandwide referendum (Trías Monge 1982: 270). The proposed Commonwealth would control most local matters: taxation, the insular budget, education, health, and so on. A common citizenship allowed free travel to and from the U.S. mainland, as is the case with goods and services, while it also made Puerto Ricans eligible for military conscription.

The Commonwealth's government functions much like a state government on the U.S. mainland. However, unlike the states the Commonwealth has no say in the presidential Electoral College, no delegation in the U.S. Senate, and only a nonvoting delegate in the federal House of Representatives. Unlike residents of the fifty states or the District of Columbia, most Puerto Rican residents pay no federal income taxes. Under the current legal and political arrangement, Puerto Rico is embraced as a domestic part of the United States while it is also marginalized (Meléndez 1993b: 42). Unlike the notorious Supreme Court case of *Plessy v. Ferguson,* there is no legal pretense here. Puerto Rico represents a "Separate and Unequal" entity (Torruella 1985).

The Eisenhower administration used the establishment of the Commonwealth to justify removing Puerto Rico from the United Nation's list of formal colonies (Trías Monge 1983: 16–17). At the international level, the commonwealth status became a fig leaf giving the federal government the leverage to reprimand others for failing to decolonize, and it freed Washington from submitting annual reports to the United Nations on Puerto Rico (Meléndez 1993a: 110–11). There is no legal mandate to augment autonomy even if desired by the local populace. Indeed, congressional refusal to expand the Commonwealth's autonomy has undermined its very legitimacy (Meléndez 1991: 122).

Commonwealth supporters were stunned when one of their own publicly stated that this is a colonial status (Trías Monge 1997: 107). "Those in the United States and Puerto Rico who still cling to the strange notion that Puerto Rico is nevertheless self-governing are simply out of step with the rest of the informed world. There is no question that in the Caribbean, Latin America, and the United Nations itself Puerto Rico is seen as a colony of the United States" (163). Worse still, there is no guarantee that this status is permanent (174). Trías Monge, a legal scholar and former chief justice of Puerto Rico's Supreme Court, was also a longtime member of the pro-commonwealth PPD and a delegate to the very assembly that drafted the 1952 Constitution. "Colonialism and citizenship remain at the heart of the relationship between the United States and Puerto Rico" (Meléndez 1993b: 43).

The Puerto Rican Party System

Observers of American politics usually ignore the overseas territories since they play no direct role in U.S. policy making. Puerto Rican politics operate in Spanish; thus there may be a language problem for students of American politics, who are often monolingual Anglophones. Americans studying nationalist movements in other countries often feel uncomfortable acknowledging that the United States has a colonial problem. Perhaps political scientists can take a cue from other disciplines that find Puerto Rico a data-rich arena in which one can test numerous hypotheses and expand upon contending theoretical perspectives.

Once every four years the mainland parties appear. Like a four-year cicada the GOP and the Democrats make noise for a few weeks and then vanish until the next presidential primary. The separation of the U.S. and Puerto Rican party systems is reinforced by the fact that Puerto Rico's only elected federal office is the post of resident commissioner. Puerto Rico's system may be accurately described as a two-and-a-half party system (Blondel 1990: 304–5).

The two largest parties are the Partido Nuevo Progresista (PNP—New Progressive Party) and the Partido Popular Democrático (PPD—Popular Democratic Party). If asked about their affiliation with the American parties, most PPD members claim to support the mainland Democrats. Luis Muñoz Marín, the PPD's founder, was a staunch New Dealer who maintained close links to the Kennedy administration. Some in the PNP also profess their loyalty to the Democratic Party. Battles over chairing the Democratic Party are vicious, but they are skirmishes between the annexationist PNP and the autonomist PPD and not conflicts over liberal or conservative policy issues. The nominal Republican Party in Puerto Rico is unquestionably a PNP bastion. Mainland Republican alliances with pro-statehood parties go back to the first years of American rule on the island. The smallest party, the Partido Independentista Puertorriqueño (PIP—Puerto Rican Independence Party), is not affiliated with any U.S. party. The PIP is a member of the International Socialist and maintains ties with Social Democratic parties, especially in Latin America and Europe.

More than any other issue these organizations are divided by their preferred constitutional concord with the United States (Meléndez 1998: 110). Differing elites promote rival status alternatives in searching for a framework that maximizes their long-term interests (Meléndez 1993a: 264). Rather than the common left-right ideological continuum found in most countries, Puerto Rican politics is fought along a center-periphery divide (Anderson, R. 1983: 13). Pro-center parties aspire to increase ties with the central government. The most militant pro-periphery parties are separatist; their polar opposites are pro-statehood.

Statistical analyses show that the status question drives Puerto Rican electoral behavior (Barreto 1995; Barreto and Eagles 2000). Starting with the most pro-center party, we find the PNP, founded by industrialist Luis A. Ferré in 1967, advocating Puerto Rican statehood.[2] Historically, pro-statehood parties were led by local elites connected to the commercial sector, in particular the sugar industry (Meléndez 1993a: 27). Statehood is still supported by a significant portion of the local bourgeoisie. Meléndez (1993a: 11) argued that many in this class feel that only a permanent U.S. presence on the island can safeguard their economic privileges. But the bulk of the PNP's voters, as with the PPD, are poor. Rank-and-file PNP and PPD supporters feel that only a close relationship with the United States guarantees their federal benefits. Indeed, the PNPs campaigned in the 1970s on the premise that statehood ultimately benefited the poor (Romero-Barceló 1978).

Traditionally, statehood advocates supported Americanization (Meléndez 1993a: 53). As late as the 1950s the PNP's predecessor, the Partido Estadista Republicano (PER—Republican Statehood Party) backed employing English as the medium of instruction in public education (Bothwell 1979b: 773). Under Ferré's leadership, the PNP moved in a more culturally nationalistic direction. A new generation of statehood supporters revived an idea from the early 1900s. Puerto Rico was the *patria regional,* or regional fatherland—a subset of the larger American homeland (Meléndez 1993a: 56). The United States was a "Republic of Republics" (Meléndez 1993a: 57). The 1960s and seventies represented the height of the American Civil Rights movement, with public discussions about diversity and multiculturalism. With its Latin culture intact, Puerto Rico could work cooperatively, according to the PNP, within the American union under the concept of *estadidad jíbara*, or Creole Statehood (Meléndez 1993a: 152). *E Pluribus Unum* referred to the acquisition of a larger identity and not necessarily the adoption of a new set of sociocultural traits.

Somewhere between the two endpoints of the center-periphery axis lies the PPD. The Partido Popular Democrático was the creation of the charismatic Luis Muñoz Marín, who founded a party in 1938 that united autonomists and separatists. Like his father, the eminent Luis Muñoz Rivera, the PPD's founder was convinced that autonomy was the most desirable relationship with the United States. From the early 1940s to the mid-1960s, Puerto Rico became a virtual one-party system. The PPD dominated Puerto Rico in much the same way as the Liberal Democratic Party dominated Japanese politics in the decades following the Second World War.

While the PPD embraced symbols of the Puerto Rican peasantry (Guerra 1998; Janer 1998), it undermined the foundations of large-scale agriculture, particularly the sugar cane industry. Not surprisingly, this economic sector was a traditional bastion of its *republicano* rivals. The PPD overthrew American commercial agro-elites by aligning itself with the American manufacturing sector. It brought together the exploited working class that labored on American-owned plantations with the disenchanted middle classes descended from the old hacienda-owning families (Meléndez 1998: 121). Such a coalition was unworkable until the 1930s, when the weakened hacienda class was secure that the masses would aim their wrath at American agro-interests (Quintero 1986: 154). While PPD followers, commonly referred to as Populares, debate Puerto Rico's ideal level of autonomy from the United States, they remain the prime defender of the current commonwealth status.

Muñoz Marín's insistence on autonomy drove a wedge between the PPD's two main camps, and in 1946 he expelled the hard-core separatist faction from the party. Led by Gilberto Concepción de Gracia, these dissidents organized themselves that year as a new party dedicated to independence from the United States by electoral means, the PIP.[3] While it is electorally the weakest of the three parties, scholars have long noted that there remains an omnipresent nationalism in Puerto Rico. "The presence of latent nationalism on the Puerto Rican political scene represents a disturbing element whose ultimate significance, while it cannot be precisely evaluated, cannot be ignored" (Anderson, R. 1965: 45). In terms of the political parties that regularly vie for office, the PIP lies at the pro-periphery end of the ideological spectrum. One of its strongholds, and even here it holds no monopoly, is among island intellectuals. Responding to their concerns, PIP Senator Rubén Berríos Martínez introduced a bill in the 1970s to establish Spanish as the island's sole official language (*Revista* 1993: 105–12). The PIP's legislative delegation, however, was too small to abrogate the 1902 law.

Ironically, we find that a higher proportion of Puerto Rican independence advocates have a stronger command of the English language than any other political grouping, including statehood advocates. A survey revealed that 38 percent of PIP supporters felt comfortable expressing themselves in English ("Gusta" 1997: 6). The same comfort level was shared by only 28 percent of those who identified themselves with the pro-statehood PNP, 25 percent who did not declare a party affiliation, and only 16 percent of PPD backers. At the opposite end of the scale the same poll revealed that 55 percent of the Populares, 46 percent of the PNP supporters, 45 percent of the nonaffiliated respondents, and 24 percent who back the PIP reported feeling uncomfortable expressing themselves in the American vernacular ("Gusta" 1997: 6). Noting this fascinating irony, Romero-Barceló said:

> These preachers of separatism denounce the teaching of English in our public schools; they call English a threat to our Puerto Rican culture. The majority of these independence advocates are themselves fluent in English, yet their sense of identity as Puerto Ricans seems not to have been weakened in the slightest. Indeed, they regard themselves as the purest of Puerto Rican patriots. (Romero-Barceló 1986: 31)

Washington lawmakers have been faced with anecdotal evidence of this paradoxical phenomenon. When Puerto Rican leaders speak before a committee on the island's status, federal senators and representatives have found that those who defend Puerto Rican independence from the United States often do so in very eloquent English. During one hearing, Congressman Dan Burton of Indiana commended PIP President Rubén Berríos Martínez for quoting a passage from Shakespeare's *Henry V* (U.S. House 1995: 53–54). At the other end of the ideological spectrum, some espousing a permanent union with the United States have been shown wanting in their command of English.

Voters must weigh the status options that best serve their particular interests. Since the establishment of the Commonwealth, Puerto Rico has, for the most part, experienced a less confrontational relationship with the United States. An exception to that rule is the controversy surrounding the

U.S. Navy and the island municipality of Vieques. In April 1999, two Navy pilots flew off course during military exercises and dropped their ordnance on a Vieques civilian. Civic, political, and religious leaders in Vieques, the main island of Puerto Rico, and even Puerto Rican communities in the United States, have used this tragedy to demand that the U.S. Navy halt all operations in Vieques.

In economic terms, Puerto Ricans are now more dependent on the American economy, which provides the lion's share of high-paying professional positions, supplies the Commonwealth government with millions of dollars of revenue, and sustains a majority of the population through a host of government programs. The Puerto Rican heart, on the other hand, engenders a cultural nationalism that pulls voters toward the "periphery."

> Puerto Ricans of all persuasions are principally cultural nationalists. The overwhelming majority consider themselves Puerto Ricans first and Americans second. Should the people of Puerto Rico feel that their native language or sense of identity are threatened by statehood, if, for example, a condition to statehood was that English would be the primary language or that public school instruction would be in English, large numbers of statehooders would surely flock to the autonomist and independence options. And, should they be further convinced that the United States has no intention of purging Commonwealth status of its colonial features and insists in preserving the status quo, independence could possibly become again the preferred status of a solid majority of Puerto Ricans, although it would take time and understanding for them to overcome their apprehensions. (Trías Monge 1997: 183)

It is important to note that Puerto Rican nationalism with its tenacious manifestations in the cultural arena is far more muted in politics, where it reveals itself in the guise of autonomism but not separatism (Morales Carrión 1983: 71). "In fact, there exists such a thing as a growing Puerto Rican nationalism, but it's a *lite nationalism,* which *has nothing to do* necessarily with the majoritarian desire to establish an 'independent' Puerto Rican state nor with the extreme chauvinism of the nationalists of the far right" (Rivera, A. 1996: 213; emphasis in the original). Absent direct federal government intervention in cultural matters, economic concerns outweigh cultural considerations when it comes to voting (Colón Morera 1993: 458).

One must also appraise various ways in which the government has influenced individual voters. "Material prosperity, coupled with repression

Table 4.1
Survey of Status Alternatives That Best Address Key Policy Problems (Percentages)

| | Status | | | | | |
Policy	S	C	I	D	NR	Imp
Control crime and drugs	31	25	5	4	37	94
Medical and health services	43	33	3	3	18	90
Quality public education	39	36	4	3	19	95
Avoid tax increases	24	42	5	4	25	n.a.
Maintain Section 936 firms	22	52	2	4	20	69
Vote for U.S. president	63	17	1	4	15	n.a.
Increase Puerto Rico's political influence in U.S.	55	26	2	5	12	n.a.
Maintain PR's Olympic team	20	51	10	4	16	60
Maintain the use of Spanish	20	49	15	2	14	70

Abbreviations: Statehood (S), Commonwealth (C), Independence (I), Do Not Know (D), the status question is Not Related to this issue (NR), not available (n.a.). Respondents were also asked whether they considered the policy issue extremely important (Imp).
Source: "Goza de aprobación" 1993: 6–7.

and intimidation, have blunted the demand for independence" (Weisskoff 1985: 121). Particularly during the Cold War, both the Federal Bureau of Investigation and commonwealth police persecuted Puerto Rican separatists (Acosta 1987, 1991; Pabón 1972). Both federal (Bosque Pérez 1997; Gautier and Blanco 1997) and commonwealth governments (Colón Morera 1997) maintained "subversive files" on thousands of independence supporters who were deemed security risks.[4] Being branded as an *independentista* could endanger one's career or employment. In a few celebrated cases, such as the *Cerro Maravilla* incident of the late 1970s, this persecution was lethal (Nelson 1986; Suárez 1987). A clear message was sent that supporting independence from the United States meant trouble. If culture made Puerto Ricans nationalistic, economics made them pro-American. Intimidation reinforced the belief that advocating independence was a risky venture.

Opinion polls highlight how the public weighs the prospects of each status option to solve major sociocultural, economic, and political concerns (see table 4.1). When asked which status alternative would best preserve the dominance of the Spanish language, 49 percent said the commonwealth status. Only 20 percent insisted that statehood would do so, and 15 percent said that independence was the best protector of the vernacular ("Goza" 1993: 6). Commonwealth was selected by 51 percent of the public as the status option most likely to maintain Puerto Rico's Olympic team, while statehood obtained 20 percent and independence 10 percent. In contrast, economic matters tended to favor statehood. About 43 percent of respondents said that statehood was more likely to provide better hospital and medical services, as opposed to 33 percent who said commonwealth would do so, and 3 percent who claimed that would be the case with independence. Statehood also won in the category of public perception on improving public education. Statehood was favored by 39 percent, commonwealth by 36 percent, and independence by 4 percent ("Goza" 1993: 6). One of the few economic areas where commonwealth beat out statehood was on the issue of taxes. About 42 percent of the island's public felt that the status quo could best avoid tax increases, while only 24 percent thought the same for statehood, and only 5 percent believed independence was capable of accomplishing the same goal ("Goza" 1993: 6). As state residents, Puerto Ricans would have to pay federal income taxes.

Of these two major arenas of public life, which is of greater importance, economics or culture? The same survey asked how many considered these to be "extremely important" issues. Health services and education were judged as extremely important by 90 and 95 percent of those surveyed, respectively. Maintaining the supremacy of Spanish and the Olympic team were considered extremely important issues by 70 and 60 percent, respectively ("Goza" 1993: 6). On an island where the overwhelming majority speak Spanish and there is no government-led assimilationist policy, culture is not usually seen as an endangered trait. In contrast, concerns about education and health care are pressing.

Similar results were found in other polls conducted that asked Puerto Ricans about the nexus between the economy and the status dilemma (see table 4.2). Respondents to this survey were asked to speculate on what would happen in five years to unemployment, the economy, quality of life, and crime rates under the three typical status options. By far statehood fared the best of the three status alternatives. More thought that unemployment would decrease (37 percent) than increase (26 percent) under statehood ("La emoción" 1997: 5). A larger segment of the population believed that the economy would strengthen under statehood (50 percent) than under the commonwealth (21 percent). Statehood fared better in the quality of life question. And almost equal numbers felt that crime would increase or decease under statehood. The most dramatic responses pertained to the independence option. Here, 53 percent believed that unemployment

Table 4.2

Survey of How Puerto Rico Would Fare Five Years from Now Under Various Status Options (Percentages)

	Status Options		
Policy	Commonwealth	Statehood	Independence
Unemployment			
Increase	17	26	53
Decrease	18	37	20
Same	63	35	24
Economy			
Strengthen	21	50	9
Weaken	17	22	69
Same	61	26	20
Quality of Life			
Increase	19	42	11
Decrease	15	23	62
Same	64	33	25
Crime			
Increase	19	24	45
Decrease	11	26	10
Same	67	47	42

Source: "La emoción" 1997: 5.

would increase, 69 percent assumed that the economy would weaken, and respondents also speculated that crime would increase while quality of life would decrease were Puerto Rico to become a separate country ("La emoción" 1997: 5).

Since the abolition of assimilationist policies, the aforementioned factors have intersected to create an electorate more supportive of closer ties to the United States (see table 4.3).[5] This is a remarkable change given the strength of separatist and autonomist parties in the 1940s. The first elections under the Commonwealth constitution represented the electoral apex of both the PIP and PPD. At this time separatists retained official opposition status. The first years of the Commonwealth witnessed radical changes. Puerto Ricans were increasingly employed by American multinational corporations, and the United States came to represent material prosperity.

Separatism's decline was matched and surpassed by the rise of the statehood movement. Some claim that statehood has seen continuous growth

Table 4.3

Electoral Support for Gubernatorial Candidates of Independence, Commonwealth, and Statehood Parties, 1952–1996 (Percentages)

Election Year	Independence	Commonwealth	Statehood	Nonstatus
1952	19.0	64.9	16.2	
1956	12.5	62.6	25.0	
1960	3.1	58.2	32.1	6.6
1964	2.7	59.4	34.7	3.3
1968	2.8	52.1	45.1	
1972	4.4	51.5	44.1	
1976	6.4	45.3	48.3	
1980	5.7	47.0	47.2	
1984	3.6	47.8	44.6	4.1
1988	5.5	48.7	45.8	
1992	4.2	45.9	49.9	
1996	3.8	44.5	51.1	

Source: Bayrón 1989: 349; Comisión Estatal 1993a: 1; Comisión Estatal 1996: 1.

in support into the 1990s (Grosfoguel 1997: 57). Electoral statistics contradict that claim and demonstrate that this movement witnessed its most precipitous growth in the 1960s (Rivera, A. 1996: 98). The period since 1968, when Puerto Rico began its current phase as a two-and-a-half–party system, has been one of remarkable electoral stability and near parity of the PPD and the PNP (Rivera et al. 1991: 178).[6] While it has not amassed more than 7 percent of the vote in decades, the PIP represents one of the conventional status options. Also, the presence of three parties makes winning islandwide races by a majority a rarity.

Modeling the Puerto Rican Electorate

While scholars noted an increase in the political relevance of nonstatus issues (Anderson, R. 1983: 25), status preferences still explain voter choices more than any other single factor (Barreto and Eagles 2000). Parties that fail to identify themselves in term of the status question—such as the Partido Acción Cristiana of the 1960s or the Partido Renovación Puertorriqueña of the 1980s—usually last an election or two. The political tug-of-war jolting society along a center-periphery divide facilitates visu-

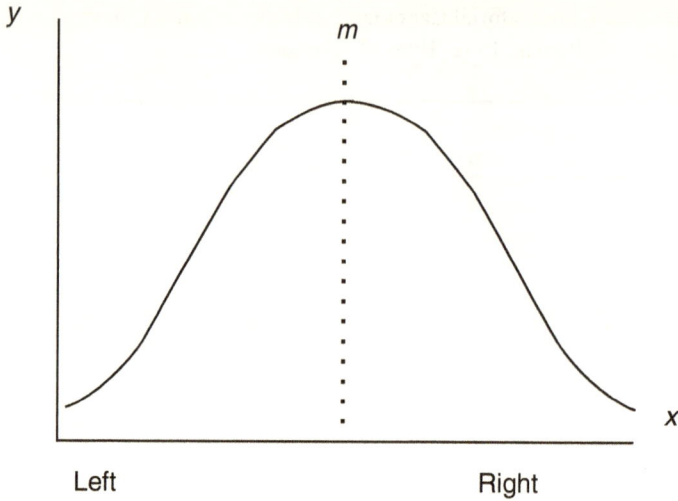

Fig. 4.1. A Downsian Spatial Model of a Unimodal Electorate

alizing island partisan preferences along a single ideological dimension. The PIP is at the pro-periphery end of the ideological spectrum. On the pro-center end we find the PNP; somewhere in the middle is the PPD. To conceptualize Puerto Rican politics we begin by reviewing some classic models.

Downs (1957: 118) described an ideal political society divided along a conventional left-right divide (see figure 4.1). Along the x-axis we have a traditional ideological spectrum, which runs from the extreme left to the far right. Using conventional terminology, these diametrically opposing ideologies would be represented by communists and fascists, respectively. The curve's height, or y-axis, represents the number or percentage of voters in an electoral system. A dashed line running down the middle of the ideological spectrum represents the locus of the centrist or moderate voters. Centrist voters in this model, the highest point in the curve, represent the largest segment of the voting public. Downs drew this representation as a normal curve. As with all normal distributions, the dashed line divides the curve into two symmetrical halves, which also represents the convergence points of all three fundamental measures of central tendency: the mode, median, and mean (Vogt 1993: 155). Moving toward the ideological extremes, the proportion of the voting public declines precipitously. Downs used this model to explain why office seekers moderate their policies. By moving toward the center, politicians endeavor to maximize their electoral appeal and thus increase their likelihood of winning elections.

Downs also postulated that electorates could be distributed in other ways. In figure 4.2, the two largest voter blocs diverge from the ideological center. Those running for office here would promote, contrary to the previous model, more extremist policies (Downs 1957: 119). Given a polarized polity, candidates will turn up the rhetoric and make more extremist statements in their quest for increased popular support. As in the previous model, the vote-chasing politician is simply responding to the existing ideological conditions. Those bucking the prevailing political winds will likely lose the next election. Electoral success dictates that candidates understand their polity.

Before attempting to model the electorate, we must understand whether partisan support in Puerto Rico is discrete or continuous. Are the status alternatives in Puerto Rico—statehood, commonwealth, and independence—specific and fixed points along an ideological continuum, or are they conventional points of reference situated along an unbroken axis? The answer to this vital question is provided by Rivera's treatise. At the heart of his opus is the maxim that in Puerto Rico *todos somos autonomistas*—we are all autonomists (Rivera, A. 1996: 54). This is not a statement of personal ideological preference, rather an observation that within the traditional ideological camps there are those who weight devotion to the island and affinity toward the United States to varying degrees.

We can begin with Rivera's survey of Puerto Rican identity. Individuals were asked to label themselves as *"puertorriqueñistas fuertes"* (strong Puerto Ricanists), pro-American, or something in between the two—a cultural hybrid (Rivera, A. 1996: 208). Presumably the strong Puerto Ricanists valued their national identity and culture more than their U.S. citizenship. In contrast, those who considered themselves politically American cherished their citizenship more than their ethnic identity. The hybrids were mixed. The majority of all respondents—56.6 percent—considered themselves strong Puerto Ricanists, 27.8 percent said they were hybrids, and only 15.9 percent claimed they were culturally pro-American (Rivera, A. 1996: 208). Certainly these public opinion survey results do not harmonize with election results during the commonwealth era (see table 4.3). If cultural factors alone determined electoral preferences, the PIP would advance from the smallest party on the island to a political machine sweeping the electoral map. These preferences were broken down on

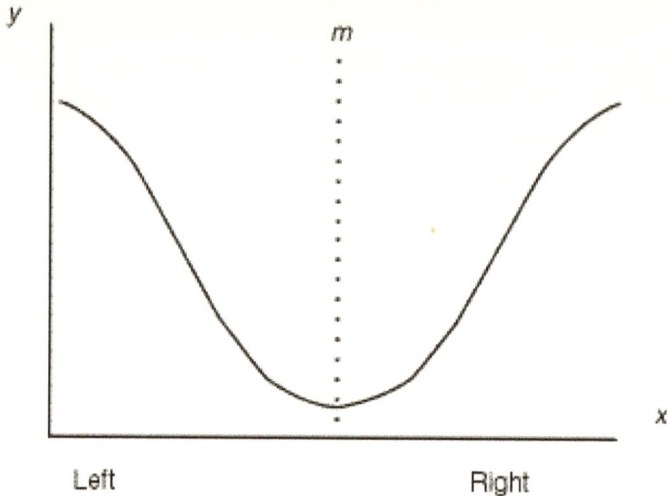

Fig. 4.2. A Downsian Spatial Model of a Bimodal Electorate

the basis of how respondents would vote in a forthcoming status plebiscite (see table 4.4).

Unremarkably, almost 80 percent of independence advocates and 61 percent of commonwealth supporters considered themselves strong Puerto Ricanists. Yet, 43.5 percent of statehood backers identified themselves as *fuertes puertorriqueñistas;* 26 percent of statehood supporters regarded themselves as politically American (Rivera, A. 1996: 209). Within the pro-statehood camp there are more cultural nationalists than cultural assimilationists. This may help to explain the electoral success of the PNP as opposed to its uncompromising forerunner, the assimilationist Partido Estadista Republicano.

Table 4.4

Relative Importance of Puerto Rican Nationhood and American Citizenship in Terms of How One Would Vote in an Upcoming Status Plebiscite (Percentages)

	Independence	Commonwealth	Statehood	Undecided
Strong Puerto Ricanist	79.2	60.8	43.5	63.4
Hybrid	11.1	27.6	30.5	27.4
Politically American	9.7	11.6	26.0	9.2

Source: Rivera, A. 1996: 209.

Fascinatingly, almost 10 percent of *independentistas* value their U.S. citizenship more than their Puerto Rican nationhood. While almost 80 percent of independence supporters classified themselves as *fuertes puertorriqueñistas*, the majority of separatists also favored maintaining their U.S. citizenship (Rivera, A. 1996: 211). Logically, PIP President Berríos Martínez asked Congress that the inhabitants of an independent Puerto Rico should be allowed to retain their American citizenship (U.S. House 1995: 54). Even among separatists there is a strong centripetal attraction that entices them away from the pro-periphery ideological endpoint.

Moving toward the middle of the x-axis we encroach on the domain of commonwealth supporters. Here we discover that 40 percent of those who believe in the Estado Libre Asociado prefer greater autonomy from the United States. On the other hand, 29 percent favor going in the opposite direction and establishing closer ties with the American government; only 26 percent support the status quo (Rivera, A. 1996: 381). Astonishingly, around 10 percent of those who vote PNP at election time select the commonwealth status during status plebiscites (Rivera, A. 1996: 104). Rivera (A. 1996: 104) suggested that many who left the PPD for the PNP in the 1960s still maintain their old autonomist leanings. These Populares who could not vote for the PER of the 1950s found it possible to cast a ballot for the more nationalistic PNP in the 1970s.

This Puerto Rican nationalism—or, using Rivera's term, *lite nationalism*—was at the heart of Ferré's *estadidad jíbara* slogan. In the words of Baltazar Corrada del Río, former PNP mayor of San Juan, "Statehood means political integration, not cultural assimilation" (Corrada 1986: 16). Former PNP governor Carlos Romero-Barceló claimed: "Our duty as Puerto Ricans is to establish beyond any doubt that yes, we want statehood, but that *neither our language nor our culture is negotiable*" [emphasis in the original] (Romero-Barceló 1978: 95). This statement, a logical appeal to an electorate prizing its cultural heritage, helped to move this statehood party closer to the median voter (Rivera, A. 1996: 266). Rivera's research supports the thesis that status preferences in Puerto Rico are continuous, not discrete.

Downs (1957: 121) suggested that societies could be unimodal and skewed, which is an appropriate option for the study of Puerto Rican politics. Models cannot represent every nuance and subtlety and they can change over time. During the early 1950s, Puerto Rico's electoral distribution could almost be described as a normal curve. But a model of post-1968 politics must show a larger percentage of the public favoring increased ties

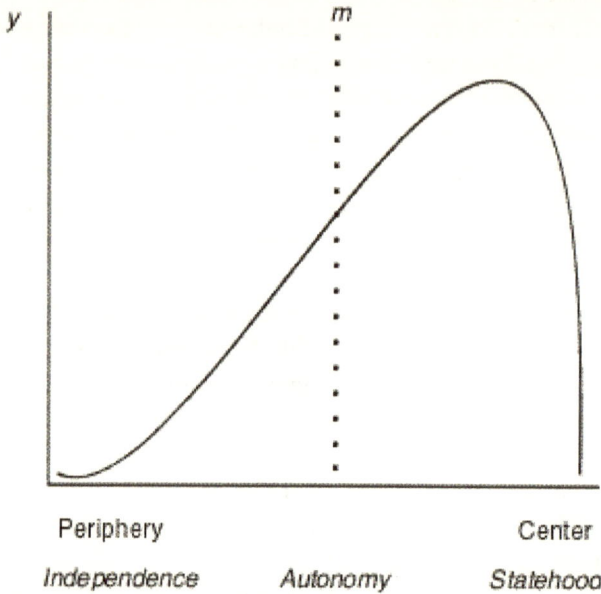

Fig. 4.3. A Spatial Model of Puerto Rican Status Preferences, 1968–1996

with the United States than with separation. Yet even among pro-American voters there is a strong autonomist pull. In sum, Puerto Rico's electorate is distributed in such a way that it appears as a peripherally skewed curve. The mode, the curve's highest peak, is located closer to the pro-center endpoint than the pro-periphery terminus (see figure 4.3).

Figure 4.3 takes into account the aforementioned conditions. How do parties compete with such a skewed electorate? We can emphasize different parts of this model, showing the political spaces where the parties compete. We now add two lines with small dashes—lines s and t (see figure 4.4). Line s, the vertical line closest to the pro-periphery end of the x-axis, represents the conceptual boundary dividing the separatist PIP from the autonomist PPD. Toward the pro-center end lies the second small-dashed line, t, separating the PPD and the pro-statehood PNP. Each party appeals to a different segment of the populace. Yet, efforts to alter a party's platforms are limited by the space already occupied by an ideologically neighboring party.

Different segments of the electorate—the areas under the curve divided by lines s and t—will be distinguished with the letters a, b, and c (see figure 4.4). Letter a connotes the electorate gravitating toward the PIP. Keeping

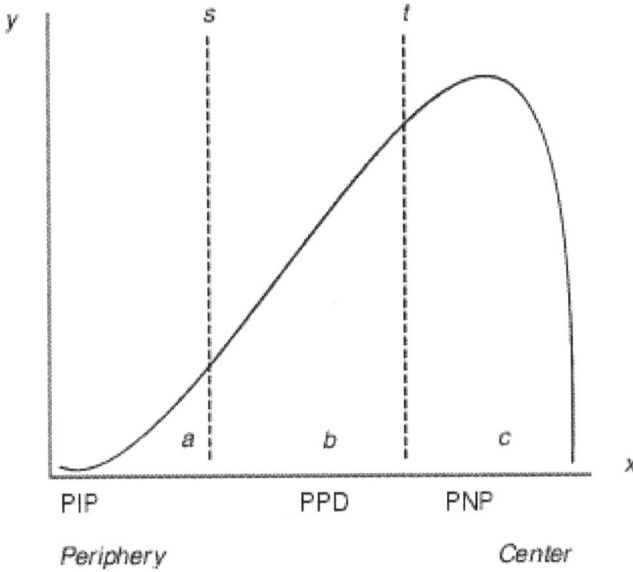

Fig. 4.4. A Spatial Model of the Ideological Distribution of the Puerto Rican Electorate and Political Parties, 1968–1996

true to Rivera's thesis, the largest share of the PIP's base (close to the *s* line) comes from separatists who want to maintain some sort of tie to the United States. We now move to *b*. As the party occupying the ideological middle ground, the PPD has the luxury of emphasizing either greater autonomy or closer links with the United States, depending on the locus of the electoral mean. Employing Rivera's theoretical construct, the area under the curve labeled *b* shows that more Populares want greater autonomy than closer ties to the United States. However, if the PPD moved in a more nationalistic direction, toward line *s*, the party would leave its pro-American faction (the segment of *b* closest to the *t*-line) exposed to a possible takeover by the PNP. In order to maintain both its very nationalist and pro-American wings in check, the PPD rarely promotes any significant changes to the status quo.

We now move to the most pro-center segment of the electorate represented—*c*—the PNP's domain. In keeping with electoral statistics, areas *b* and *c* are roughly equal. Notice that the majority of the PNP's supporters are ideologically closer to the *t*-line than to the pro-center endpoint. Rivera's thesis explains the electoral success of the PNP. Appealing to this electorate required the PNP to insist that political union via statehood and cultural autonomy—*estadidad jíbara*—were compatible.

In the late 1980s PPD Governor Rafael Hernández Colón was presented with the option of abolishing the 1902 bilingualism law and declaring Spanish the only official language. This would be seen as a staunchly nationalistic move and leave the PPD vulnerable to PNP accusations that Popular Democrats were toying with separatism. Downsian notions assert that Governor Hernández Colón should leave the old language law alone. He weighed these consequences in a complex political calculus with implications far beyond his tenure in office.

5

Reviving the Language Debate

Debate over language policy declined significantly after Americanization was eliminated in 1949. However, the 1902 law establishing English and Spanish as official languages remained on the books. To a large degree this statute was essentially forgotten. The commonwealth government and its municipalities, whether under Popular (PPD) or Novoprogresista (PNP) administrations, continued to operate almost exclusively in Spanish. Federal agencies on the island, which were never affected by the 1902 law, continued to perform their duties in English.

After 1949, public schools established a curriculum in Spanish, while many private schools opted to use English as an auxiliary or even the primary medium of instruction. Puerto Ricans live very diglossic lives, employing different languages for disparate functions. Language patterns are shaped by American popular culture, the socioeconomic mobility associated with speaking English fluently, and the need to communicate with English-dominant family members on the U.S. mainland. The merger of these idioms is the patois commonly referred to as *Spanglish*.

Still, language remains a potent political issue. Lacking a tradition of transpartisan teamwork, policy making essentially becomes the purview of the ruling party. Separatist parties usually stood at the forefront of protecting and promoting insular culture. Had the PIP been a formidable electoral force, *independentista* legislators might have been able to advance a new language policy. New Progressives claimed that statehood with Spanish as an official language was possible. Yet, the PNP was certainly not about to eliminate the American vernacular as an official language, whether or not the majority of the island's population could speak it. Combining the PIP's legislative feebleness with the PNP's timidity, changes in language policy would have to come from the autonomist Popular Democrats.

On several occasions the PPD had the opportunity to enact a new language policy and each time the party declined. Attempts to change language policy were met by PNP charges that unilingualism was a covert attempt to promote separatism. Yet, by the late 1980s there were signs that the PPD might consider adjusting this stance. Language became a tool in the larger conflict over Puerto Rico's relationship with the United States.

Attempts to Change Language Policy in the 1970s and 1980s

Where language reinforces ethnic membership, nationalists frequently attempt to revisit language policies. We find cultural nationalists leading these symbolic battles. Basque, Catalan, and Québécois separatists spearheaded drives to change their respective society's cultural policies. Beyond state minorities, nationalistic sentiments are also found among ethnic majorities. A dominant group—the *staatvolk*—often couch cultural agendas in ways that ostensibly promote the state's interests (Connor 1994: 201). The federal government's Americanization program in Puerto Rico was one such example.

Parties may not have the electoral strength to pass their legislative agenda; nonetheless, they often find drafting symbolic bills worthwhile. Even if a new cultural policy fails to win approval, or even emerge out of a legislative committee, the ensuing public discussion refortifies social norms, cultural myths, and hegemonic beliefs. Additionally, such measures frequently serve to publicly reinforce the bond between a party and the defense of the local culture.

Months before the United States celebrated the bicentennial of its revolution, PIP leader Rubén Berríos Martínez introduced a bill in the territorial Senate to rescind the 1902 language law. The bill's long preamble recounted the historic struggle to protect the Spanish vernacular (see appendix 2). His bill would have proclaimed Spanish the official medium of government operations and the island's symbolic language and mandated the use of Spanish in various private sector arenas, and it would have formally established Spanish as the medium of instruction in the public and private schools. The reach of this proposal is reminiscent of a more famous bill that became law in 1977—Quebec's Charter of the French Language, also known as Bill 101 (Barreto 1998: chap. 9). The Berríos Martínez language bill quietly passed away in the Asamblea Legislativa without serious debate.

Did the Spanish language need any special protection in 1976? According to a noted PPD political activist, Puerto Rico's culture proved its resilience by surviving the furor of the Americanization policy (Benítez 1976: 7A). In 1976 the PPD was unwilling to support Berríos Martínez's proposal. Rather than chastise the PIP, the ruling Popular Democrats simply ignored the entire legislative enterprise. Barring PPD support for the Berríos Martínez initiative, the PNP did not attempt to link the Populares with the PIP's language proposal.

Two figures affiliated with the Partido Popular Democrático stood out in the attempt to alter language policy. One was Senator Sergio Peña Clos and the other was Education Secretary Awilda Aponte Roque. Senator Sergio Peña Clos was one of the most radical autonomists within the PPD. For a brief stint in the early 1980s he served as senate vice president. By the late 1990s, Peña Clos switched partisan affiliations and joined the ranks of the pro-statehood PNP. In spite of such a momentous change, Peña Clos claimed that he remained a staunch autonomist. Commenting on his ideological leanings and his assessment of the commonwealth status, he said that "all my life I have been a sovereigntist. I have believed in the freedom of my people—in statehood or independence. What I cannot believe in is the colony and this [commonwealth] is a colony" (Peña Clos 1998).[1]

Early in 1982, Senator Peña Clos introduced two language bills. He felt that the Spanish language needed the protection of the local government. The first would have prohibited the use of English as the medium of public school instruction (see appendix 3). A second would have applied the same regulations to private schools (Fernández, I. 1982: 8). Under the two proposed statutes English remained a part of the curriculum in both public and private schools. Reflecting on these matters almost two decades later, Senator Peña Clos still refers to the Spanish language in very passionate terms: "Well, I have always believed that children learn more and better in the language they suckle from their mother's bosom, that which is spoken in their home" (Peña Clos 1998).[2] Language reform was but one component in Peña Clos's autonomist agenda. At about the same time, he suggested that the federal courts on the island should be dissolved and that the constitutionality of any language law should be determined by the island's judiciary (Castro Pereda 1982a: 10).

Soon after Peña Clos announced these initiatives his opponents launched a counteroffensive. His detractors celebrated the benefits of knowing both English and Spanish. They also accused him of hypocrisy, noting that Senator Peña Clos had attended the University of Missouri. He would have been unable to study in the United States were it not for knowing English (Licha 1982: 27). Attorneys for the Asociación de Escuelas Privadas de Puerto Rico (AEPPR—Puerto Rico Association of Private Schools) claimed that the Peña Clos bill was meant to restrict the use of English in private schools. This was, they contended, bad public policy and unconstitutional according to the U.S. Supreme Court's decision in *Meyers vs. Nebraska*[3] (Castro Pereda 1982b: 28).

Adding to the fray, statehood supporters attacked Senator Sergio Peña Clos and his pro-commonwealth party. According to statehood activists these proposals were separatist in inspiration, and a veiled attempt was made to derail their annexationist movement (Miranda 1982: 31). For statehood supporters, meddling with the role of English in the classroom was an affront to their movement. Gestures are important, and the PNP feared that even a symbolic language law could be seen in Washington as a show of defiance and emphasize to federal legislators, most of whom knew little about Puerto Rico, the cultural distinctiveness of this Caribbean territory. Concerned that Peña Clos's bills would be seen as radical policy making, the PPD-led Senate dropped both of his proposals (Castrodad 1982: 18). Rhetorically, statehood proponents branded any change in official bilingualism proposed by Populares as a first step toward independence. Given the low level of support for separation, such an insinuation could spell electoral trouble.

A few years later the language controversy resurfaced in a different form. Awilda Aponte Roque was the secretary of education in 1986 during Rafael Hernández Colón's second term as governor (1985–1989). (Hernández Colón served a four-year term as governor in the early 1970s.) Secretary Aponte Roque discussed a number of educational reforms; one sought to *puertorriqueñizar* (Puerto Ricanize) the public education system. Studies found schoolchildren lacking basic skills, including proficiency in their mother tongue. She proposed delaying the teaching of English until the fourth grade, while Spanish was reinforced and new courses on Puerto Rican history were introduced at all levels (Olavarria 1986a: 3).

With enthusism the AMPR endorsed this plan (Olavarria 1986b: 11). As the island's largest teachers' union, the AMPR's endorsement carried considerable weight in pedagogical circles. Soon thereafter the rival Federación de Maestros de Puerto Rico (FMPR, Teacher's Federation of Puerto Rico)—the island's second largest teachers' union—also gave this proposal its seal of approval (Sánchez, L. 1986: 5). Private schools reacted differently. The Puerto Rican Episcopal Conference expressed a profound concern with extending the new policy to Catholic schools (Varela 1986b: 5). Bishop Fremiot Torres Oliver said that, if enacted, this reform would "create very serious problems" for parochial schools (Torres, I. 1986: 3). Again the AEPPR proclaimed that it would challenge this policy just as it had fought Senator Peña Clos's proposal four years earlier (Ortiz 1986: 5). As was the case with Peña Clos's 1982 education bills, statehood supporters attacked the PPD for attempting to impair their movement. In a flutter of Cold War rhetoric, the PPD was accused of sympathizing with *independentistas* and communists (Fernández, I. 1986: 41).

Legislative reaction to Aponte Roque's proposal varied by partisan affiliation. Sergio Peña Clos supported the secretary's initiative (Penchi 1986: 10). Yet, Gladys Rosario de Galarza, PPD member and chair of the Senate's Education Commission, opposed the Aponte plan. Senator Rosario, a former public school teacher, stated that "we cannot fortify Spanish by debilitating English" (Varela 1986c: 10). It was also rejected by the Popular Speaker of the House of Representatives José Ronaldo Jarabo—commonly known in political circles as "Rony"—and it was censured by San Juan's PNP mayor Baltazar Corrada del Río (Varela 1986a: 11). In the eyes of Corrada del Río, this was a "separatist" plan motivated by the government's desire to "indoctrinate" the island's youth (Estrada Resto 1986: 5). After assessing the reactions of various sectors, this PPD administration decided to drop the Aponte Roque plan entirely (Quiñones 1986: 3).

Aponte Roque's attempt to institute school reform died early in 1986. Later that spring, Senator Sergio Peña Clos tried once more to change language policy. Rather than focusing on the medium of instruction, he, along with fellow PPD Senator Antonio Fas Alzamora, drafted a new bill that simply declared Spanish Puerto Rico's official language (see appendix 4). It had the advantage of overturning the 1902 Official Languages Act while leaving educational policy untouched. While acknowledging that Spanish was Puerto Rico's unquestioned vernacular, Governor Hernández Colón flatly rejected this bill ("RHC rechaza" 1986: 16). Popular Democrats treated language reform like the plague in the 1970s and 1980s. They were not philosophically opposed to such a measure.

While the Peña Clos bills and the Aponte proposals were debated, Miguel Hernández Agosto led the Popular Democrats in the Asamblea Legislativa's upper chamber. Looking back at these initiatives, the former senate president remarked:

> In fact, other bills were presented. And I believe that the other bills did not move forward to the point of becoming law because of a kind of political sluggishness in the sense they not be understood as a nationalist transition, a goal. And that was attributed to fears within the then-governing party [the PPD]—the party that I belong to. In fact, it's curious that one of the authors of a bill establishing Spanish as the [official] language is the current Senator Sergio Peña Clos. And that

bill was not dealt with fundamentally due to political fears that came from the highest leadership of the party—in other words, from Governor Rafael Hernández Colón himself.[4] (Hernández Agosto 1998)

Governor Hernández Colón concurred with the former senate president. The former leader of the Partido Popular Democrático acknowledged that electoral concerns prevented the party from diving into the language controversy. "From the [nineteen] forties until ninety-one, when the law you referred to was passed, well, there were a number of bills that were presented before the Legislative Assembly to make Spanish the only official language. None of these bills flourished because it was understood that it was better—more politically convenient for the government in power— not to touch the topic" (Hernández Colón 1998b).[5]

If the PPD avoided the language issue for so long, why did it plunge into the quandary in the early 1990s? Changes in attitude resulted from the 1988 U.S. elections and the federal government's commitment to address the status question. Governor Hernández Colón would face an administration in Washington that was less than sympathetic to his cherished commonwealth status.

The 1988 U.S. Presidential Elections

Toward the end of his second term as governor, Rafael Hernández Colón contemplated tackling the status predicament. This was a fairly risky endeavor, since the end result of a status referendum might not bode well for the PPD's preferred constitutional arrangement. However, members of the Partido Popular Democrático began to publicly criticize the level of autonomy accorded to Puerto Rico under the 1952 Constitution. Logically, Hernández Colón did not want to ask Washington for more autonomy than it was willing to concede. Doing so could prove humiliating and it might cast further doubts on the legitimacy of the Commonwealth, thus making the "colony" label stick more conspicuously than before. Moreover, requests for autonomy could be interpreted as a move toward separation. Hernández Colón did not rule out convening a constitutional assembly.

Governor Hernández Colón wanted to modify the Estado Libre Asociado, not substitute it. Thus he categorically rejected the semisovereign "Associated Republic" status accorded to the former trust territories of the Marshall Islands and the Federated States of Micronesia (Varela 1988: 6).

The governor implied that expanding the Commonwealth's authority would be much easier with a Democrat in the White House (Viseras 1988: 8). The PPD's de facto spokesman in Washington, Resident Commissioner Jaime Fuster, categorically affirmed that his party's plans to revisit the status question were tied to the fortunes of the Democratic Party's presidential nominee—Governor Michael Dukakis of Massachusetts (Berríos, N. 1988a: 8).

The relationship between governors Dukakis and Hernández Colón, one that started when the two worked together in the National Governors' Association, was a decisive factor in the actions of Puerto Rico's delegation to the 1988 Democratic National Convention. Despite the fact that insular Puerto Ricans cannot vote in the U.S. general elections, the two major mainland parties hold presidential primaries in the territories, which send delegations to their respective national conventions. In 1988 Jesse Jackson upset Michael Dukakis and won Puerto Rico's Democratic presidential primaries (Suárez 1988b: D31).

This was a nonbinding primary. Bypassing the primary's outcome, the top leadership of the PPD—including Governor Rafael Hernández Colón and Senate President Miguel Hernández Agosto—came out forcefully behind the Dukakis candidacy. Only days before the primary, Hernández Agosto won the local leadership of the mainland Democratic Party in a bitter race against his pro-statehood contender, former governor Carlos Romero-Barceló (Suárez 1988a: D22). That victory gave the PPD leadership the muscle to shape the island's delegation to the Democratic National Convention. Not surprisingly, the overwhelming majority of Puerto Rico's delegation to the Democratic National Convention backed Dukakis over Jackson ("Dukakis" 1988: D26).

Strong backing of the Dukakis candidacy led some to perceive the Massachusetts governor as a zealous proponent of the island's commonwealth status. Governor Dukakis did envision this status as an arrangement between the peoples of Puerto Rico and the United States. He admired the close relationship between the PPD's founder, Luis Muñoz Marín, and President John F. Kennedy. The Massachusetts governor was confident that this Spanish-speaking territory could facilitate U.S.–Latin American relations (Dukakis 1998). In contrast to Reagan's belligerent policy toward Latin America—as the conflicts in El Salvador, Grenada, and Nicaragua attest—Dukakis foresaw his administration fomenting greater cooperation with its neighbors.

Good relations with Hernández Colón did not imply, however, that Dukakis's support for the status quo was absolute. Without a doubt Governor

Dukakis was open to the possibility of enhancing Puerto Rico's autonomy, but only if it were supported by the island's electorate. Discussing Governor Hernández Colón's autonomist proposal, Michael Dukakis commented: "I obviously would have wanted to be reasonably assured that he was reflecting majority opinion in Puerto Rico" (Dukakis 1998). At the same time he had no problem with admitting the island as a member state of the union. Touching on Puerto Rico's distinct culture and its relationship to the United States, he said, "why the linguistic issue should in any way block statehood if the people of Puerto Rico wanted statehood, has always been a mystery to me" (Dukakis 1998). Both George Bush and Michael Dukakis were open to the idea of admitting Puerto Rico as the fifty-first state. The biggest difference between the two was their willingness to expand the Commonwealth's autonomy. Dukakis saw no problem with this, given evidence of popular support, while George Bush was firmly entrenched in the pro-statehood camp.

Following the 1988 elections, Luis A. Ferré—the PNP's founder and head of the island's Republican Party—met with President-elect Bush. Ferré announced that George Bush intended to ask Congress for a federally backed referendum on the status question (Berríos, N. 1988b: 4). It was rumored that an emissary from the presidential transition team delivered a message to Hernández Colón outlining Bush's plans (Luciano 1989: 4). At his third inaugural speech, in January 1989, Rafael Hernández Colón stunned the public and the PPD leadership by announcing his support for a status plebiscite in the coming term (Meléndez 1998: 164). Hernández Colón reiterated his desire to maintain a permanent relationship with the United States and his opposition to an "Associated Republic" status (Luciano 1989: 4).

Senate PNP leader Roberto Rexach Benítez and former governor Carlos Romero-Barceló felt that Hernández Colón was pressured into a status plebiscite by George Bush (Berríos, N. 1989: 6; Penchi 1989: 8). To this day, most Puerto Ricans are convinced that the president-elect's announcement was the prime catalyst for launching the 1989–91 quest for a federal plebiscite. It is possible that Bush's investiture was the last straw pushing Hernández Colón into status deliberations. Yet, it would be disingenuous to discount the governor's input.

Recalling a conversation with Governor Hernández Colón during his run for the White House, Michael Dukakis noted that his Puerto Rican counterpart was already contemplating a status plebiscite. "I believe we had some conversations at that time about a prospective plebiscite in which he was going to place this enhanced Commonwealth in the ballot. The statehood people would put their proposal up there, and the *independentistas* would put their proposal there. And I think he was reasonably confident at that point that he could win substantial support" (Dukakis 1998). While he may not have publicly voiced his ideas, Dukakis confirmed that Hernández Colón seriously considered the issue long before the 1988 general elections.

Act One—A Proposed Federal Referendum

Thanks to Hernández Colón's speech, Puerto Rico was already abuzz with talk about the status question. For the American public the news came in George Bush's first address to the Congress as president, when he said: "I have long believed that the people of Puerto Rico should have the right to determine their own political future. Personally, I favor Statehood. But I ask the Congress to take the necessary steps to let the people decide in a referendum" ("Bush's Address" 1989: 278). Some suggested that his statehood endorsement was less a genuine backing of this ideal and more of an easy way to repay his Puerto Rican supporters. In the end Congress would define the referendum's parameters in keeping with an assessment of how these alternative constitutional arrangements would affect long-term U.S. interests (Meléndez 1998: 166). A study of the 1989–91 plebiscite process proposed that Congress was alarmed with the perceived growth of the island's statehood movement (Colón Morera 1993: 167–68).

The U.S. Senate began holding hearings on the proposed referendum in the summer of 1989. Language, as a component of the status debate, came up on the first day of the hearings. PIP President Rubén Berríos Martínez wasted little time in outlining some basic facts that Congress could not ignore when discussing Puerto Rico's status. Distinguishing the linguistic plight of ethnic Puerto Ricans living on the U.S. mainland from their insular brethren, Berríos Martínez pointed out that on the whole, insular Puerto Ricans were not bilingual (U.S. Senate 1989a: 186). His comments were backed by federal census data.

Berríos Martínez's comments were followed by a heated exchange between Carlos Romero-Barceló and Rafael Hernández Colón. The two protagonists laid a series of charges against one another in a vicious style that has, sadly, become the norm in Puerto Rican politics. PNP leader Romero-Barceló tried to portray his supporters, in contrast to the PPD, as loyal Americans. Romero-Barceló acquainted Congress with the proposal by Hernández Colón's secretary of education to eliminate the teaching of English in the first grades (U.S. Senate 1989a: 188). He also brought up Peña Clos's language bills. Romero-Barceló said: "There are legislators in his [Hernández Colón's] party who have submitted bills precisely for making Spanish the only official language in Puerto Rico. So, what they would like to do is eliminate English and create a greater difference between Puerto Rico and the rest of the nation" (U.S. Senate 1989a: 188).

If Romero-Barceló tried to portray the Populares as less than loyal, Hernández Colón attempted to depict the PNP as less than honest. Governor Hernández Colón asserted that the PNP was trying to peddle one image of statehood in the United States and a different one in Puerto Rico. Like Berríos Martínez, Governor Hernández Colón reminded senators of the federal government's attempt to culturally assimilate the island via Americanization earlier in the twentieth century, a historic period frequently overlooked by statehood supporters (U.S. Senate 1989a: 188). The PPD leader also pointed to PNP assertions that even after statehood, Puerto Rico could maintain its separate Olympic team and the primacy of Spanish would be ensured (U.S. Senate 1989a: 212).

Chairing these hearings was Senator J. Bennett Johnston of Louisiana. On the second day of the hearings he drilled Carlos Romero-Barceló on the official language controversy (U.S. Senate 1989a: 364–65). As a delegate from a state with a long-standing interest in language issues, Johnston wanted to clarify Romero-Barceló's proposal.[6] In keeping with his admonitions from the 1970s (Romero-Barceló 1978), the PNP leader wanted to phrase the congressional definition of statehood in such a way that it guaranteed the role of Spanish in Puerto Rico (U.S. Senate 1989a: 366). PNP founder Luis Ferré reemphasized Romero-Barceló's point: "Spanish would have to be one of the official languages of Puerto Rico if Puerto Rico became a state of the Union" (U.S. Senate 1989a: 369). Senator Johnston asked Romero-Barceló what the reaction would be to a clause in the referendum bill stating that henceforth English would be Puerto Rico's official language. Romero-Barceló responded: "That would be unacceptable to me" and "it would be unacceptable to the people of Puerto Rico" (U.S. Senate 1989a: 369).

Insistence by statehood leaders on protecting the island's vernacular confirmed the strength of cultural nationalism in Puerto Rico. Language and Puerto Rican identity were inextricably linked to a degree that could be described in Gramscian terms as culturally hegemonic (Barreto 1998: 124). It also reinforced the Riverist thesis that in Puerto Rico, *todos somos autonomistas*—"we are all autonomists." But Senator Johnston had a different interpretation of Romero-Barceló's request: "Isn't the real effect of this designed to protect Puerto Rico from a future amendment, either to the Constitution or to the laws, that would specify English as the official language?" (U.S. Senate 1989a: 368).

Whether he realized it or not, Senator Johnston shifted the discussion's focus from an analysis of Puerto Rican identity and its impact on the United States to divulging certain aspects about American identity and Puerto Rico's compatibility with that cultural model. Outside of government spheres, ideals live and thrive in civil society. Norms are cherished, protected, and conveyed to future generations with no need for directives from the authorities. At times such beliefs persevere *despite* government officials. There was a strong American identity, and Senator Johnston noted: "While it may be unacceptable in Latin America and in Puerto Rico to say English is the official language, it may be unacceptable to a lot of people up here to say Spanish is the official language which leads me to ask if there is not much in this debate, why not just be silent on the question, just leave it out altogether" (U.S. Senate 1989a: 370).

It is rather fascinating to see how a small clause in a federal statute dealing with an overseas U.S. territory had the potential to ignite such a contentious debate. This was a controversy that Senator Johnston wanted to avoid. His primary mission was to secure federal backing for a status referendum. Whether or not it was a slip of the tongue, Senator Johnston revealed that to be Latino or Hispanic is to be one of "them" and not one of "us." As this senator from Louisiana noted: "by putting it in this legislation, then you get the whole focus of debate in the Congress and out in the 50 states about how different Puerto Rico is and that it is Hispanic. It doesn't want to be American. They want to insist on their separateness. I think it just emphasizes separateness" (U.S. Senate 1989a: 371).

When weighing strategies that fulfill long-term goals, one is apt to reassess the tactic of the moment. The goal of the pro-statehood movement on the island was, and remains, Puerto Rico's full and permanent incorporation into the American federation. Selling statehood in Puerto Rico was one concern. Yet these same leaders could not ignore the fact that any statehood petition had to pass both houses of Congress. Guaranteeing a secure place for the Spanish language under statehood was a fundamental element in the PNP's *estadidad jíbara* thesis, but the issue was exceedingly contentious in Congress (Meléndez 1993a: 270–71). Attempting to appease Congress, Romero-Barceló agreed with Senator Johnston's recommendation to omit references to an official language under statehood (U.S. Senate 1989a: 370). Acting Deputy Attorney General Edward Dennis agreed that silence on the language issue was the best course of action (U.S. Senate 1989c: 64).

Not all statehood proponents agreed. Miriam Ramírez de Ferrer insisted that some reference to language was indispensable—even if only a symbolic reference tucked in the bill's preamble:

> We appreciate Senator Johnston's recommendations in the June 2 hearings regarding that the language issue presented this way could affect smooth passage of legislation. This, however, has been the target of anti-statehooders who have misconstrued the incident and as you can see by the Newspaper headlines included in the Annexes, it is claimed that under Statehood, the people of Puerto Rico would not be able to speak Spanish. . . . Since we also share your desire that this process move forward smoothly, we suggest placing this language in the preamble Bill S.712, as it appears in our proposal. (U.S. Senate 1989b: 266)

Leaders of other parties and organizations were adamant that the issue would have to be faced directly and spelled out explicitly. Legislation does not exist in a vacuum and an integral part of history is the forlorn Americanization policy. Reminding senators of this initiative, Resident Commissioner Jaime Fuster insisted that: "There is no way that a meaningful referendum can be held in Puerto Rico without squarely addressing the question of Federal intervention and influence regarding the Spanish language under statehood" (U.S. Senate 1989b: 8).

On the American domestic front, organizations dedicated to making English the official language of the country also insisted on clearly defining the statehood option and its linguistic responsibilities. In justifying this requisite condition for permanent union, these groups cited congressional precedence. Representing the group U.S. English, Luis Acle told the Senate: "we feel it would be badly misleading for the people of Puerto Rico to vote in the plebiscite thinking that any language other than English can be the official language of a State in the Union" (U.S. Senate 1989c: 365). His group wanted to emphasize that proficiency in the English language represented a substantial move toward fully integrating into American society (U.S. Senate 1989c: 405). The diplomatic tone of U.S. English's statements contrast with more alarmist assertions made by other groups. On behalf of the group English First, Gerda Bikales warned Congress that with Puerto Rico as a state there existed the real possibility of official bilingualism down the road. As far as this organization was concerned, official bilingualism could become as divisive and destabilizing an issue in the United States as it was in Canada (U.S. Senate 1989c: 377). Political union did not preclude sovereigntists from winning provincial elections in the Francophone province of Quebec over a century after the birth of the Canadian Confederation in 1867. Well into the 1990s, analogies to Quebec resurfaced every time Congress addressed Puerto Rico's status.

Act Two—A Federal Plebiscite

Johnston's referendum bill—S.712—died in the 101st Congress. According to Johnston one of its primary failings was its self-executing clause. If passed, the Puerto Rican people would trigger the enactment of one status option or another. Clearly many in Congress were not willing to give up that power and even less so to the inhabitants of an overseas territory. In an attempt to avoid another failure, Senator Johnston proposed a replacement—S.244 (U.S. Senate 1991: 1). Replacing a referendum with a nonbinding plebiscite changed a meaningful election into, essentially, a glorified beauty contest.

Even eliminating the self-executing language, many of the same issues continued to haunt Senator Johnston's new bill in the 102nd Congress. Concerns over the economic costs of statehood were discussed, as were the consequences of a culturally distinct state with an active separatist movement. Could Puerto Rico become a destabilizing factor in American political life? Warning the U.S. Senate about the possible consequences of a culturally distinct state, PIP leader Rubén Berríos Martínez asked senators to examine current events in a host of countries undergoing ethnic strife: Yugoslavia, Ireland, Spain's Basque region, and Quebec (U.S. Senate 1991: 145). As far as English First was concerned, Puerto Rico was the American counterpart to the Canadian province of Quebec (U.S. Senate 1991: 330). As Berríos Martínez said, the real focus of this debate was the impact that a new status could have on the United States, not on Puerto Rico:

> The real issue for the United States is what type of juridical and political relationship is it willing to venture with the people who constitute a historically distinct nationality inhabiting a separate and distinct territory who speak a different language, who aspire to maintain a separate identity, and who happen, through no choice of their own, to be citizens of the United States. (U.S. Senate 1991: 141)

By this time, straightforward opposition to Johnston's second bill came from within the Senate. Representing the state of Oklahoma, Don Nickles pronounced categorically:

> I will be very open in stating I have some reservations concerning the statehood option. I am not sure that many people in the United States have seriously considered whether having Puerto Rico join the Union as a State is something that we want to do. . . . We have significant differences right now with Puerto Rico, economic differences, cultural differences, geographical differences, language differences that need to be considered, need to be discussed. (U.S. Senate 1991: 105)

Senator Nickles voiced a concern that many of his colleagues shared. Johnston's endeavor to salvage a plebiscite, even omitting the controversial self-execution language, was not enough. As Senator Moynihan of New York noted: "However, despite the urging of President Bush that Congress provide for a referendum which will enable the citizens of Puerto Rico to make such a choice, Congress has not been willing to do so. Congressional resistance arises largely from the question of whether the island should have the option to choose statehood whilst retaining Spanish as an official language" (Moynihan 1993: 73).

Many in the United States opposing statehood fear that to publicly voice their opinion leaves them vulnerable to accusations of racism (Benítez 1998a: 22). Concerned with possible allegations of cultural and ethnic prejudices, many find it easier to attack statehood on economic grounds. Of the three status options, statehood was treated the worst in the 1989–91 congressional deliberations (Rivera, A. 1996: 105). The commonwealth status won, but only by default (Colón Morera 1993: 351). Still, the Popular Democratic leadership was convinced that statehood presented a real threat (Rivera, A. 1996: 379). Assuming that the PPD wanted to cripple the statehood movement, the question was how far to go and whether attacking the PNP's statehood prospects would jeopardize the PPD's chances of electoral success.

6

The Official Language Act of 1991

In this chapter we explore the events surrounding the PPD's decision to repeal the 1902 bilingual act. A member of the legislature, Héctor López Galarza, drafted a symbolic statute declaring Spanish the island's only official language. From the beginning he struggled to convince his fellow party members of the bill's merits. From the beginning there were concerns with the electoral consequences of such a measure. The PPD's leadership chose a go-slow approach. The decision to take the bill out of committee and present it to the governor was tied to congressional deliberations over a federal status referendum. Key members of the ruling PPD wanted to attract congressional attention and they succeeded. What they did not count on was an international spotlight boosting the new language policy statute.

Outside the PIP, a few Populares wanted to undo what they considered a historic anomaly. These individuals saw no logic in an official language law dating back to the early 1900s that gave co-equal status to English, denying Puerto Rico's linguistic reality and cultural identity. Electoral outcomes were not always an integral part of the political calculus of these legislators. Debates over a new language bill in Puerto Rico in the late 1980s corresponded with discussions over federal sponsorship of an islandwide status referendum. Popular wisdom was reaffirmed in this case, where observers of the political scene can say that, unquestionably, *timing was everything.*

The López Galarza Proposal

While Congress debated the island's fate, Héctor López Galarza pondered changing language policy. He was a lifelong member of the Partido Popular Democrático, and his largely rural district included his hometown of Utuado in the central highlands. First elected to the Commonwealth's House of Representatives in 1980, he waited until the spring of 1989 before introducing his language bill. As Representative López Galarza emphasized: "It is not a law of the Popular [Democratic] Party. This should be clear. This is a concern I have had since I was a high school teacher early in the '70s" (López Galarza 1998).[1]

The Spanish language holds a special place in the Puerto Rican pantheon of cultural icons. Political leadership on the island is based on one's ability to communicate in Spanish, not English. Referring to the PNP administration of Pedro Rosselló, governor at the time this interview was conducted, López Galarza (1998) commented: "And Spanish is the official language of Puerto Ricans because as far as I am concerned the official language is that which the government [uses to] communicates with its people. . . . In Puerto Rico even Rosselló does not dare deliver a speech in English."[2]

Héctor López Galarza could not take for granted the support of his party's leadership. Previous attempts to change language policy were turned down by Popular Democrats fearful of the potentially negative electoral consequences. The one forum that Representative López Galarza could count on was the House Commission on Education and Culture—a legislative committee that he chaired.

> Then on March 27, 1989 I submitted a bill which is House Resolution 417. . . . It stays there [in committee] for a while, but I said: no, look, excuse me, I am not doing what was done on previous occasions. Bills dealing with language were proposed only to store them away. And then I decided that we were going to press ahead [with] that bill since I chaired the Education and Culture Commission in the House of Representatives. . . . When I was about to go ahead with it I consulted the speaker of the House of Representatives and then we decided to speak with the governor. (López Galarza 1998)[3]

Bill 417 sought to overturn the status of English as an official language of the Puerto Rican government. Repealing this nearly century-old bilingual statute was also a goal of the proposed Berríos Martínez language bill in 1976 and the Peña Clos–Fas Alzamora language bill submitted a decade later. According to these bills' authors, a government staffed by Spanish-speaking Puerto Ricans did not need to bequeath an official status to any other language. Regardless, those failing to heed the public will often find themselves soon out of office.

López Galarza's proposal did not mandate the government's use of Spanish in all matters. Article 3 allowed the island's government to use languages other than Spanish when necessary or convenient as long as the agency or department in question had the governor's consent (see appendix 5). This provision gave the executive branch maximum flexibility to implement the policy. Bill 417 could be a purely symbolic measure, making few if any changes in the daily operations of the Puerto Rican government. On the other hand, extremely few "Article 3" exceptions could be conferred, making the statute a potent legal instrument affecting the government-to-government relationship between Puerto Rico and the United States.

Not surprisingly, López Galarza's critics sarcastically derided Bill 417 as "Spanish Only" in an attempt to rhetorically juxtapose it to the "English Only" laws passed in numerous mainland jurisdictions. Those opposing Bill 417 also compared it to the legislative agenda of fellow-PPD member Sergio Peña Clos, and they charged López Galarza with a hidden agenda of eliminating English in island schools. The lawmaker categorically rejected these allegations: "We believe, and I am a firm believer, in the need to improve the teaching of English in Puerto Rico. And not only that it [English] be taught but also French and other languages" (López Galarza 1998).[4]

Unlike Peña Clos's proposals, educational reform was not Bill 417's aim. To the contrary, at about the same time lawmakers contemplated López Galarza's initiative, the legislature clarified the role of English as a second language in the public school system, a move backed by all three political parties. Former house speaker Jarabo said:

> In 1990, as a matter of fact, we came back to the language of education in the educational reform bill which was known as the organic act of the Department of Education. There was a joint commission—House and Senate—and the chairmanship of this commission alternated between the House speaker and the Senate president. So in 1990 I was the chairman of the joint commission and we got this very important piece of legislation approved with the votes in the House. The three parties voting for the law. . . . So we established by law that Spanish would be the language of the public school system in Puerto Rico. We also established that one of the prime objectives of the system was that students had to learn, read, and write English. (Jarabo 1998)

Despite this measure's explicit stipulations safeguarding English in schools, the impending debate latched onto the nexus between education, language, socioeconomic status, and the island's relationship with the United States.

The Start of Public and Legislative Debate

Bill 417, introduced in 1989, was finally debated in the House of Representatives the following year. Several noted intellectuals strongly encouraged Representative López Galarza to proceed with hearings (Colón Martínez 1990: 46; Delgado Cintrón 1993: 19; Torres, I. 1990a: 16). However, taking this bill to the next stage was not an easy decision. As López Galarza (1998) noted, "even my advisors told me: that does not politically benefit you."[5]

Since this language bill was penned by a lone lawmaker, there was some question as to how much support it had among the PPD's leadership, the party's backbenchers in the legislature, and the party's rank and file. In the summer of 1990 López Galarza claimed to have the support of the House leadership (Candelas 1990a: 12). Fellow House member Severo Colberg Ramírez—a well-known PPD cultural nationalist—was an early backer (Colberg Ramírez 1990: 27). From outside the legislature a fellow Popular, San Juan Mayor Héctor Luis Acevedo, publicly supported the bill (Torres, I. 1990b: 14). Even with the House's backing there was still the matter of securing Senate approval.

Simultaneously, there was a debate as to whether the bill would be presented as a simple statute or if the proposal should become a constitutional amendment. In 1990 Speaker Jarabo and PIP Representative David Noriega preferred a constitutional amendment (Luciano 1990a: 10). If entrenched in the constitution, the Spanish language proposition would enjoy greater symbolic value than would be the case with a statute. Furthermore, once enshrined in the constitution, future administrations would find changing or eliminating language statutes very difficult. Both Jarabo and Noriega understood that constitutional amendments in Puerto Rico need the support of two-thirds of both legislative chambers and popular approval in a referendum. The very obstacles that deterred overturning a constitutional amendment also made it more difficult to pass in the first place.

A poll conducted in July 1990 showed that statehood was backed by 48 percent, the commonwealth option could count on only 41 percent of the electorate, and independence had the support of about 8 percent ("Al frente" 1990: 5). Two months later, another survey showed statehood unchanged, commonwealth support rose to 44 percent, and about 7 percent wanted independence ("Avanza" 1990: 1).[6] Add to these numbers a July 1990 survey showing that around 43 percent would leave Puerto Rico if it became a separate country ("Miedo" 1990: 5). The PPD leadership knew that fear of independence was a potent tool in the hands of its primary political rival, whose motto was *Estadidad, Seguridad, Progreso*—Statehood, Security, Progress. Bill 417 opponents were ready to brand the PPD as a separatist organization (Luciano 1990b: 22).

On cue the PNP attacked the López Galarza bill soon after the measure was introduced. At first the comments were somewhat muted. Pedro Rosselló, the PNP's vice president at that time, called the bill unnecessary and compared it to the English Only laws in the United States (Cordero 1990: 12). A few days later a Novoprogresista House member used Bill 417 to accuse the Popular leadership of holding "separatist longings" (Fernández, I. 1990: 53). Despite the fact that Bill 417 had no impact on school policies, Carlos Romero-Barceló (1990: 67) charged that López Galarza's bill would downgrade English in public schools and contribute to the widening gap between the public and private school systems. Romero-Barceló also divulged that this bill could encumber the statehood cause in Washington (Cabán, L. 1990a: 8). This PNP leader categorically stated that if elected governor he would undoubtedly work to repeal Bill 417 (Luciano 1990d: 10).

Perhaps these are some of the very reasons why the PIP supported the López Galarza bill in the first place. PIP President Rubén Berríos Martínez was concerned that the status bill debated in Washington did not protect or even recognize Puerto Rican culture under any status alternative (Berríos Martínez 1990: 59). Even Governor Hernández Colón pointed out that the definitions of the statehood option under congressional review made no explicit cultural guarantees (Hernández Colón 1990: 66). Thus, PIP Vice President Fernando Martín suggested that the language bill before the territorial House of Representative could impact the congressional status debates (Delgado, J. 1990: 12). PPD leader Jarabo agreed with Martín's assessment (Luciano 1990c: 5). PIP Representative David Noriega claimed that, if passed, López Galarza's bill would "constitute an inescapable political obstacle for the Statehood movement" (Andreu 1990: 8). Given this possibility, PNP leaders tried to convince legislators that this bill could ignite deep divisions in Puerto Rican society (Cabán, L. 1990b: 10).

Even with the support of the House leadership, Bill 417 needed Senate support. Senate Majority Leader Gilberto Rivera Ortiz refused to endorse the López Galarza initiative (Penchi 1990: 15). Ironically, Senator Sergio Peña Clos, the author of several language initiatives in the 1980s, urged a postponement of the language debate (Candelas 1990b: 8). Peña Clos's lack of enthusiasm caused a furor within the PPD's ranks. PPD Representative Severo Colberg Ramírez accused Peña Clos of betraying his autonomist ideals and inching toward a new partisan affiliation with the PNP (Fernández Colón 1990: 19). Moreover, Representative Colberg Ramírez threatened to run against Senator Peña Clos in the next elections. Indeed, a few years later Peña Clos abandoned his PPD membership and joined the pro-statehood PNP. In the fall of 1990 the PPD was far from a united party on this issue.

At this juncture Governor Hernández Colón refused to give this proposal his seal of approval. Nonetheless, he gave his party's legislators the green light to debate the measure (Luciano 1990c: 5). Hernández Colón, while flatly rejecting any substantive changes in pedagogical language policy, was open to altering the symbolic status of English (Martínez 1990: 11). The PPD leadership wanted the language game to play itself out and they could observe the unfolding results without the risks associated with a public endorsement. Some suggested that the governor could use a language law to antagonize Congress to slam the door shut on statehood (García Passalacqua 1990a: 73).

While the PPD deliberated Bill 417, a rather interesting compromise emerged from the other side of the aisle. PNP Representative Gilberto Moreno Rodríguez drafted what he considered a happy medium between the 1902 law and Bill 417 ("Proyecto" 1990: 18). He proposed declaring Spanish Puerto Rico's "first" official language and English the "second" official language (see appendix 6). Interestingly, San Juan's PPD mayor, Héctor Luis Acevedo, praised Moreno Rodríguez despite the fact that Acevedo backed the López Galarza initiative (Adames 1990: 10). The PPD could now decide to proceed with López Galarza's bill, advance Moreno Rodríguez's alternative, or drop the language matter entirely.

Congressional Plebiscite Deliberations

Just as debate on the language issue escalated, the House leadership in San Juan decided to suspend deliberations on this matter in September 1990 so as not to interfere with congressional status discussions. On September 19 the federal House of Representatives voted 37 to 1 to send its status bill out of committee. At this point Speaker Jarabo suggested that there was not enough time to debate the López Galarza language bill (Luciano 1990e: 6; Varela 1990: 11). Other PPD legislators stated, off the record, that they were worried about how hearings on the language issue in Puerto Rico could affect status deliberations in Congress (Luciano 1990f: 12).

The federal status bill established no cultural safeguards for Puerto Rico under any status option, nor did it spell out any preconditions for any status options (González, M. 1991a: 2). In response, various Puerto Rican organizations presented Congress with a petition. Cultural guarantees topped their agenda. Regardless of the island's final juridio-political relationship with the United States, these groups insisted that Spanish remain Puerto Rico's language and they wanted the federal government to recognize this ("Reafirmarán" 1990: 3A). Leaders of the PIP and PPD penned an open letter to this effect. Remarkably, one of the signatories was PNP Vice President Pedro Rosselló. This was not a popular decision with all statehood supporters, some of whom chastised Rosselló for supporting a PPD- and PIP-led initiative ("Fustigan" 1990: 6A).

What some considered strengths in the federal House bill, ambiguities that facilitated the bill's exodus from committee, others considered flaws. In October 1990 Senator J. Bennett Johnston, chair of the Senate committee deliberating on the Puerto Rican status bill, announced that the House bill, H.R. 4765, was unacceptable. He urged his colleagues to pass a status bill clearly outlining the definitions of the three status options. Johnston could not sway his colleagues to follow suit. Political pundit Juan M. García Passalacqua (1990b: 77) speculated that Senator Johnston resisted the House status bill due to a lack of support from Senate conservatives. Citing several problems, the senator from Louisiana announced that he would wait until the start of the next Congress before introducing another plebiscite bill (Skelly 1990: 4).

The Language Debate Resumes

A requiem for the federal plebiscite bill turned into a joyous bar mitzvah for the López Galarza language initiative. As the chairman of the Commonwealth's House Committee on Education and Culture, Héctor López Galarza announced that his language bill was leaving committee (Luciano 1990g: 12). The House leadership decided not to debate Moreno Rodríguez's ranked-languages plan. Not surprisingly, many Novoprogresista legislators were angry. During the House debate, a PNP delegate voiced his opposition to the proposed statute by delivering remarks in English (Luciano 1990i: 4). In a symbolic counterattack, Speaker Jarabo ruled that legislator out of order for using English. Noting that local speech was riddled with Anglicisms, statehood advocates mockingly asked whether the López Galarza bill was a first step toward *decontam-*

inating Puerto Rican Spanish (Salas 1990: 9A). It was at this stage that, finally, Senator Sergio Peña Clos publicly backed the López Galarza bill (Pastrana 1990: 4).

The Senate's president, Miguel Hernández Agosto, made clear that his chamber would not vote on the language controversy until hearings were held (Luciano 1990h: 10). What were the Senate president's views on language prior to this debate? "We are also proud of our linkage with the United States; English is our second language, and we have conscientiously adapted the best democratic institutions of the United States. But we are not willing to relinquish Spanish as our first language or to change our Hispanic culture for the 'American way of life'" (Hernández Agosto 1986: 29). Preferring a more cautious approach, Miguel Hernández Agosto used the Senate to apply legislative brakes.

There was good reason for concern. A poll published in September 1990 revealed that 77 percent of Puerto Ricans supported two official languages, 22 percent favored declaring Spanish the exclusive idiom, and 1 percent preferred to make English the island's only official language ("'Sí' a los dos" 1990: 1A). Even 70 percent of PPD supporters wanted two official languages. Among statehood supporters, only 10 percent wanted to declare Spanish the sole official language. A second poll released two weeks later by a rival newspaper confirmed that about 76 percent of the Puerto Rican public preferred maintaining two official languages ("76%" 1990: 5). Among PNP supporters, 85 percent opposed the López Galarza bill. What the PPD did not count on was that 72 percent of its own supporters did not want to eliminate English as an official language. Surprisingly, among those who professed to support the separatist PIP, 55 percent objected to the López Galarza bill ("76%" 1990: 5). A clear majority of the island's population wanted to bestow the English language with official language status, in spite of the fact that most could not speak it. Thus, with a parliamentary majority the PPD could unilaterally proceed with a language statute but not a constitutional amendment that required popular approval in a referendum.

The Puerto Rican Senate resumed debate on the language bill following its winter recess. In the first months of 1991, federal officials had little interest in Puerto Rico's status. They were far more concerned with Operation Desert Storm and the Persian Gulf War. Charles Untermeyer, the Bush administration's advisor on Puerto Rico, said there was still time to debate and pass a plebiscite bill (Galib 1991d: 8). Despite his optimistic outlook, by March it was rather obvious to most observers that the Senate would fail to pass it (Colón Morera 1993: 252). On March 5, 1991, the Puerto Rican Senate approved the López Galarza language bill and sent it off to the Fortaleza for the governor's signature (Luciano 1991a: 19). At this late stage there were still doubts as to whether Governor Hernández Colón would sign the bill (González, M. 1991b: 2). PNP leaders, including Luis Ferré and Pedro Rosselló, pleaded with Rafael Hernández Colón to veto the measure (Martínez 1991: 12). According to Hernández Colón's former secretary of education, the death of the federal plebiscite bill was the sign the governor was waiting for (Benítez 1998a: 23).

Legislative passage of the language bill caught many on the mainland by surprise. Groups such as English First pointed to this act when arguing that Puerto Rican statehood would be problematic for the United States (Galib 1991c: 5). Conservative commentators Pat Buchanan and George Will used it to argue that cultural differences between Puerto Rico and the United States made statehood an undesirable outcome (Galib 1991b: 8). If passed, said Bush advisor Charles Untermeyer, the language law should be interpreted as an attempt to scare Washington rather than an assertion of cultural militancy (Galib 1991e: 4). One of the most severe reactions came from Pennsylvania Representative Richard Schulze. This Republican lawmaker proposed punishing Puerto Rico by eliminating the federal tax exemptions enjoyed by U.S. firms on the island (Galib 1991a: 5).

In the words of Carlos Chardón, a former education secretary under the Romero-Barceló administration, Governor Hernández Colón was fixated less on electoral concerns and more with transmitting a symbolic communiqué: "He wanted to convey the message that Puerto Ricans were a distinct people. So distinct that they could not be a permanent part of the USA. And this was a way of driving that idea through. . . . This was all a very carefully orchestrated campaign to convey the message that Puerto Ricans could not be Americans in the sense that Americans think of themselves as Americans" (Chardón 1998). Concurring with this assessment was PNP Representative Angel Cintrón García.

Therefore, to destroy the 1902 law was to fundamentally imperil Puerto Rico in a process of nationalization, of sociological separation from the United States, with the intent of later obtaining eventual political separation which defied the interests of the majority of our people. . . . Therefore, that 1991 law was not only a language law. It was . . . part of a scene being constructed by then-governor Hernández Colón and his government to little by little lay the groundwork for changes in Puerto Rico, to rupture social relations or separate Puerto Ricans from Americans. (Cintrón García 1998)[7]

Another pro-statehood voice echoing the thesis that there was a separatist objective behind the language law was PNP Senator Enrique Rodríguez Negrón (1998): "Frankly I believe that it was a carefully developed agenda to distance Puerto Rico from American influence. I have no doubt about that."[8] PNP leader and former Senate president Roberto Rexach Benítez (1998) worried how it would affect congressional attitudes toward Puerto Rico: "First, it was creating the wrong impression about Puerto Rico in the U.S. Congress—giving the impression that these people [Puerto Ricans] . . . wanted to distance themselves from the United States when these people have always wanted a closer relationship with the United States, whether through a commonwealth or by way of statehood."[9]

Rafael Hernández Colón's adversaries clearly warned him that they would use the language law against the PPD in the next electoral campaign. On their side were public opinion surveys indicating that most islanders disagreed with this law. Until this point the chief executive avoided publicly committing himself one way or the other. In the end the real choice was whether the symbolic message was worth more than the potential electoral losses the PPD could face in November 1992. Popular Democrats had to choose between a strategy to maximize electoral support or one bent on inflicting harm on the statehood cause in Congress.

Repealing Official Bilingualism

On April 5, 1991, Rafael Hernández Colón signed the López Galarza bill into law and in so doing repealed the eighty-nine-year-old statute that gave English an official status in the Puerto Rican government. At the signing ceremony at the Centro de Bellas Artes in the Santurce district of San Juan, the governor proclaimed that: "With the signing of this law we reaffirm this country's determination to endure. We declare our mother tongue our most precious sign of identity" (Estrada 1991a: 4).

For many Spanish-language activists, the early 1990s represented a cultural renaissance. They found pride in their legislative accomplishment and the activities surrounding a noteworthy anniversary. The early 1990s coincided with festivities commemorating the 500th anniversary of Columbus's arrival in the Americas. Recalling the events of the early

1990s, former Senate president Hernández Agosto said: "With the celebration of the fifth centennial of the discovery of America and Puerto Rico it was as if the country was developing pride in its own things—a little different from what we had in previous years" (Hernández Agosto 1998).[10] Although it was now law, PIP President Rubén Berríos Martínez suggested putting the matter before the public in order to elevate the language law to the rank of a constitutional amendment (Estrada 1991c: 13). Aware of the polls showing feeble popular support for this law, the administration decided to leave well enough alone. The government was proud, but not foolhardy.

Soon after the new language measure was signed, concerns arose about implementation costs, given that some commonwealth agencies and offices conducted their affairs in English (Núñez and Mier 1991: 4). In order to alleviate such fears, Governor Hernández Colón began dispensing linguistic waivers (Ferré Rangel 1991: 10). Thus, unlike its famous counterpart in Francophone North America—Quebec's Bill 101—Puerto Rico's Bill 417 would have relatively little impact on the day-to-day operations of the commonwealth government (Barreto 1998: 129). With no significant Anglophone community to speak of, outside of military bases and tourist areas, there was little chance of a legal challenge on civil rights grounds. One area where the administration denied exemptions was contracts; they had to be drafted in Spanish (Mier and Núñez 1991: 12). By invoking several "Article 3" exceptions, Governor Rafael Hernández Colón demonstrated that his primary goal was symbolic and not to institute radical change.

In a rare display of multipartisan adulation, the secretary general of the separatist Partido Socialista Puertorriqueño (PSP—Puerto Rican Socialist Party), usually a staunch critic of PPD policies, praised Governor Hernández Colón (Gallisá 1991: 11). *Independentistas* referred to the measure as a triumph for all Puerto Ricans (Torres Rivera 1991: 30). "The passage of Bill number 417 culminates an almost centennial struggle for the defense and conservation of the Spanish language in Puerto Rico" (Delgado Cintrón 1991: 588). It was even celebrated by ethnic Puerto Ricans on the U.S. mainland as an act of cultural affirmation (Cornell 1991: 8). If the praise of separatists was predictable, so was the condemnation by annexationists.

Before the ink was even dry on the governor's signature, the PNP threatened legal action (Covas 1991: 6). Pedro Rosselló insisted that, if elected governor in 1992, he would abolish the new language law and put the measure before voters (Estrada 1991b: 5). Some in the PNP were threatening civil disobedience by using English in an official capacity. Resisting the Official Language Act was possible but likely limited. The socialist and separatist weekly newspaper *Claridad* published the results of its phone survey of some pro-statehood municipal governments. Outside of the larger municipalities, few functionaries could answer basic questions in English (Coss 1991: 5). Again, many aspiring to make Puerto Rico the fifty-first state of the United States were caught defending a language that most could not speak.

A key administration concern was how the law would be perceived in the United States. The PPD leadership did not want to go so far that its legislation would be seen as anti-American. For example, the American flag was clearly visible and in close proximity to the Puerto Rican flag during the bill's signing ceremony (*Revista* 1993: 502). Throughout this event there were numerous references to the United States. The governor stated that Puerto Rican participation in the Persian Gulf War was evidence of the island's "union" with the United States (Hernández Colón 1993: 133). He also made more than one reference to a common citizenship that linked Puerto Ricans to Americans (Hernández Colón 1993: 134–35). In an open letter published in the *New York Times* the governor explained: "So as we reaffirm our Spanish language and culture today, we also reaffirm our unity with the United States" (Hernández Colón 1991b: A25). While he wanted to transmit a "culturally nationalistic" message, Hernández Colón did not intend to convey an *overly* nationalistic message.

Beyond the American public, the Puerto Rican government was also concerned with how Congress viewed the language initiative. As a member of the ruling PPD the island's resident commissioner, Jaime Fuster, explained his party's decision on the floor of the U.S. House of Representatives. This law "merely restates the obvious: That the predominant language in Puerto Rico is Spanish" (*Congressional Record* 1991: E1152). The law did not: restrict individual rights, impede any federal agency's use of English, stop private firms from operating in the language of their choice, or eliminate the teaching of English in public schools. Nor was it a pre-declaration of independence.

> Now, Mr. Speaker, let me explain what the new law does do. It is essentially a symbolic gesture in part to correct historic mistakes and inequities and to clarify any misunderstandings that may exist in both Puerto Rico and the mainland United States. The purpose of the law is to reaffirm the incontestable fact that Spanish is the language of

Puerto Rico, and to avoid any confusion regarding its predominance. It is not intended to defy; it is intended to clarify. (*Congressional Record* 1991: E1152)

Hernández Colón also sent a letter to every member of Congress explaining the purpose behind the new law (Galib 1991f: 28). While the governor focused on the U.S. front, the López Galarza law attracted unanticipated international attention.

Passions mounted when Puerto Rico was nominated for the Principe de Asturias (Prince of Asturias) Award in Letters. This prize, named after the heir to the Spanish throne, is given "to the person whose creative labor represents an important contribution to the enrichment of the common language of Hispanic peoples and their cultural patrimony" ("Tributo" 1991: 5). This represented the first time that an entire people were nominated for an accolade typically given to particular individuals (Leal 1991: 4). Highlighting that the López Galarza initiative was never approved in a plebiscite, Carlos Romero-Barceló asked the award committee to reconsider their nomination (Luciano 1991b: 26). To no avail; the committee unanimously voted to give the honor to Puerto Rico (Leal 1991: 4). In response, the PNP lashed out at the award's committee (Ferré, L. 1991: 45).

Critics asserted that Governor Rafael Hernández Colón was afflicted with "Spanishization" fever (Fernández I. 1997b: 49). Referring to the governor's home city of Ponce, former PNP education secretary Carlos Chardón said, "he [Hernández Colón] developed a fatal attraction towards Spain. He suddenly became a friend of the King [Juan Carlos] and like all people in the tropics they found a royalist in their heart. . . . And suddenly he was an aristocrat. People used to kid in Puerto Rico that he would be called the Duke of Ponce" (Chardón 1998). If Spain inspired Hernández Colón, perhaps, as some argued, his policies were a reflection of deep-seated Eurocentrism.

In Puerto Rico, the politics of "Spanish Only" represents the recycling of the Hispanophile tradition and of the colonial state's (and traditional *independentista's*) concurrent reductions of culture to language, culture to a relatively fixed organic entity, and language to a homogeneous dead vernacular. This fictive language of the "ideal nation" not only displays its Eurocentrism by defending the language of the old empire against the language of the new master but also negates that at this point in our history the various idiolects that Puerto Ricans speak oscillate between different combinations and permutations of the Spanish and English languages. (Lao 1997: 178; emphasis in the original)

Historically, Puerto Rican statehood supporters aligned themselves with the mainland Republican Party. One is hard-pressed to categorize the U.S. Republican Party, with its fiscal and social conservatives, as a progressive movement. Meanwhile, mainstream separatists in Puerto Rico were forging alliances with social democrats in Western Europe and Latin America via the International Socialist. More militant Puerto Rican separatists during the Cold War built bridges with communist parties in Eastern Europe and Latin America. This is not the first time that annexationists, the most conservative of political actors in Puerto Rico, have employed leftist rhetoric. With the demise of the old Partido Estadista Republicano and the rise of the Partido Nuevo Progresista, many statehood supporters condemned the commonwealth status as a "colonial" relationship. While accurately describing Puerto Rico's current status it remains, nonetheless, a term more frequently associated with those on the Left.

Regardless of their ideological leanings, these critics pointed to the governor's "flirtation" with Spain as a variable explaining the promulgation of the Official Language Act of 1991. When it came to explaining the ruling party's decision to proceed with this legislation, other hypotheses were suggested. Most share a contention that Rafael Hernández Colón and the PPD leadership went ahead with a culturally nationalist agenda despite the electoral consequences. As we see in the next chapter, that very notion challenges the long-held idea that politicians only seek to maximize electoral gains.

7

Rational Politics

We now turn to a theoretical discussion of the factors motivating political action. This study assesses the Puerto Rico case from one of the most frequently employed approaches in the field of politics—Rational Choice. Presumably, parties and their candidates bend to the public will to increase their prospects of holding office. After outlining the ideological distribution of the Puerto Rican electorate we are left with a rather stunning paradox. This approach, used in numerous political analyses, suggests that when it comes to language policy Puerto Rican politicians are an exception to the rule. Perhaps Puerto Rico is far too unique to assess with mainstream theories. On the other hand, a study of this island might shed light on a significant flaw in mainstream political analyses. If so, then conceivably this case can also improve our study of other societies unsettled by the national question.

Theory and the Study of Puerto Rican Politics

The Partido Popular Democrático, the focus of much academic attention from the early 1940s until the late 1960s, has received remarkably little scholarly study in recent years (Meléndez 1993a: 91). Among recent studies of Puerto Rican parties few dealt with theories of political parties as such (Meléndez 1995: 57; 1998: 36). Some exceptions are marxist and other class-conflict analyses (Maldonado-Denis 1972; Meléndez 1993a; 1998; Quintero 1986). Outside of a handful of mostly island-based scholars, the mainstream political science community has largely ignored Puerto Rico. In contrast, other social sciences have long found this island a consummate laboratory to test hypotheses.

Its unique status as an American commonwealth leaves Puerto Rico outside the conventional parameters of domestic U.S. politics. A point that cannot be ignored is that this Caribbean territory represents an embarrassment to the United States. This country, proud of its democratic traditions, finds itself one of the few remaining colonial administrators in the twenty-first century. Lack of familiarity with Spanish also hinders the study of island politics among North American scholars. As Janda (1993: 163) noted, "[b]ecause of scholarly ethnocentricity, much of the comparative parties literature escapes the attention of American academics." Concurrently, its colonial status also excludes Puerto Rico from most Latin American political analyses.

If this Caribbean island represents such an anomaly, it begs the question whether mainstream theories in the discipline are applicable. Perhaps societies are so unique that the search for generalizable theories or paradigms should remain a secondary goal to the traditional pursuit of descriptive analyses that seek insight through detailing the nuances distinguishing people and places. Meléndez argued against this viewpoint, noting that the methodologies used in many social sciences are not innately exclusive. "While the historian looks to reconstruct the historic moment and its particular elements in their totality, the tendency of the social sciences—particularly in Political Science—is general and all-encompassing interpretation, without paying much attention to historic depth and peculiarity. These concepts should not be exclusive, but complementary" (Meléndez 1998: 77). Taking his advice to heart, this study explores Puerto Rican politics through a theoretical lens.

Once one decides to embark on a hypothesis-testing enterprise, the next question to answer is what theory to test. As noted above, among the few studies that examine Puerto Rican politics in terms of grand theory, marxist and class analyses are common. The popularity of this approach, especially among scholars in developing countries, was augmented by the rise of Dependency Theory in the 1960s (Chilcote 1994: 235). While Dependencia focused on developing societies, a related hypothesis based on class conflict—Internal Colonialism—generated a great deal of interest among those researching advanced industrial democracies.

The most celebrated work employing this approach to nationalism was Hechter's (1975) study of the United Kingdom. He argued that nationalism in Britain's Celtic fringe resulted from capitalism's development in the Anglo-Irish isles. An English industrial "core" dominated and exploited its Celtic "periphery." The geographically uneven development and spread of industrial capitalism created a "Cultural-Division-of-Labour" that sparked resentment against the core region and fueled nationalist passions in the periphery. In later years, Hechter (1985) noted problems with his original Internal Colonialism thesis.

Investigations of dependent class conflict analyses start with the economic class as their basic unit of analysis. Individual behavior should be primarily determined, they argue, by one's relationship to the means of production. Yet a paradox that could not be solved within the Internal Colonialist camp was the presumably irrational behavior of key nationalists. In their pursuit of economic and social equality, it makes sense to see the peasantry and proletariat at odds with the bourgeoisie. Where there is a strong Cultural-Division-of-Labour it is logical to see the subaltern and exploited ethnic group in conflict with the dominant ethnic group. Interestingly, the further one studies nationalism the more one cannot avoid contending with a profound paradox. Frequently, leaders of nationalist movements, the struggle of the downtrodden, are themselves members of the bourgeoisie. Regionally based elites often join their lower-class ethnic brethren in a liberation struggle against elites from the core. If individuals behaved in terms of their class interests, we should not see such blatant interclass cooperation. Perhaps individuals behave contrary to their class interests.

Hechter's research shifted its focus, taking on a new direction that recognized the explanatory power of the Rational Choice approach and its applicability to the study of ethnic conflict and collective action (Levi and Hechter 1985; Hechter 1986; 1987). Indeed, scholars studying ethnolinguistic politics in other societies have found Rational Choice an extremely useful tool (Colomer 1990; Laitin 1988; 1989; 1993; 1997). Many legislative studies derive their premises from Rational Choice, whose origins can be traced to the ideas of Hobbes, Grotius, Condorcet, and others. The work debuting it to the social science community was Von Neumann and Morgenstern's (1953) *Theory of Games and Economic Behavior.* Of all the branches of the social sciences economics is, by far, the one to employ this theory's tenets with the greatest of frequency and intensity. Before diving into this approach and discussing how it could improve our understanding of Puerto Rico, we must first understand its fundamental philosophical tenets.

Utilities and Rationality

Whereas studies of Internal Colonialism use large groups (classes) as their fundamental units of analysis, Rational Choice focuses on individuals and their motivation. According to philosopher Jeremy Bentham, behavior is affected by one's sense of pain and pleasure—the foundation of his "Utility Principle" (Bentham 1988: 25). This standard covered everyone and he made a special reference to legislators (Bentham 1988: 29). Individuals seek to maximize their pleasure and minimize their pain. The pleasures or pains involved could be physical or material. On the other hand, the rewards or punishments could be social or psychological. People motivated by greed look for ways to augment their personal fortunes. The typical *homo economicus* is driven by a lust for money and finds pleasure in amassing material wealth or possessions. Parting with these things is painful, but a rational individual might do so if a short-term investment has the potential to produce a long-term net gain. Pecuniary maximization is a basic premise in most economic analyses.

Avarice motivates the *homo economicus;* social prestige, social status, honor, and the like drive the *homo sociologicus.* This individual is content to sacrifice material possessions if it helps maximize social rewards. The most extreme manifestation of this phenomenon is the martyr who gives up the ultimate material possession—physical existence—for the cause or community. Pleasure here is measured not in coins of the realm but in joining the pantheon of society's most noble, its saints. Downs (1957: 5) clarified that "the term *rational* is never applied to an agent's end, but only to his means" (emphasis in the original). In this sense even the martyr is behaving rationally, given that the sacrifice achieves the desired end. Pain is associated with humiliation or dishonor. Regardless of the particular motivation, both the prototypic social and economic individuals are rational according to Bentham's utility principle.

Before embarking on a course of action, rational individuals naturally assess not only the reasons favoring a particular action but also those against it (Nozick 1993: 71–72). Downs enumerated five basic characteristics of all rational individuals:

> A rational man is one who behaves as follows: (1) he can always make a decision when confronted with a range of alternatives; (2) he ranks all the alternatives facing him in order of his preference in such a way that each is either preferred to, indifferent to, or inferior to each other; (3) his preference ranking is transitive; (4) he always chooses from among the possible alternatives that which ranks highest in his preference ordering; and (5) he always makes the same decision each time he is confronted with the same alternatives. All rational decision-makers in our model—including political parties, interest groups, and governments—exhibit the same qualities. (Downs 1957: 6)

Note that Downs treats collectives as if they were individual actors, so long as the membership shares the same preferences or has an institutional mechanism for imposing the majority's or the leader's preferences on dissenters (i.e., party caucuses, group conventions, legal procedures, gentle persuasion or repression).

The first step for a rational being is to distinguish alternatives: alternatives x and y are not the same. Focusing on legislators, let us discuss x and y as if they were alternative pieces of legislation. Proposal x could be a bill to declare Spanish the only official language of Puerto Rico. Its counterpart y might be a proposition to establish both Spanish and English as the two official idioms. The order of the x and the y is not important. What is significant is that the two proposals are understood to be different. If Puerto Rican politicians are rational actors, they must be able to distinguish between the two. Symbolically we could write this inequality as: $x \neq y$.

Next, our rational actors must be able to compare alternatives and rank them. Symbolically, preferences are often represented with a capital letter P. A feeling of indifference between a couple of selections is frequently depicted with a capital letter I. The preferences or indifferences of a given individual are designated with a lowercased and subscript p or i. We can say that individuals prefer x to y (xP_iy); inversely, they can favor y to x (yP_ix); or an individual could be indifferent (xI_iy) to the two choices (Shepsle and Bonchek 1997: 25–26). Using the same examples, our rational politicians in Puerto Rico may prefer a unilingual Spanish policy to a bilingual policy of Spanish and English (xP_iy). Perhaps they back official bilingualism over official *unilingüismo* (yP_ix). Or our Puerto Rican elected officials could be simply disinterested in which alternative became government policy (xI_iy).

Third, our rational actors must have transitive preferences. The choices individuals make will be consistent with their most preferred options. Using the same examples from above, we add a third legislative alternative—z. If x and y were Spanish unilingualism and Spanish-English bilingualism, respectively, then z could represent an English unilingual policy. Assuming that an actor prefers x to y (xP_iy) and also prefers y to z (yP_iz), then this person will select x over z (xP_iz). A Puerto Rican politician favoring Spanish unilingualism over Spanish-English bilingualism, who also considers Spanish-English bilingualism a better choice than English unilingualism, would rationally pick a policy of Spanish unilingualism over one declaring English the sole official language. The same principle applies to indifferences.[1] Finally, as Downs mentioned, given the same choices over time a rational individual will always take the same course of action.

Rationality does not imply that actors have an unlimited set of choices to pick from. Especially when talking about politics it is understood that rational actors are boxed into a finite number of alternatives. Looking at reelection down the road, politicians in democratic polities are constantly concerned with facing the electorate. Thus, they try to avoid unpopular stances on key issues of the day. But there are also institutional constraints. An ordinary member of a legislative body will be bound by the formal rules of that polity's law-making processes. These controls are imposed both by the chamber's operating rules and the country's constitution. With rank comes certain privileges. Different sets of restrictions apply to committee chairs or even heads of parliamentary bodies—speakers, chamber presidents, or prime ministers—whose posts give them a wider degree of latitude and therefore far more choices. As Tsebelis notes, "Each actor will try to maximize his objectives while remaining inside the institutional constraints" (1990: 96). Operating outside institutional constraints is the hallmark of coups and revolutions.

Rational actors assess not only their preferences among a limited set of alternatives but they also assign them *utilities*. Calculating utilities is based on weighing the value of that alternative in terms of the probability of its occurrence.

> Players are assumed to be able to evaluate and compare the consequences associated with the set of possible outcomes and assign numbers, called utilities, to each outcome indicating a *preference* relationship among them. When these numbers are judged to reflect only a rank ordering of the outcomes, they are called *ordinal* utilities; when they indicate both order and intensity of preference, they are called *cardinal* utilities. (Zagare 1984: 12; emphasis in the original)

Many economic studies, using a given currency as the basic unit of analysis, have the luxury of calculating cardinal utilities.[2] This is rarely the case in the other social sciences, where we generally deal with preferences, such as different language policies in this case, that cannot be quantified. Each actor is weighing or assigning different utilities to the various options. By its very nature this is a highly subjective process. Thus, with our ordinal utilities we can say that an actor prefers x over y but we cannot say by how much.

Politicians use a similar approach when evaluating political choices. Citizens assess the expected utility of voting for their favorite candidate in light of their chances of actually winning the next election. An expected utility calculus may reveal that the most preferred candidate was the best choice. On the other hand, the low probability of victory might alter the voter's calculus in such a way that casting a ballot for the second most preferred candidate seems the most logical alternative. Those acquainted with Puerto Rican politics will be very familiar with this kind of expected utility calculation.

To those who are not versed in the island's colorful political jargon, an often amusing and puzzling political term is *melón*—watermelon. This is not a literal reference to fruit but a figurative allusion to partisan colors and affiliation. Each political party on the island is associated with a distinct color and symbol. The pro-statehood PNP uses a blue palm tree as its emblem. Publications and posters issued by the pro-commonwealth PPD recall the party's original base of support among rural communities and the peasantry; they use the red silhouette of a Puerto Rican peasant wearing a straw hat, or *pava*. If you see a green flag with a white cross you are looking at a PIP ad.

A *melón* is someone who, like a watermelon, is green on the outside and red on the inside. This refers to someone who sounds separatist and makes pro-independence statements (green on the outside) but nonetheless votes for the autonomist PPD (red on the inside). While there are potentially many reasons why an independence sympathizer might vote for an autonomist candidate, the most common justification is that *independentista* candidates usually garner around 5 percent of the popular vote. The worst scenario for many separatists would be the victory of the PNP. Weighing electoral preferences in terms of probabilities of victory leads some Puerto Rican separatists to forgo their most preferred option. Their expected utility calculus assigns a higher ordinal utility to voting for their second-best option, voting PPD.

While the Rational Choice approach has been used extensively in many political studies, this does not imply in any way that it is universally accepted. Some suggest that "the weaknesses of rational choice scholarship are rooted in the characteristic aspiration of rational choice theorists to come up with universal theories of politics" (Green and Shapiro 1994: 6). These critics argued that Rational Choice could benefit from dropping universality in favor of "partial universalism," which could include rational strategizing as one factor among several that explain political phenomena (Green and Shapiro 1994: 69).

Theory testing requires scholars to be aware of what the theory predicts in the first place (Green and Shapiro 1994: 38). Sadly, many using Rational Choice fail to spell out specifically what data is needed either to confirm or reject a particular hypothesis (36). Much of the approach's explanatory power comes from assumptions about individual preferences. Of course, measuring these preferences or beliefs can be difficult (150). In their zeal to promote this approach, some scholars have collected evidence selectively, in a way that makes the theory stand out, while perhaps discarding evidence that refutes their hypothesis (42). Perhaps this study of language policy and nationalist politics in Puerto Rico can remedy these shortcomings.

First, we must explore what the Rational Choice approach says about political behavior and the reactions of rational political actors. Many rely on the postulates of Anthony Downs and his models that make specific predictions about how actors should behave depending on the spatial distribution of the electorate. However, some contend that "the elaboration of spatial models has had only a tenuous connection with empirical application" (Green and Shapiro 1994: 172). We compare these predictions with our evidence and assess the usefulness of Rational Choice as a tool in the analysis of Puerto Rican language policy.

Downsian Spatial Models

In his celebrated *Economic Theory of Democracy*, Downs unequivocally incorporated Rational Choice assumptions into his general thesis of behavior. Politicians in democratic systems are indeed rational actors, and Downs's definition of a political party integrated this notion. He described a party as "a team of men seeking to control the governing apparatus by gaining office in a duly constituted election" (Downs 1957: 25). It is important to differentiate parties in democratic regimes from their counterparts in authoritarian systems. Dictatorships are frequently one-party systems or no-party states. Assuming that this designation is de facto and not de jure, the outcome of multiparty elections is predetermined. Under these circumstances parties may consider violence and revolution as more certain avenues to holding power than the ballot box.

In democratic systems political parties have but one priority—to become the ruling party (Downs 1957: 7). Winning elections is a party's primary goal, not enacting legislation. Referring to political parties, Downs stated:

> We assume that they act solely in order to attain the income, prestige, and power which come from being in office. Thus politicians in our model never seek office as a means of carrying out particular policies; their only goal is to reap the rewards of holding office *per se*. They treat policies purely as means to the attainment of their private

ends, which they can reach only by being elected. (Downs 1957: 28; emphasis in the original)

Parties aspiring to govern usually need to accumulate more votes than their opponents. An exception is found where a minority party becomes a power broker in a multiparty system. It could amass tremendous power, even if it lost votes, so long as it held enough parliamentary seats to christen the next ruling coalition. Using Rational Choice terminology, we would say that political parties are vote-maximizing organizations.

How do they attract votes? Commonly, political parties draft long and detailed platforms enumerating their policy wish list. For scholars interested in penetrating analyses of partisan preferences, these declarations represent an abundance of data. On the other hand, this same information offers headaches for the average voters. Long ago Michels noted that voters turn to political experts because of information overload. Few individuals have the time, formal education, or patience to scrutinize party platforms and complex policy issues (Michels 1959: 83–88). Parties have a solution to this problem—political labels. The party's name and symbol are usually associated with a diminutive set of policies or perhaps even one significant issue.

> Political labeling, in fact, seems an almost inescapable feature of elections, allowing policy debates to be carried on in a form of short-hand that frees voters from the need to be highly informed about each candidate's positions on a broad range of issues. Given the lack of incentive for voters to acquire information about the candidates, political labels become an ideal method of communicating with the voter. (Enelow and Hinich 1984: 38)

This certainly applies to Puerto Rican parties that openly and emphatically identify themselves on the basis of their preferred status option. As mentioned above, these policies are popularly linked with specific colors and particular symbols. Beyond promises of a future postelection agenda, party labels remind voters about preceding events and successes (Popkin 1993: 24). They prompt voters to recollect what the party did in the past and the failings of their electoral rivals. However, this is far from an objective undertaking (Enelow and Hinich 1984: 40).

Clearly there are no legal obligations compelling politicians to adhere to their party platforms. Slogans and labels, hallmarks of parties as well as individual politicians, could promise programs and initiatives that are later ignored or even reversed following an election. Publicly an office seeker could endorse a given policy position while secretly favoring an alternative policy (Shepsle and Bonchek 1997: 112). It is common in American politics for challengers who laud term limits to change their minds once in office. What prevents politicians from going back on their word? It may be hard to believe, but most politicians value their reputations. "Perhaps voters believe policy promises because they know that politicians know that a reputation for deception and misrepresentation is a serious electoral obstacle in future electoral campaigns" (Shepsle and Bonchek 1997: 112). Concern with a reputation is no exercise in vanity but a matter of political survival. An individual known for changing policy positions, or "flip-flopping," is seen as untrustworthy. Such a stigma could spell disaster for that party's or that politician's future electoral viability (Downs 1957: 107–8).

At this point we combine our general discussion of rationality with our earlier discussion of Downs's spatial models of electoral distribution from chapter 4. Downs's (1957: 115) idea of spatial competition in politics came from Hotelling's (1929) work in economics. Competition for customers leads to an equilibrium whereby merchants locate their establishments near one another in order to accrue the largest market segment possible. Over time their prices begin to resemble one another's. These market principles could apply to politics.

> The competition for votes between the Republican and Democratic parties does not lead to a clear drawing of issues, an adoption of two strongly contrasted positions between which the voter may choose. Instead, each party strives to make its platform as much like the other's as possible. Any radical departure would lose many votes, even though it might lead to stronger commendation of the party by some who would vote for it anyhow. Each candidate "pussyfoots," replies ambiguously to questions, refuses to take a definite stand in any controversy for fear of losing votes. (Hotelling 1929: 54)

Politicians try to resemble one another; however, concerns over losing their electoral peripheries prevent parties from moving into the exact ideological middle (Smithies 1941).

Let us return to a spatial model first introduced in chapter 4, one symbolizing a normally distributed electorate. The height of the curve represents the number or percentage of voters. In this configuration, the single largest concentration of voters is aggregated in the ideological middle. What does this kind of electoral distribution suggest to liberal or conservative candidates? If they want to be elected they should moderate their policies and gravitate toward the center. "Viewed in the simplest spatial terms, the voter casts his vote for the candidate 'closest' to him in a space that describes all the factors that are of concern to the voter" (Enelow and Hinich 1984: 3).

Parties do not always converge in the ideological center. That depends upon the shape of a society's electoral distribution. For example, how do politicians behave if the electorate is bimodal, rather than unimodally distributed? Under those circumstances parties espouse diametrically divergent policies (Downs 1957: 118). While the convergence property described by Downs applies to unidimensional spaces, it rarely holds in bidimensional spaces (Ferejohn 1993: 109). Regardless of the exact shape of the electoral distribution, vote maximization is at the heart of politicians' activities in a democratic polity. Indeed, Ordeshook referred to this as a "postulated preference"—a political axiom (1986: 15).

Rational Party Strategies in Puerto Rico

How should politicians in Puerto Rico behave given the distribution of the island's electorate? Rather than employing a left-right continuum, which is standard in many polities, Puerto Rican politics is best described in terms of a center-periphery electoral distribution. The status question—the debate over the island's relationship with the United States—dominates the Puerto Rican political scene (see figure 7.1). Again, areas "a," "b," and "c" represent the portions of the electorate that the PIP, PPD, and PNP appeal to, respectively. Since the late 1960s, the island's electorate has spread out in such a way that the median voter is located not in the ideological middle but leaning toward the pro-center side of the spectrum. The shape of the distribution implies a different tactic for each party.

Let us commence with the separatist PIP. Most PIP voters hold what could be designated as quasi- or semi-autonomist beliefs rather than pure separatist principles. More PIP voters are concentrated at the s-line in figure 7.1 than at the pro-periphery end touching the y-axis. How does that translate into party policies, given that even many *independentistas* want to maintain some ties with the United States? Logically, the Partido Independentista Puertorriqueño should call for policies such as dual citizenship after independence. Maintaining American citizenship remains a recurring theme in PIP presentations before congressional committee hearings. Currently, people, capital, and products travel freely between the United States and Puerto Rico. The PIP should also take a cue from its

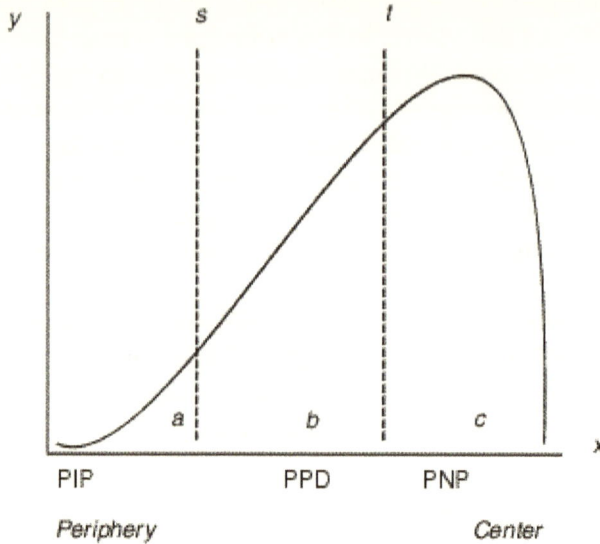

Fig. 7.1. A Spatial Model of the Ideological Distribution of the Puerto Rican Electorate and Political Parties, 1968–1996

separatist counterparts in western Europe. Many of these parties call for economic unity hand in hand with political sovereignty.

While this is far from an exhaustive enumeration of PIP policies, it reveals that this party's leadership is attuned to its electoral appeal and has made efforts to expand its support base to include otherwise PPD voters. Were the PIP to stake out policies too far from its pro-periphery roots it would risk exposing itself to an incursion from other separatist parties such as the Partido Socialista Puertorriqueño. In contrast, if the PIP becomes too resolute in its separatist positions—calling for an end to free trade and travel to and from the United States—the party stands to lose voters to the autonomist PPD.

At the other end of the ideological spectrum is the PNP. While the party favors incorporating the island as a member state of the American federation, it finds itself with a fascinating paradox. More of the party's support is located at the *t*-line than at the pro-center endpoint. Even the most pro-American political party has members who can best be described as *cultural nationalists*. Given the shape of the Puerto Rican electorate, what kind of policies should the PNP rationally espouse? According to Downsian principles, New Progressives should promote the idea that cultural autonomy is compatible with the other states in the federation. In fact, cultural autonomy lies at the heart of Ferré's *estadidad jíbara* thesis and at the root of comments by Romero-Barceló, insisting that the island's vernacular is not negotiable. One of the features distinguishing the Partido Nuevo Progresista from its predecessor—the Partido Estadista Republicano—is the PNP's culturally nationalistic stance. In contrast, the PER continued to promote cultural and linguistic assimilation as necessary steps toward statehood.

Finally, what are rational policies for the PPD? The Partido Popular Democrático captivates the segment of the public in area "b." Parties in the ideological middle attempt to portray themselves as pillars of moderation. Over the past few decades, the PPD focused its attacks on the PNP. In contrast, the PPD of the 1950s was far more interested in denouncing the PIP. Parties in the middle of the ideological spectrum have the advantage of tilting their rhetoric toward one side or the other, depending on the prevailing political winds; yet, they have major disadvantages. Parties in the ideological middle must constantly fight on two fronts. Were the PPD to portray itself as "too pro-American" by trying to cross the *t*-line, it could leave its pro-periphery flank vulnerable to an incursion from the PIP. Turning the equation around, we find the same thing could happen if the PPD attempted to promote policies perceived to be quasiseparatist. By shifting party policies over to the *s*-line, the Populares would leave their more pro-American supporters exposed to alluring messages from the PNP.

Logically the PPD, if presenting changes to the Commonwealth's status, should suggest alterations that give the island greater autonomy from the United States while at the same time bringing it closer. As a result of fighting simultaneously on two fronts, the PPD must submit seemingly contradictory and even schizophrenic policies. Given the island's electoral distribution, the PPD should advocate the status quo and avoid the perception that it is moving toward either ideological endpoint.

Interestingly, the PPD knew many would perceive the promotion of the Official Language Act of 1991 as a move toward the pro-periphery end of the ideological spectrum. How did the PPD's behavior, particularly in light of its controversial decision to proceed with a new language policy, correspond with Downsian expectations of rationality? Were Governor Hernández Colón and the rest of the PPD leadership behaving irrationally? Perhaps there are problems with the applicability of Rational Choice models to Puerto Rico. On the other hand, perhaps the Puerto Rican case can shed light on the motivations behind nationalist policies.

8

Culture, Policy, and Nested Games

Traditional Rational Choice analyses claim that politicians are ultimately concerned with vote maximization. How well did the PPD's language policies harmonize with this theoretical expectation? In the 1970s and 1980s, the PPD's leadership refused to back several Spanish-language initiatives. The Populares were weary of how their PNP rivals would portray such a cultural policy to an electorate leaning toward the pro-center side of a center-periphery ideological continuum. Until the early 1990s, Popular Democratic language policy followed standard Downsian expectations. Interviews with key PPD leaders indicate beyond a shadow of a doubt that this organization was well aware of the potentially negative electoral consequences of enacting a unilingual language policy. What could have caused the party to alter course and adopt such an *irrational* strategy?

Some argued that the governor had a personal fascination with Spain and that closer ties to Madrid was his true intention. Others suggested that the party simply miscalculated both the public mood and the perspective of the PPD's rank and file. After exploring these alternative explanations, we consider an unorthodox approach within the Rational Choice camp. This *Nested Games* approach proposes that under certain circumstances politicians forgo electoral expediency in favor of a vital objective or policy concern. In Puerto Rico, as in other societies where the *national question* is a major concern or the central focus of partisan debate, political actors might be willing to make electoral sacrifices as long as it advances their preferred status option. Parties might forfeit votes if the legislative action sabotages the goals or aspirations of their adversaries.

Fulfilling Downsian Expectations, 1970s and 1980s

The Popular Democratic leadership decided in 1991 to establish Spanish as the sole official language, thus departing from party precedent. In the 1980s Senator Sergio Peña Clos was a PPD cultural nationalist. When

Senator Peña Clos proposed his language bill in 1982, Carlos Romero-Barceló was governor. No one seriously expected a pro-statehood governor to back a measure perceived as symbolically distancing the island from the United States. Statehood advocates were adamant that Peña Clos's bill was a signal of his party's hidden *independentista* agenda. How did the PPD respond to charges of flirting with separatism? With a gubernatorial veto all but assured, the PPD's central committee backed away from Peña Clos's initiative. The Partido Popular Democrático's behavior was rational and consistent with a Downsian vote-maximization strategy.

What happened to the other language bills? Senators Berríos Martínez of the PIP and Peña Clos of the PPD introduced language legislation in 1976 and 1986, respectively. Unlike the 1982 legislative proposal discussed above, these bills were drafted when the PPD was in power. Rafael Hernández Colón won his first four-year term as governor in 1972. Losing reelection bids in 1976 and 1980, he retook the governorship in 1984 and was reelected to a third term in 1988. During his three terms in office, Hernández Colón enjoyed a PPD majority in both chambers of the Asamblea Legislativa. Strong party discipline in Puerto Rico translates into little interparty parliamentary cooperation. Also, once the leadership has given a proposal either its blessing or its condemnation, legislators usually step in line. Governor Hernández Colón had the opportunity in 1976 and 1986 to back these language initiatives. Again, he and his party wanted to avoid the separatist label.

Until the early 1990s the PPD's hierarchy demonstrated a clear understanding of the Puerto Rican electorate. Their decisions on language policy were thoroughly in line with standard expectations of rational behavior. Yet, in a radical departure from previous stances, Governor Rafael Hernández Colón decided to back Representative Héctor López Galarza's initiative in 1991. Despite his support for the measure, former house speaker Jarabo clearly understood the potential harm it could inflict on his party. "You had to be blind not to realize that there was a political risk involved because if the national factor is a *matrix fact* of Puerto Rican politics there are other factors that are [just] as important. And one of them is whether you are getting closer to the United States or you are separating from it" (Jarabo 1998).

Rafael Hernández Colón decided against seeking a fourth term in 1992, thus opening the door for Victoria "Melo" Muñoz Mendoza to run as the PPD's candidate for governor. Senator Muñoz Mendoza was a daughter of the Commonwealth's founder, Luis Muñoz Marín. The PNP nominated physician and political activist Pedro Rosselló as its standard bearer for the November elections. Restoring English as an official language was one of Rosselló's campaign promises ("Ratifican" 1992: 18). Other PNP leaders reiterated the same goal. Referring to the PPD's unilingual law, former Senate president Roberto Rexach Benítez said: "there was a commitment on our part to repeal this law. Furthermore, we pointed it out since 1991 when the law was enacted" (Rexach Benítez 1998).[1] The PNP's statement on a future language policy was clear and the party apparently felt that publicly voicing its goal would enhance its own electoral base.

The 1992 Elections

Language policy was not at the heart of the 1992 election. Nevertheless, the PNP used the 1991 language statute as "evidence" that the PPD was distancing Puerto Rico from the United States. In an editorial published only days before the elections, Rosselló clumped together the PPD's cultural agenda and their failed 1991 plebiscite—one that asked voters to endorse a list of democratic rights in the form of a constitutional amendment. One of them was the right of self-determination. Attempting to link separatists and autonomists, Rosselló claimed: "Instead of fleeing, we stood up to them, alone against two parties, alone against the gigantic machine of an incumbent party, alone against separation and deceit" (Rosselló 1992: 55).

Some of the PNP's campaign advertisements directly targeted the language issue. A Senator Kenneth McClintock Hernández newspaper advertisement was topped off with a fluttering American flag and promoted the fact that "Los populares, ya te quitaron el inglés"—The Populares already took English away from you ("Los populares" 1992: 38). Another example was an advertisement for gubernatorial candidate Pedro Rosselló. His "*Sólo uno*" ad (1992: 37) attempted to forge a link between language policy, the PPD's 1991 plebiscite, and separatism.

Based on this publicly available information, the PPD should have reconsidered its language policy. Opinion polls were showing Rosselló clearly ahead of his rivals in early September ("Los jóvenes 1992: 4), and he maintained this lead straight through the fall campaign ("Rosselló mantiene" 1992: 4). Certainly the PPD had time to alter its policies to "prove" its greater loyalty to the United States. The Populares could have reconsidered the Moreno Rodríguez ranked language bill—Spanish would have been declared the first official language and English the second language. In the end the PPD lost the 1992 elections, and the very first bill introduced in the

1993 legislative session concerned the restoration of official bilingualism. Despite his party's defeat, Hernández Colón claimed that the 1991 Official Language Act was one of his greatest accomplishments (Varela 1993: 12).

Rival Explanations

In terms of vote maximization, establishing the local vernacular as the sole official language was a disaster. Not only did the PPD lose the 1992 elections, it also lost the following elections in 1996. As mentioned above, the PPD was presented with opinion polls published before Bill 417 was signed and they showed public opposition to changing language policy for fear of repercussions from Washington. In contrast, the PNP showed a keen understanding of the spatial distribution of the Puerto Rican electorate. They promised that both statehood and cultural autonomy were possible. Rhetorically, New Progressives attempted to portray their primary adversaries as separatists and thus drifting away from the average voter. Most Puerto Ricans want to maintain the right to travel freely between the mainland and the island, keep their U.S. citizenship, and benefit from the federal coffers. To the outside observer these policies may seem contradictory but they reflect the island's electoral preferences.

Perhaps Governor Hernández Colón was beset by a severe case of His-panophile-*itis*. After all, one cannot ignore four centuries of Spanish rule and a half-millennium of cultural ties with Iberia. This hypothesis falls into the same category as various others suggesting that the governor successfully imposed his personal preferences on the party. Even if it were an accurate reflection of Hernández Colón's thinking, this would still violate Downs's fundamental notion of political expediency. Additionally, even charismatic leaders must convince the party faithful that their path is the right one. Other PPD leaders, rational actors themselves, could have opposed this bill from the start.

Perhaps the governor yielded to the influence of intellectuals and Spanish-language activists (Vélez and Schweers 1993: 127). Once more we find the same problems here as in the first hypothesis. Fulfilling the aspirations of a small segment of the island's electorate would violate basic Downsian premises. In addition, we discover here a more fundamental problem. Island intellectuals endorsed the López Galarza bill since it was publicly announced in 1989. Yet Hernández Colón refused to back this proposal until almost the very day that he signed it into law. Spanish-language activists had no idea until 1991 whether the governor was a friend or a foe.

If the governor truly favored official unilingualism, why did he fail to initiate a change in language policy? Héctor López Galarza drafted Bill 417. Governor Hernández Colón never made a public or intraparty appeal for this statute, nor did any other member of the PPD leadership. One of Hernández Colón's cabinet secretaries in his last administration, Celeste Benítez, attested to the fact that in her view such a statute was unessential. "I never thought that law [Bill 417] was necessary. I did not think it was necessary because it was saying that the sun rises in the East and sets in the West. The underlying socio-economic reality is that Puerto Rico is a country with an Hispanic culture—a Spanish-speaking country" (Benítez 1998b).[2] Benítez made it abundantly clear in this interview that she was not a member of the PPD's decision-making inner circle while she was education secretary. During the entire debate Hernández Colón was publicly silent on the matter.

What was the sentiment of PPD's base? For an insight into this dimension we turn to Rafael Alicea Vázquez, a lifelong PPD activist in Lares—a traditional stronghold in the island's western highlands. This retired mathematics teacher was a member of the Lares Municipal Assembly for much of the 1970s and 1980s. In the late 1970s he was the president of the town assembly. His position in the party's grassroots gives us some insight as to what the party's base was thinking throughout these debates.

Alicea Vázquez voiced his opinion that the bill's approbation represented an emotional boost to many in the teaching profession; the bill was an affirmation of the island's unique culture and identity (Alicea Vázquez 1998). Teachers were deeply concerned with matters of culture and language in Puerto Rico. After all, teachers led the battle against the federal government's Americanization policy in the first half of the 1900s. It was also a teacher—Héctor López Galarza—that introduced Bill 417 to the insular House of Representatives. As a loyal member of the Partido Popular Democrático, "Rafo" supported his party's decision and lauded the legislative triumph of his personal friend, Héctor López Galarza. However, was the language bill promoted from the party's base or its leadership?

Frankly I should say that it was more something steered by the leadership of the Popular [Democratic] Party . . . than a call from the people. . . . Clearly, when the situation later arose it became an issue among the people. Then the people awoke. . . . The people began to concern themselves and talk about language. But naturally it's our language. It's the vernacular. Well, the only ones bothered are those people that assert other political ideologies [statehood supporters] alien to Puerto Rican's idiosyncracies. (Alicea Vázquez 1998)[3]

One interview does not constitute a thorough survey of the PPD's base, but it does represent the views of a local party activist and former office-holder. Alicea Vázquez's view coincides with public opinion polls, which demonstrated low levels of grassroots support for the initiative in 1990, only months before the bill was signed into law. Unlike in the U.S. main-land, strong party discipline is a commonly observed hallmark of Puerto Rican politics. Once the leadership decided to back the bill, many of the party's frontline militants gave it their solid support.

Perhaps the PPD could have mounted an effective campaign explaining to the public its reasons for pursuing language reform. Speaker Jarabo not-ed that at PPD leadership meetings his requests for educational campaign funds focusing on the Spanish-language bill were turned down (Jarabo 1998). Celeste Benítez commented: "Frankly the political leadership of the Popular [Democratic] Party did not make a concerted nor serious effort to offset that propaganda from the New Progressive Party. Later that Spanish law became embroiled in a political controversy that harmed the Popular [Democratic] Party" (Benítez 1998b).[4]

Members of his own party felt that López Galarza's language law could hurt the Partido Popular Democrático. A former PPD Senate president noted that electoral maximization did not top the party's agenda at that time. "Afterwards, it could have been prejudicial from a partisan point of view. But I think that at that time it was created the political impact was not weighed—neither beneficial nor prejudicial" (Hernández Agosto 1998).[5] One PNP leader concluded that the López Galarza bill was simply a foolish proposition. Former Senate president Rexach Benítez said: "Yes, from a partisan standpoint really the bill was stupid since it did not provide the Popular [Democratic] Party that promoted it a political advantage. To the contrary, it inflicted political harm because in Puerto Rico far more than 70 percent of the people want permanent union with the United States" (Rexach Benítez 1998).[6] Clearly and intentionally, the PPD's leadership ambled down a legislative path filled with electoral dangers. There does not seem to be any way to reconcile this political decision with Downsian expectations of rational behavior.

Sending a Message

Representative Héctor López Galarza made it clear why he wrote the language bill. The cultural goals of the bill's author in no way imply that others shared his particular preferences. When asked to suggest reasons why Governor Hernández Colón supported his bill, he speculated that his proposal was linked to the concurrent status debates in Congress. He said: "Rafael Hernández Colón also saw that law as a way to deal with the status question" (López Galarza 1998).[7] Celeste Benítez also believed that attacking statehood was the underlying reason for Hernández Colón's support for the López Galarza bill (Benítez 1998a: 24). According to opponents of the Official Language Act of 1991, the language question hit the statehood movement "at its weakest point" (Vélez and Schweers 1993: 124).

The PPD spearheaded the creation of the commonwealth status. Party leader Rafael Hernández Colón was committed to protecting the status quo against challenges from any alternatives. With popular support in the single digits, independence was not perceived as an impending menace by the PPD, but the statehood movement was a different matter entirely. Héctor López Galarza noted that the status question and the language debate were linked:

I believe that one of the obstacles to statehood is precisely language. . . . I believe that the United States would not accept a state whose official language and whose mother tongue were Spanish. . . . There are [undoubtedly] a variety of cultures in the United States. But in the United States there is still a sense of national unity and English gives that sense of national unity even though other languages are spoken. (López Galarza 1998)[8]

López Galarza's conviction that the language issue adjoined the status dilemma was one shared by activists in the PNP and the PPD. Governor Hernández Colón stated that the language law and the 1991 plebiscite on democratic and political rights were reactions to congressional inaction over the federal status referendum bill (Hernández Colón 1996: 483). Referring to the failure of the death of the congressional status bill, he remarked:

Well, when the legislation in Congress was not approved, we then felt the need to take some steps over here to clarify what we wanted to jointly clarify with Congress. And one of the subjects that we wanted to clarify was the matter of Puerto Rican identity. And so we can say the moment to produce an act of linguistic affirmation, an assertion of Spanish as an affirmation of our identity, as an affirmation of our being had arrived. But at the same time [we had] some linguistic intentions in the country with the aim of fortifying, enriching, and improving the use of our language which had become impoverished in a pronounced manner over many years. And we took the step. (Hernández Colón 1998b)[9]

When asked about whether he suspected that the PNP would charge his party with promoting separatism, Hernández Colón (1998b) answered: "I knew they were going to allege that. But that did not worry me. I knew where I clearly stood. Their political demagoguery never worried me to the point of moving me to inaction. I take it into consideration, well, to keep things clear before the people. But it does not paralyze me."[10]

Independence supporters backed the López Galarza initiative from the start. As previously noted, the PIP's leader, Senator Rubén Berríos Martínez, called for the proposal's insertion in the commonwealth constitution. Separatism was not a label that the PIP feared in the least. Quite the contrary, for the PIP it was a badge of honor. *Independentistas* knew that they did not have the parliamentary strength to unilaterally promulgate a new language law. Now that the PPD was taking the initiative, the PIP could join in.

Undoubtedly the Partido Independentista Puertorriqueño was aware that there was more to the López Galarza bill than just declaring an official language. At the time Bill 417 was debated, Víctor García San Inocencio was an assistant to then-PIP representative David Noriega. Currently the PIP's lone member in the lower house, García San Inocencio focused on the party's expectations of how Congress would react to the language bill. "But that declaration of that which is obvious, that which is evident, in Puerto Rico also constituted in political terms a difficult declaration for the United States Congress to digest and chew" (García San Inocencio 1998).[11] Former PIP senator Fernando Martín said: "Certainly, we saw that dimension as an important dimension; there is no doubt" (Martín 1998).[12] Regardless of its additional features, the former senator pointed out that it was still an act of cultural affirmation.

No, no, that the United States would perceive the [cultural] difference and that this would trigger the debate over the role of language in Puerto Rico—the obstacles to statehood and the Latin American character of Puerto Ricans—even to the point that a government of Puerto Rico, though colonial, could say that Spanish is the official language of Puerto Rico—supported a bit our thesis reminding Americans that—for those who do not know it—Puerto Rico is a distinct nation from the United States, that it has a different language, and that the majority of the people in Puerto Rico do not understand English. (Martín 1998)[13]

The language game was, in fact, being played out simultaneously in San Juan and Washington. Amassing votes was not central to the PPD's strategy in this venture.

Downs's traditional model of vote-maximizing political actors does not apply to cultural legislation in Puerto Rico. Perhaps there is a serious flaw in the approach. Maybe Puerto Rico is simply so unique that mainstream theories of political behavior do not apply. Another possibility is that this particular case was an aberration or onetime deal. Before running to any of those alternatives we have one more option. Tsebelis lays the groundwork for a conceptualization that addresses these paradoxes within a Rational Choice framework. At times actors are engaged in conflicts in two arenas, thus giving the impression that they are behaving irrationally. Without assessing the relative values of each arena we fail to see the larger and more complete picture and, more important, comprehend the utility that our actors are trying to maximize.

Tsebelis's Nested Games Model

We assume that actors will, using Bentham's terms, try to increase their pleasure and decrease their pain. Perhaps we misunderstand the gratification being sought. Reiterating a point from the previous chapter, we realize that the classic *homo economicus* has one set of goals while the *homo sociologicus* harbors radically different inclinations. While different, their actions are nonetheless rational given their respective priorities. If we assumed fiscal maximization, socially oriented individuals would appear to behave in less than rational ways. Our perception of irrationality is not a result of our theoretical approach but a problem with our focal point. As observers we focus on one arena while completely overlooking the other foci of concern. Scholars concentrate on the "principal arena" when in fact our actors are interested in an alternative arena (Tsebelis 1990: 7). "The observer fails to see that the formulation of preferences in the arena of interest is conditioned by simultaneous political interaction in other arenas" (Batty and Danilovic 1997: 95).

Others suggest, contrary to Downs, that party leaders may forego vote maximizing when the policy being promoted is highly cherished (Wittman

1983; 1990). "To have policy goals does not mean that the politician is ideo-logically dogmatic, unconcerned with winning, or values platform positions as an end itself, but rather that candidates, like voters, are interested in policy implementation" (Wittman 1983: 142). Others who study political parties understand that these institutions do not always strive to amass votes at the cost of sacrificing policies. Page and his co-authors classified vote-maximiz-ing parties as "ambitious parties," while those more concerned with policies were labeled "ideological parties" (Page et al. 1993: 162). But even ideological parties cannot escape electoral reality. If they want to hold office they must shift their policy postures closer to the median voter (172).

Tsebelis employed a Nested Games approach to help explain what out-wardly appeared to be irrational behavior in Belgian politics—an example of a consociational democracy. The most famous example of a consocia-tional democracy is the Netherlands, thanks to Lijphart's renowned study. Deep social cleavages in Holland based on class and religion divide society into *zuilen* or blocs (Lijphart 1968: 17). At the mass level, interbloc an-tagonisms discourage cooperation across the socioreligious divide (Tse-belis 1990: 164–65). This means that voters have a dominant strategy of noncooperation. Based on Downsian principles, politicians responding to the vox populi avoid cooperating in Parliament. In light of the fact that no bloc constitutes a majority of the electorate, the inevitable consequence of responding to voter preferences would be legislative deadlock. Political elites realize the negative repercussions of always acquiescing to the will of the people and choose to cooperate on key issues and in so doing cross bloc boundaries.

How does this affect a political actor's assessment of pain and pleasure? We can combine our discussion of pain and pleasure and talk about a *pay-off* that we represent as PO. In order to specify an individual's payoff we use a subscript i—(PO_i). The greater one's pleasure the higher the payoff, the worse one's pain the lower the payoff. Downs's prototypical rational individual is concerned only with prevailing in elections. Tsebelis denot-ed the individual's electoral payoff with a subscript ei—(PO_{ei}). As far as Downs was concerned, an individual politician's payoff was the same as their electoral payoff: $PO_i = PO_{ei}$.

Tsebelis pointed out, however, that in Belgium legislators at times valued the payoff from passing key laws despite the popular will to forego cooper-ation. This payoff is generated in the "parliamentary arena" and is located, therefore, outside the sphere of electoral politics. Parliamentary inaction led to a legislative stalemate that some political actors considered an extremely negative proposition. He represented this, the individual's payoff from the parliamentary arena, with the subscript pi—(PO_{pi}). Electoral politics fall into the category of "visible" politics, whereas parliamentary interaction was part of the "invisible" political scene. What determined the degree to which politicians deviated from a vote-maximizing strategy is the influence of the masses on the decision-making process (Tsebelis 1990: 167–68). To represent the relative weight of mass influence on political payoff calculations, Tsebelis used the letter k—variable in the [0,1] interval. So it could be worth one, zero, or any decimal between those two numeric endpoints. Combining all three elements—the electoral payoff, the parliamentary payoff, and the relative weight of popular input—Tsebelis (166) employed the following algebraic equation:

Equation 8.1: Tsebelis's Dual Arena Nested Games Model

$$PO_i = kPO_{ei} + (1-k)PO_{pi}$$

Notice that the variable k has an antithetical impact on the electoral and parliamentary payoffs. The higher the value of k the greater the importance of the electoral payoff.[14] Flipping the coin, the inverse would be true if voters had no impact on that policy issue. A k between zero and one could sway a politician to move in either direction—favoring either electoral expediency or the rewards of parliamentary action—depending on the value of k and the relative weights of the two payoffs. In the end the value of k will be determined by the amount of information the public has about the issue and the reasoning behind elite behavior (Tsebelis 1990: 168). It also depends on whether the party held a "monopoly of representation" (ibid.).[15] Voters holding these beliefs or ideological positions may have nowhere else to turn for parliamentary representation.

Nested Games—Creole Style

Now we modify Tsebelis's original Nested Games model to suit Puerto Rico and cases of nationalist politics. The model developed here is generalizable to any polity where one of the primary issues of the day is the region's relationship to the center or the *national question*. In societies where peripheries question the degree of local autonomy, self-determination is usually at the apex of political issues and controversies. As a result, such an issue should be regarded as a separate arena.

First, others suggested that there might be more than one arena in Puerto Rican politics. Regarding discussions over a possible federally sponsored status plebiscite in Puerto Rico, "there are two different logics involved in this process: the metropolitan logic and the Puerto Rican elite's logic. The two major actors expect different results from the plebiscite" (Meléndez 1991: 117). Parties may attempt to portray themselves as liberal or conservative. Perhaps they want to show concern for the poor and ordinary workers. They might argue that their platform would improve Puerto Rico's investment climate. But the one issue parties cannot escape is the status question.

Since the establishment of the Commonwealth, parties failing to take a clear stance on this point perish. We need only look at the Christian Democratic Partido Acción Cristiana of the 1960s or the promises of good and clean government offered by former San Juan mayor Hernán Padilla and his Partido Renovación Puertorriqueña in the mid-1980s. Taking a position in favor of one status alternative is no guarantee of electoral success. That was made apparent with such cases as the autonomist Partido del Pueblo in the late 1960s and the separatist Partido Socialista Puertorriqueño that ran candidates in the late 1970s and early 1980s. Without staking a clear status position, commonwealth-era parties do not survive for long.

As it is an unincorporated American territory of the United States, Congress ultimately determines Puerto Rico's status. The evidence presented here indicates that one of the reasons why the Hernández Colón administration backed the 1991 language law, despite the electoral costs, was to send a message to Washington. The status game is the secondary arena in Puerto Rican politics. Thus, we can replace the parliamentary arena in Tsebelis's original equation with a *nationalist* arena. With a nationalist arena we now have a *nationalist* payoff (PO_{ni}) and a new dual arena model that is applicable to cases of nationalist politics:

Equation 8.2: A Dual-Arena Model of Nationalist Politics

$$PO_i = kPO_{ei} + (1-k)PO_{ni}$$

Electoral payoffs in both models are the same. The variable k now represents the balance between the electoral and constitutional arenas. The value of the last variable, k, is determined by the center's insistence on maintaining the status quo since it is the center that ultimately determines the periphery's status.

Where the metropolitan power declines to seriously consider changing the periphery's status, the value of k is high (approaching one). Politicians in the periphery seek only to maximize votes. This was clearly the case with the language bills debated in the 1970s and 1980s. Congress, the final arbiter of Puerto Rico's status, did not consider any fundamental changes to the commonwealth status. No status plebiscites were passed either by Congress or the Puerto Rican legislature. Thus, there was no nationalist payoff to be enjoyed.

In electoral terms Popular Democrats assessed the potential political fallout from changing the 1902 language law. They were aware that a larger percentage of the island's electorate was on the pro-center side of the ideological midpoint than on the pro-periphery side. Once these bills or proposed policies became common knowledge the PNP, acting as a rational institution cognizant of Puerto Rico's ideological spatial distribution, immediately began its rhetorical attack, labeling such bills as key components of a hidden separatist agenda. Responding rationally, the PPD leadership behaved the way that Downs would have predicted and denied the bills their endorsement.

Nested Games models make allowances for changes in circumstances that free political actors to maximize payoffs other than those found in the electoral arena. In cases where the k drops, say, to zero, Puerto Rican politicians shift their attention to the nationalist payoff. Assuming a low k, Governor Rafael Hernández Colón embarked on an electorally dangerous path, but one that was completely rational given that he and the PPD were trying to maximize a nonelectoral payoff. The value of k dropped because Congress was willing to genuinely consider altering the island's status. When Washington sincerely discusses Puerto Rico's status, thus opening the possibility of instigating a fundamental change in Puerto Rican–U.S. relations, the result in Puerto Rico is a disruption in the electoral maximization strategy of island politicians.

Yet, how could the PPD reap a benefit from the *nationalist* arena? After all, Puerto Rico has no effective congressional representation. One possibility was to symbolically crown Spanish as the sole official language, thus highlighting Puerto Rico's cultural distinctiveness vis-à-vis the United States. Such a move was premised on a connection between American identity and the English language.

9

Congress, the English Language, and American Identity

Assume that Governor Rafael Hernández Colón and the leadership of the Partido Popular Democrático were trying to maximize a "nationalist" payoff. How could this be achieved? Arguably the only American territory with an impact on federal policies is the District of Columbia. First, its status as the seat of the government is symbolic, which in and of itself does not afford its residents much influence. Second, thanks to the Twenty-third Amendment, this is the only nonstate jurisdiction with a delegation to the Electoral College; but this Democratic Party stronghold has only three electoral votes. The GOP ignores this jurisdiction, while Democrats take it for granted.

The territories do send delegates to the federal House of Representatives, and these legislators are allowed to vote in committees and subcommittees. Nonetheless, their ineligibility to vote on measures presented on the House floor consigns these House members to the de facto status of publicly financed territorial lobbyists. Furthermore, there are no territorial envoys in the Senate. On continental North America, white settlement, territorial incorporation, and statehood were preordained trajectories for virtually all of the territories (Leibowitz 1989: 8). Thus, the federal constitution did not create the institutions, such as a cabinet-level ministry or agency, that specialized in their plight. In the executive branch, territorial matters are routed through the Interior Department. Federal authority over the territories is practically indistinguishable from its control over parks and wildlife sanctuaries. In contrast to the federal government's relationship with the various Indian reservations, there are no treaties governing federal-territorial affairs.

What could Puerto Rico do to influence congressional action when the island had no voting power in the federal legislature? For the PPD the logical strategy was to highlight Puerto Rican identity, reinforce the uniqueness of its culture, and remind federal lawmakers that these U.S. citizens spoke and cherished a different vernacular. Such a tactic depended on the understanding that the American people and its Congress revered the English language. In order to *threaten* American identity, the Puerto Rican government waved the island's own culture in a bid to frighten Congress into rejecting Puerto Rican statehood. All it took was a mere statute to serve as a catalyst. Presumably cultural conservatives in the United States would take care of the rest. This chapter explores how the PPD could use culture to safeguard the incumbent commonwealth status.

American Identity and Language

Civil society is a robust forum for the preservation and promotion of beliefs independent of those promulgated by the state. Government authorities have at their disposal the power of state agencies, police, and other law enforcers. Outside the bureaucracy, society also imposes its rules, norms, and views. This decentralized collectivity can use shame, humiliation, praise, and gossip to keep its members in line. Defectors risk being ignored, socially isolated, and alienated. While the state and nonstate spheres are distinct, they clearly influence one another. In an effort to imprint state values on society, governments have turned to education departments and ministries that now perform many of the same mythmaking functions executed by elders and clerics in earlier eras and in more traditional societies (Anderson, B. 1983; Hobsbawm 1990; Weber 1976).

Ethnic and national groups need not identify themselves on the basis of language or another particular cultural trait. As mentioned in chapter 2, group identification with language is but one example of *objectification*. In a specious attempt to emulate the methodological approaches used in the natural and applied sciences, ethnic groups and their leaders attempt to *prove* their distinctiveness by pointing to concrete cultural traits such as language, racial or physical characteristics, religious beliefs, folk traditions and fashions, and others (Handler 1988: 13–15). Conceptualized in this manner, group identities are portrayed as the spontaneous and natural outgrowth of the cultural characteristics themselves. This process of articulating group boundaries is a task usually undertaken by elites. Defining the collective on the basis of one trait, or set of traits, maximizes their grip on society (Barreto 1998: 38–39). Of course, in the modern era segments of the bourgeoisie do have various forms of popular media at their disposal, through which they can disseminate particular views. However, the elites most involved in this undertaking are members of the intelligentsia—society's prime mythmakers. Eloquence and high levels of formal education give their opinions respect and great weight (Maldonado-Denis 1972: 219).

Indeed, the successful promulgation of laws declaring the American vernacular the official language of various states, counties, and towns indicates how firmly entrenched language is at the grassroots of U.S. society. Surveys indicate that the connections between the English language and American identity go beyond partisan preferences, socioeconomic status, and racial categories. Frendreis and Tatalovich (1997: 360) discovered that English Only initiatives were strongly supported by those affiliated with both major political parties, although support was stronger among Republicans and those who ideologically identify themselves as conservatives. Likewise, most respondents endorsed this policy initiative across all income brackets, although among those with higher incomes there was a more enthusiastic voice of approval. Finally, among major ethno-racial categories, the English Only ideal was accepted by convincing majorities of whites, blacks, Asians, and even Latinos, although support among Latinos was the weakest of these groups (Frendreis and Tatalovich 1997: 360).

As with many social and political issues, there is quite a bit of scholarly disagreement about what triggered the current wave of English language initiatives in the United States. Some suggest that it was a reaction to demographic changes. Fluctuations in birth rates and immigration patterns increase the frequency and intensity of contacts between different linguistic groups, leading to conflicts over control of social and economic spaces. Perhaps the most noted exponent of this hypothesis is Laponce (1984; 1987), with his cultural-contact/cultural-conflict thesis. In keeping with this line of thinking, Arington (1991: 326) suggested that the recently enacted English First or English Only laws were drafted in reaction to large numbers of immigrants from Latin America and Asia. In contrast, others suggested that the movements backing these initiatives were representative of something larger and deeper. Tatalovich (1995: 54) found that support for these official English initiatives was not correlated with areas heavily populated by Latinos. This study of Puerto Rican language policy does not provide enough evidence to answer that particular controversy. However, it is clear that the language-identity link in the United States is deep-rooted.

Even before secession from Great Britain, the North American colonies accommodated a heterogeneous mixture of peoples. Some Anglo-Irish settlers lived in close proximity to Dutch residents in cities such as New York. English-speaking colonists also lived near German immigrants in Pennsylvania, and there was a myriad of indigenous communities throughout the continent. Despite the omnipresent cultural diversity in the United States, there is an implicit notion that language delineates the domestic from the alien (Baron 1990: 5; Citrin 1990: 96).

The origins of this delineation predate the founding of the American Republic. Eighteenth-century political leaders employed language to reinforce social differences between British subjects and German immigrants (Baron 1990: chap. 3). American society considered English a superior language to others, and this attitude extended to those who spoke it (Barreto 1998: 47–61). Eighteenth-century stereotypes about immigrant intellectual inferiority flourished. Such social conventions were embraced by the lower classes of the newly anointed dominant group, who were assured that their speech, while considered inferior to the variant spoken by Anglophone elites, was nonetheless evidence of their preeminence over non–English speakers. Over time this attitude created a paradox in American society. Proving loyalty to the country obliged immigrants to learn English; yet, immigrants and their English-dominant descendants are subsequently encouraged to learn other languages in order to fortify the country's position in global commerce (Baron 1990: 15).

Identities and hierarchies in the United States have always encompassed more than language. African slavery played an even stronger role in instituting socioeconomic hierarchies based on race (Ignatiev 1995; Omi and Winant 1994). Some scholars argue that the paradigmatic model American citizen is based on an "Anglo" archetype, implying that both language and phenotype help to establish "in-group" membership (Oboler 1995; Urciuoli 1998). Despite the unequal ways in which different ethnic groups are treated, any lack of socioeconomic ascent is blamed on alleged defects in a group's cultural mores. "Ethnicizing discourses are modeled after what is now the classic European immigrant success myth, in which all groups are assumed to start from the same point and move on to success or failure depending on each group's 'value system'" (Urciuoli 1998: 22). In this way, ethnic Puerto Ricans living on the U.S. mainland are very often "blamed" for their standing in the lower classes. This should not be surprising, given the attitudes some government officials held toward their Caribbean subjects (Barreto 1998: 89). While deficient in the eyes of American administrations, presumably Puerto Ricans could be saved thanks to the supposed superiority of the English language and American cultural norms (Carroll 1975: 58–59).

Congressional Precedents

Again, it is important to reemphasize that the United States has no official language policy. Nonetheless, the preeminence of English is extremely pervasive throughout society. This may explain why President Roosevelt, in a 1937 letter to Puerto Rican Education Commissioner José Gallardo, stated that "English is the official language of our country" notwithstanding the lack of any constitutional provision, statute, or government directive to that effect (in Osuna 1975: 377). Beyond social norms and attitudes, the connection between language and American identity also sustains a foothold in government policies and past practices.

Precedents are patterns of past behavior that individuals and institutions use to judge subsequent cases in similar situations. Depending on the institution, the use of precedents may be mandatory or merely suggestive; regardless, they are always open to interpretation. Over the past couple of centuries, the U.S. Congress has created various linguistic precedents that affect discussions of Puerto Rico and its relationship to the federal government. The status alternative most affected by these cases is statehood. When it comes to admitting new states into the union, a report commissioned by the U.S. Congress reported that "The history of statehood admissions is one of both tradition and flexibility" (Comptroller General 1980: 20). This frees the federal legislature to admit the territories it wants under any conditions it sets while allowing Congress to boast of openness.

There are several precedents used to assess a territory's candidacy for statehood, but two specifically affect Puerto Rico's bid. One is the requirement that permanent union be accepted by a clear and convincing majority of the population—a "super majority" (Barreto 1991). The reasoning is straightforward. Statehood is considered a permanent status—a marriage without divorce. Under those circumstances, one wants to be absolutely certain, or as convinced as possible, that the applicant wants statehood. Lacking a prescribed or fixed number, Congress can set the plebiscite's threshold at any level it chooses.

Achieving a super majority remains problematic for the pro-statehood movement in Puerto Rico. In the 1990s the PNP was barely able to crack the 50 percent mark. The last time a political party could count on overwhelming majorities was in the mid-1960s. Under its founder, Luis Muñoz Marín, the PPD usually garnered around 60 percent of the popular vote. At that time the Populares could also count on winning clear majorities of the municipal governments. Recent plebiscite results demonstrate that when it comes time to voting for status options, rather than parties or candidates, support for statehood stabilizes at around 46 to 47 percent. Not surprisingly, pro-statehood leaders do not subscribe to the need for stronger popular support. While former governor Luis A. Ferré is one of many PNP leaders who insisted that a "super-majority" is not required for statehood, U.S. Senate Majority Leader Trent Lott disagreed (Mulero 1996d: 8).

Beyond electoral support lies the question of culture and language. Federal officials have long been aware of the connection between the Spanish language and Puerto Rican identity. A congressional report pointed out that "all status participants, intensely proud of their Puerto Rican heritage, are adamant about preserving and enhancing the island's culture and Spanish language" (Comptroller General 1981: ii). But how does that identity and attachment to language blend into the American political fabric? The first statehood applicant with a significant non–English-speaking community—excluding Indian reservations—was Louisiana in 1812. Congress accepted the territory of Orleans into the union on the condition that English become the state's official language and the medium of legislative debate and judicial affairs (Serrano and Gorrín 1979: 524). As Louisiana bordered other English-speaking states, it was clear that over time migrants from neighboring states would help to transform Louisiana into a state with an English-speaking majority. In the words of Senator Moynihan (1993: 73–74) from New York: "In two centuries, the United States Congress has admitted thirty-seven new states to the original union of thirteen. But always a stated or unstated condition was that English be the official language."

Language was a concern with three other statehood candidates: Arizona, New Mexico, and Oklahoma. Arizona was admitted on the proviso that its future state legislators and chief executive be fluent and literate in English (Serrano and Gorrín 1979: 524). In two remaining states Congress went much further. New Mexico and Oklahoma were ordered to establish English as the medium of instruction in their public school systems (Comptroller General 1980: 13–14). As Senator Moynihan (1993: 74–75) summarized: "The United States Congress has never accepted the idea of a state with an official language other than English."

Hernández Colón and the Linguistic Nexus

American society and its governments have established a linguistic hierarchy that is not always spelled out explicitly. Most American politicians want to avoid being labeled racist, anti-Latino, or xenophobic. Nonetheless, the language-identity bond persists, allowing observers to describe linguistic preferences in the United States. In order to support the hypothesis that Rafael Hernández Colón and the PPD leadership were playing a Nested Game, it is not enough to demonstrate the presence of a connection between the English language and American identity. Analogizing to multiple choice examinations, it is possible to come up with the right answer for the wrong reasons. We must show that the former governor was aware of the language-statehood connection before he signed the López Galarza language bill, and that safeguarding the commonwealth status was a top priority.

Based on his speeches we are clearly led to believe that the PPD leader had faith in autonomy as the most beneficial path for Puerto Ricans. Autonomy's apex, according to Populares, was found in a Puerto Rican commonwealth. Arguments in favor of commonwealth status extol the virtues of a system that its adherents believe preserves local culture and identity while maintaining open access to American markets and unfettered travel to and from North America. "Despite 81 years of cultural interaction with the United States, our culture and our language have preserved their clear autochthonous profile. These are firm bases for our autonomy and our Puerto Rican identity" (Hernández Colón 1986: 6). Meléndez (1998: 131) noted that the centerpiece of PPD policy since the Commonwealth's founding in 1952 was to safeguard this status option and try to fine-tune or "improve" it rather than fundamentally overhaul it. Governor Hernández Colón exclaimed: "We start with the premise that the Commonwealth has served Puerto Rico well, but that it has to adjust itself to new federal and international realities" (Hernández Colón 1986: 48).

Politicians, not very different from many ordinary Puerto Ricans, have extremely strong inclinations toward their preferred status option. Puerto Ricans have been wrestling with the status question since the nineteenth century. One has only to start a conversation on the streets to realize how passionate islanders are about the status question. Particularly to American eyes and ears unaccustomed to this kind of political fervor, the enthusiasm in a Puerto Rican's gestures and the intensity of his or her speech are emotional displays more commonly associated with religious zealots. Island politics are not just about holding office; they reflect one's identity and how one views being Puerto Rican. To those who study ethnic and nationalist politics in other societies, this description will not seem all that foreign. In the United States such emotions are usually reserved for a handful of volatile policy issues such as abortion, gay rights, or gun control.

Even then, usually only small segments of the electorate use these issues as a litmus test when assessing the candidate of their choice.

In light of this discussion, how should we assess the views of Puerto Rican politicians? Political figures represent an elite unto themselves; they are also members of other key groups. In most societies elected officials, even those championing the cause of the masses, usually arise from more privileged homes and are ordinarily more educated than the average citizen. Elites at all times and in every place strive to preserve and promote their privileges. We might be best served by viewing Puerto Rican politicians as members of various key elites—whether they represent a faction of the bourgeoisie, intelligentsia, or other groups—who support the status alternative most likely, in their estimation, to maximize their long-term interests.

Politicians have peddled their favored status option to the masses arguing that it would provide ordinary citizens with great financial rewards. Funding for these benefits emanates primarily from Washington and depends on the island remaining under U.S. sovereignty. Thus autonomist and annexationist political actors cultivate their roles as middlemen supplying American funds to the Puerto Rican people. The difference between them, one could argue, is whether these political elites consider themselves an entity unto themselves (in the case of autonomists) or whether they regard themselves as a portion of a larger elite (in the case of annexationists). In contrast, the PIP's arguments based on cultural pride resonate with the party's leadership and its most consistent source of electoral support—both proceeding from the most progressive segment of the insular intelligentsia. Understanding that Hernández Colón truly supported the commonwealth status, we can appreciate his disdain for the alternatives, especially statehood since it posed the most immediate threat.

Prior to the start of public debates over López Galarza's language bill, this former PPD governor felt that PNP allusions to the possible admission of a Spanish-speaking state ran counter to congressional precedents. In *La Nueva Tesis* Hernández Colón reproached the statehood movement for distorting historic precedents. Traditionally, Congress saw statehood and a common language walking hand in hand (Hernández Colón 1986: 50). Arguably the boldest statement he made on this topic was in a speech delivered in Ponce more than two decades before backing the López Galarza proposal. In December 1969 he exalted the role of Spanish as a defining element of *puertorriqueñidad* and categorically insisted that Congress would not allow any language other than English to hold an official status following statehood.

The reality is that the statehood leadership is trafficking in demagoguery: Before the people cultural defense is espoused knowing that the people want to defend their culture. The people are not responsibly told that the tradition and firm policy observed for over 160 years by the United States Congress counters that [the Spanish] language, that is the culture's soul, may endure as an official language under statehood. (Hernández Colón 1991a: 37)

Cultural identity remains one of the critical factors guiding the growth and changes in Puerto Rican–United States relations. "Puerto Rican nationhood has been the principal factor determining and continuing to determine the nature of relations between Puerto Rico and the United States" (Hernández Colón 1998a: 31). For Populares, the PNP's *estadidad jíbara*, or Creole Statehood thesis, was an admission that Puerto Ricans rejected cultural assimilation.

Creole Statehood is nothing more than the acknowledgment that cultural Americanization is electorally unviable. Even though it's a question of demagogic electoral manipulation, Creole Statehood accepts the victory of Puerto Rican nationhood over the assimilative efforts carried out during the first half [of the twentieth] century by the government of the United States. (Hernández Colón 1998a: 43)

If statehood was an option that the PPD wanted to avoid, the insurance policy against it was Puerto Rican culture itself. This was not an opinion Hernández Colón publicly voiced during the language law debates or even during Washington's 1989–91 hearings on the island's status. Governor Hernández Colón understood that the United States was an English-speaking federation. Latinos and Latin American immigrants live there in the millions, but in no state do they constitute a majority; in no state could they challenge the linguistic hierarchy that favored the English language and, by implication, English speakers.

The 1989–1991 Status Deliberations

Language and culture became important topics of discussion in the congressional debate over Puerto Rico's status during George Bush's term in the White House and Rafael Hernández Colón's last term in the Fortaleza. From the beginning there were tensions between the two executive offices. President Bush was a longtime and well-known supporter of Puerto Rican statehood, while Governor Hernández Colón sought to preserve and possibly expand the limited autonomy enjoyed under the common-wealth constitution. In spite of these differences, Hernández Colón felt that cooperation with the Bush White House on this issue was the best approach (Hernández Colón 1996: 436–37). He underscored that "The solution to the Puerto Rico status problem has been one of my greatest concerns throughout my life" (Hernández Colón 1996: 434). Most of the time legislators in Washington are concerned with other matters and forget that the federation has sovereignty over millions living in overseas terri-tories and partial sovereignty over the hundreds of thousands who live on reservations and in indigenous nations. The 1989–91 hearings were different because Congress was actually taking a serious look at the status problem. "The encounter with Congress to discuss a plebiscite that took place between the years 1989 and 1991 is unique in history. For the first time since U.S. troops landed in Guánica, Congressional leaders faced the Puerto Rican people with the serious intent of allowing them to exercise their right to self determination choosing among the three political status alternatives" (Hernández Colón 1996: 434).

Good intentions are not enough to implement any policy initiative, and this certainly applied to the Puerto Rican status deliberations. Even with White House encouragement, Congress failed to furnish President Bush with a federal status plebiscite bill to sign. Of course, the insular govern-ment could always plan its own status referendum or plebiscite. But with the island's sovereignty in Congress's hands, such a special election would amount to little more than an electoral beauty contest—one that imposed no obligation on Congress even to acknowledge the plebiscite results, let alone act upon them.

Governor Hernández Colón was convinced that the statehood move-ment impeded this process. The most difficult issues touched on how the United States would adapt to such a unique addition to the federation. Among the controversies that were analyzed repeatedly was Senator John-ston's admonition to Carlos Romero-Barceló. The Louisiana Democrat asked Romero-Barceló to drop his language amendment—one that would have included cultural and linguistic guarantees under statehood. When faced with the responsibility of defining statehood and the terms under which Congress would even consider admitting the island as a member of the union, the federal legislature balked. "The reason why Congress resist-ed this procedural mechanism is that it is not prepared to risk conferring Statehood on Puerto Rico. No important problems were presented with the Commonwealth or with Independence" (Hernández Colón 1996: 481). Rafael Hernández Colón reinforced the connection between culture and status in a speech he delivered the day after signing the López Galarza language bill into law. At a meeting of the PPD's General Council in Caguas, he said:

> After two years of analysis and study, the [federal] senators and representatives of the relevant commissions came to a new understanding of the serious economic, social, and cultural damage that Statehood would inflict on Puerto Rico and, consequently, to the United States. They have understood that we are a distinct people, proud of our centenary culture and own personality and that we are not willing to assimilate. (Hernández Colón 1991a: 338–39)

Hernández Colón was attempting to maximize a payoff in the "nationalist arena." He attacked statehood by alarming Congress, the one body that could change the island's status. His ideological opponents accused the PPD leader of directly energizing the most right-wing, racist, and bigoted elements of American society (Negrón Muntaner 1997: 266).

If a majority of federal senators and representatives simply do not want to admit the island as a state, would it not make more sense for Congress to simply say that statehood is out of the question? After all, according to some scholars, American interest in Puerto Rico has always been focused on the island's strategic location and its value as an extension of the mainland U.S. economy (Cabán, P. 1993: 20). Assuming that this hypothesis is correct, honesty could carry dire consequences. The alleged impediments to statehood are its costs to the federal treasury, given the island's higher rate of poverty, and its distinctive culture. To openly express these views is to risk being labeled racist or anti-Latino.

For many walking through the corridors of power, the best strategy is simply to say nothing in opposition to Puerto Rican statehood and decline passing any plebiscite legislation. If the commonwealth government marches ahead with its own plebiscite, fine. No one is obligated to act on its outcome. And given the results of the past few elections, there is little chance that any option would secure an overwhelming majority of the electorate. In the end, this benefits the commonwealth status by default (Colón Morera 1993: 410–11).

By passing a simple and symbolic unilingual law the PPD hoped to influence Congress. Only hindsight will illustrate how well this strategy worked. Regardless of its success or failure, we can say that the PPD was engaged in a risky and sophisticated venture to safeguard its preferred constitutional order. Why did the PPD wait until 1991 to play this card? Congress was focused on the Puerto Rican case at that time, and promulgating a language law would virtually guarantee an alert audience. The rest shall be left for speculation or until the principal actors in this drama pen their memoirs.

Rafael Hernández Colón was, we are led to believe, considering the 1988–1992 term his last one in office and may have wanted to leave a historic legacy. Also, public opinion polls were showing that the PPD could lose the 1992 elections. With the specter of a PNP-led government, Hernández Colón could act then and there or, as the cleric says, forever hold his peace. Out of office his input into policy making would evaporate. Add to that the popularity of President Bush in 1991. George Bush's public approval ratings were at an all-time high following the Persian Gulf War. This made a Bush reelection a very likely scenario early in 1991. So, the prospects of a pro-statehood government in Puerto Rico and a pro-statehood president could not have sat well with the PPD. In many ways this law was a preemptive strike against statehood. In the next chapter we see that the PNP employed many of the same tactics and strategies following its 1992 victory.

10

Restoring Official Bilingualism

In 1993 the Partido Nuevo Progresista was sworn into office. Foremost on the party's agenda was holding a status plebiscite. If ever there were any doubts as to the enduring connection between language and status, the events of 1993 laid them to rest. This chapter explores the Rosselló administration's effort to build support for Puerto Rican statehood in the halls of Congress by enacting a local statute reestablishing English as an official language. However, in 1993 a couple of U.S. lawmakers with connections to the English Only movement stepped into the fray and openly campaigned against the statehood movement. Out of power and low on campaign funds, pro-commonwealth forces succeeded in playing the "language card" with the help of American politicians who were unwilling to separate the issues of language, cultural compatibility, and loyalty to the United States.

Plebiscites and Language Bills

After two consecutive terms in office, the PPD went down in defeat in November of 1992. The PPD lost the governorship, control of both houses of the legislature, and a majority of the island's municipal governments. Without question, the biggest disappointment for the statehood movement was the defeat of their ally George Bush. Even before taking the oath of office, Governor-elect Pedro Rosselló was discussing a status plebiscite (Luciano 1992: 4). The new governor was concerned with removing any barriers to his statehood movement. In that light the 1991 unilingual law was reconsidered. Language and status became inseparable issues and Rosselló was determined that Puerto Rican identity not become a significant issue in congressional deliberations on the matter (Meléndez 1998: 237–38).

In early January 1993 Roberto Rexach Benítez, the new Senate president, announced the creation of a special commission to study holding a status plebiscite (Cordero 1993: 20). During the previous four-year period, the Popular Democratic majority had consulted the PNP, the PIP, and, more important, Congress. At a minimum there was input from outside of the ruling party's inner circle. This time the ruling party, the PNP, decided to push ahead with a local plebiscite without Congress's formal approval, nor did the New Progressives seek a consensus with the two opposition parties (Bauzá 1993: 19).

Separatist parties often look forward to status plebiscites. The PIP did boycott the 1967 status plebiscite; however, it was an active participant in the 1989–1991 congressional hearings. Part of the PIP's strategy in recent decades has been to participate in order to highlight what they see as irreparable flaws in the commonwealth structure—a system they see as inherently colonial. By undermining the status quo, *independentistas* seek to delete one of the three traditional status options. Assuming that statehood is an unacceptable status alternative to Congress, as the PIP does, impairing or eliminating the commonwealth alternative brings the island closer to sovereignty. Nonetheless, in 1993 Governor Pedro Rosselló was not focused on separatists but on autonomists.

At the same time that the PNP was hammering out a plebiscite bill it was also working on a substitute for the 1991 language law. During the first week of 1993 Governor Pedro Rosselló asked the Asamblea Legislativa to reinstate English as an official language (Martínez 1993a: 4). Reactions to this announcement were mirror images of the responses given during the 1990–1991 language debates. PIP Senator Rubén Berríos Martínez accused the PNP of trying to send the incoming Clinton administration a false and misleading message (Estrada 1993a: 5). Separatists long ago pointed out that, regardless of the existence of a bilingual language law dating back to 1902, Puerto Rico was not a bilingual society. The PIP's delegate in the House of Representatives, Víctor García San Inocencio (1998), insinuated that the parliamentary majority aimed "to project Puerto Rico as something that could be assimilated in the eyes of the United States."[1]

PPD interim leader Victoria Muñoz Mendoza lashed out at this "assimilationist" proposal (Estrada 1993b: 13) intended to sneak statehood through the back door (Martínez 1993b: 13). While the PNP had inculpated the PPD with a hidden separatist agenda in 1991, the tables were now turned. Popular Democrats incriminated the New Progressives in a covert plot to bring in statehood and reintroduce a late twentieth-century version of Americanization. Indeed, Renan Soto Soto, president of the AMPR, suggested that a new bilingual law today would precede a new pro-English educational policy tomorrow (Estrada 1993c: 8). In hindsight his words now seem prophetic.

On the other side, PNP activists asserted that Spanish was the de facto language of the majority, therefore needing no special protection. Since the late 1940s there was no government directive to challenge the island's vernacular. For PNP members, López Galarza's 1991 language bill was an unnecessary measure laced with dubious motives (Fernández, I. 1993: 35). Moreover, the reestablishment of English as an official language was necessary to dispel any doubts on the mainland as to Puerto Rico's loyalty to the United States (Ferré 1993: 529). Like the PPD majority before them, some PNP leaders suggested that the language measure should become a constitutional amendment (P. García 1993: 7).

The dilemma for the PNP was what kind of language law would replace Bill 417. Official bilingualism, as described in the 1902 law, meant that either English or Spanish could be used equally in any branch, agency, or department of the Puerto Rican government. Yet the new House speaker, Zaida "Cucusa" Hernández Torres, suggested a compromise between the unilingualism of the 1991 Official Language Act and the strict parity of the two languages under the 1902 law. Under her proposal Spanish would be declared the island's "first language" and English would become the "second language" (Penchi 1993a: 13). Speaker Hernández Torres's proposal was, in fact, a revival of the 1990 Moreno Rodríguez proposal (see appendix 6). PIP Representative David Noriega praised PNP lawmakers Gilberto Moreno Rodríguez—the author of the 1990 alternative bill—and Jorge Luis Navarra Alicea for their endeavor to find some middle ground in the language debate (Penchi 1993b: 18). Three years later the PPD's gubernatorial candidate, Héctor Luis Acevedo, would endorse such a two-tiered policy (Bauzá 1996: 20).

Hopes for a compromise ended early. The PPD pondered over the unilingual law for months, and until the bitter end there were doubts whether Governor Hernández Colón would sign Bill 417. On the contrary, the PNP held only four days of hearings and pushed the bill out of committee with lightning speed (Delgado Cintrón 1993: 43). Héctor López Galarza, the author of the 1991 law, had had to persuade and challenge his party's establishment every step of the way. In contrast, the 1993 bilingual bill was overseen by the PNP's central committee. There was one significant change agreed to in the bill's final version (Luciano 1993b: 19). That clause would have mandated the delivery of an English-language translation of this territorial statute to Congress.

Journalists described the hearings as intense and it became apparent that any expectations of a rapprochement among the three parties was unrealistic (Luciano 1993a: 12). Rosselló administration supporters pointed out that a new language policy was one of the governor's 1992 campaign promises (Baumgartner 1993: 69). Statehood activists and sympathizers considered the law a triumph for maintaining the "doubleness" of Puerto Rican identity (Grosfoguel et al. 1997: 16). Despite earlier promises, Rosselló did not present the language measure before the public in a referendum or plebiscite (Estrada 1991b: 5).

Outside the capital building in San Juan protesters voiced their indignation with the new administration's language proposals (Estrada 1993d: 20). Upping the ante, the PIP organized a rally opposing the PNP's bill ("A defender" 1993: 18). Estimates vary as to the size of the crowd, but newspaper accounts reported that there were around 100,000 participants (Pérez 1993: 8). It was without a doubt one of the largest demonstrations ever held in Puerto Rican history and it even caught the attention of the American media, which rarely covers Puerto Rican political debates ("Inglés No" 1993: A12).

The Official Languages Act of 1993

On January 28—only three weeks into the new legislative session—the PNP majority passed House Resolution 1, which was not only the first bill of the 1993 legislative session but also the very first law promulgated under the fledgling Rosselló administration (see appendix 7). In Bayamón's Sciences Park, Pedro Rosselló signed the bill into law surrounded by hundreds of schoolchildren bused in for the event (Martínez 1993c: 8). His speech reiterated his 1992 campaign slogan that his administration would guarantee "two flags, two anthems, two languages" (Rosselló 1993: 146, 148). Interestingly, the various mainland organizations advocating the establishment of English as the primary or sole official language in the United States made no public statements.

The 1993 law did not mandate the use of any particular language. It merely stated that any government agency, department, or dependency *could* use English. Likewise, government affairs at the municipal level could be carried out in either one of the official languages. Like the 1991 unilingual law before it, the 1993 statute clearly stated that there was no attempt to repress or limit the rights of any individual to speak in the language of his or her choice. Neither the 1991 nor 1993 laws attempted to institute any substantive changes in government operations.

This bilingual law, like its unilingual predecessor, was more a symbol than an instrument of policy change. At least one PNP legislator openly concurred with this analysis. Referring to the 1993 language law, Repre-

sentative Albita Rivera noted that the PNP's electoral landslide, in terms
of the number of posts won, gave the measure an added edge.

> Rather, I think that the decision . . . of Governor Rosselló was the same as
> Rafael's [Hernández Colón] but in reverse. Rather, it demonstrated to the
> United States, *look,* here we not only rejected what Rafael [Hernández
> Colón] said—that we do not want to separate from you—but also that
> it comes from a statehood party overwhelmingly controlling the House
> and Senate and almost all the municipalities. . . . And now I am going to
> tell you that I have a mandate from the people to again restore the two
> languages. (Rivera Ramírez 1998)[2]

Another member of her party, former education secretary Carlos Chardón,
concurred with the assessment that message sending was at the apex of the
PNP's agenda, as it was with the PPD. Cutting to the chase, the former
cabinet secretary said of the 1991 and 1993 language laws: "Well, first of all,
it was equally symbolic. It changed nothing in Puerto Rico. The first one
changed nothing in Puerto Rico; the second changed nothing in Puerto
Rico" (Chardón 1998). Some on the other side of the partisan aisle agreed.
Former PPD house speaker Jarabo stated:

> So they [the PNP] did exactly the same thing that Hernández Colón tried
> to do with the '91 law—exactly. Send a message. So the language laws be-
> came pawns on the chessboard of the status debate. In '91 the determining
> factor to go ahead with the law in spite of the red flags that were popping
> up . . . was a gain in the parliamentary procedures in Congress. That was
> the green light. (Jarabo 1998)

An element deleted from the original 1993 bill was the requirement that
a translation be sent to Congress. As it turned out, that was not necessary.
Former governor and founding PNP member Carlos Romero-Barceló
was elected resident commissioner in 1992. As the island's sole delegate to
the House of Representatives, he announced the change in Puerto Rican
language policy less than a week after Bill 1 was signed. Furthermore, he
requested that a copy of the territorial statute, in English, be included in
the *Congressional Record* (1993: H329–30). Before his House colleagues
Romero-Barceló praised the law as an avowal of the bonds between Americans and Puerto Ricans:

> This, the first major act of our new Governor and our territorial legisla-
> ture, signals the intent of the people of Puerto Rico to reaffirm a principle

stated in the preamble of our territorial Constitution—and that is our special commitment as American citizens to the coexistence in our island of the two great cultures of the American hemisphere. (*Congressional Record* 1993: H328)

The 1993 law, Romero-Barceló argued, stood in sharp contrast to its antecedent. Fortifying Puerto Rican–American relations and congressional support for statehood was the goal of the 1993 law. He claimed that: "The Spanish-only law was imposed as an obstacle to equality and our achievement of full political rights in our Nation" (*Congressional Record* 1993: H328). Puerto Ricans had, in his view, earned that equality. (A justification often used by statehood activists is what can be called *blood equity*— the sacrifices Puerto Ricans have made in American wars and overseas conflicts.) Afterward Romero-Barceló brought up the topic of the island's status and a future vote plebiscite or referendum:

> Mr. Speaker, the issue of resolving Puerto Rico's status is complex—it is often controversial and it is one which will require the careful and serious attention of Congress if it is to be resolved. I am certain that my fellow colleagues will make available their patience, understanding, and attention when this issue is put on the table, following the outcome of the referendum. Your fellow U.S. citizens deserve no less. (*Congressional Record* 1993: H329)

The PNP could not even begin to take up the status issue until the unilingual Spanish language law was repealed. Underscoring just how important this measure was to the PNP in terms of its relationship with Washington, former Senate president Roberto Rexach Benítez (1998) stated: "Well, it had to be seen in Congress as a step in the right direction. Rather, we are eliminating something that does not represent the feelings of the Puerto Rican people."[3] In the same interview the Senate leader also pointed out how the measure helped the PNP, in electoral terms, during the 1992 campaign. "It helped us a great deal in the eyes of the U.S. Congress and it helped us a lot here in Puerto Rico. Obviously that one [the 1991 law] supplied us with a very powerful electoral issue against the Popular [Democratic] Party" (Rexach Benítez 1998).[4]

The PNP's opposition was very aware of the message the party wanted to send to Washington. Discussing the PNP's intentions behind the passage, former PPD Senate president Hernández Agosto (1998) said:

> the passage of the language law under the Rosselló administration says: *look*, we have changed the separatist course that the Partido Popular

Democrático was [embarking] on . . . for a route towards union with the United States. We defended statehood and made English an official language. Early on we eliminated a problem that could exist for Puerto Rico's admission into the union.[5]

Former PIP senator Fernando Martín (1998) said the government's position, while predictable, was absurd given the number of islanders fluent in English.

Well, the '93 law obviously responds to the change in the balance of power in Puerto Rico and . . . the PNP acknowledged that the '91 law stuck a finger in their eye. The first thing they did upon arrival was to rescind it. Certainly, the repeal [of Bill 417] on the part of the PNP—predictable and from their point of view perfectly understandable—always has the problem and defect of being ridiculous. Because making a language that the majority of the people do not understand an official language in your country always has something ridiculous about it. (Martín 1998)[6]

As with the 1991 law, some questioned the degree to which the PNP's grassroots championed the 1993 law. Yes, it was a campaign issue that Rosselló ran on in 1992. But did the party's base spearhead the measure in any significant way? In chapter 8 we report on the results when we asked a PPD activist and former officeholder about the nexus between the 1991 law and the party's base. We asked the same thing of a local PNP activist and former officeholder. A pharmacist by training, Félix Méndez Soto was a member of the Guaynabo municipal assembly for the PNP from the late 1960s through the late 1970s. Before that he was president of the Juventud Estadista Republicana—Statehood Republican Youth—in San Juan in the late 1950s and early 1960s. Annexationist sentiments played a major role in his family. His paternal grandfather, Aurelio Méndez Martínez, along with such notable figures as José Celso Barbosa, was a founding member of the Partido Republicano Puertorriqueño (Puerto Rican Republican Party) in 1899, Puerto Rico's first pro-statehood party under American rule.[7]

While he personally favors Puerto Rican statehood, Félix Méndez Soto understood that the final decision on whether or not to fully annex the island would be made in Washington. In terms of determining any statehood prerequisites he said: "who is going to impose conditions is the American Congress" (Méndez Soto 1998).[8] Among the reservations that the federal legislature could invoke was language. This was done earlier with statehood applicants such as Louisiana and New Mexico. Public policies in Puerto Rico are often influenced by how local leaders assess the congressional mood, and this applies particularly to the status question. Discussing the nexus between language, status, and the top-down nature of many of these policies, Félix Méndez Soto (1998) responded: "I believe that these movements for change, for example the Spanish-only in '91 by Rafael Hernández Colón and later on the two languages by Pedro Rosselló, are movements by leaders to secure what they envisage as the final [status] formula for Puerto Rico."⁹ Apparently the leadership of the two largest parties directed and employed changes in language policy for their own purposes. This helps to explain why the PNP and PPD resisted elevating the official language statutes to constitutional amendments. Such endeavors would leave the fate of linguistic matters directly in the hands of the public—a move neither party wanted to venture.

The PNP's Political Calculus

Apparently the Rosselló administration was concerned with Congress more than winning votes. Opinion polls showed that the majority of the island's public favored having two official languages. However, an analysis of newspaper reports and the interviews conducted for this study indicate that vote maximization was not foremost on the PNP's agenda. Granted, Governor Rosselló's linguistic agenda was scheduled early in his term of office. Assuming that the public turned against the Partido Nuevo Progresista for passing this law, the party had almost four years to make amends with the electorate. Still, the PNP's decision to change the 1991 language law as quickly as possible, and before proceeding with a status plebiscite, shows that the pro-statehood party was concerned much less with the electoral arena than it was with appeasing Washington.

Whether they were annexationists, autonomists, or separatists, political leaders in Puerto Rico were aware of the connection between the English language and American identity. These same leaders also knew that Puerto Ricans were proud of their culture and their vernacular and recalled the Americanization process undertaken by the federal government in the first half of the twentieth century. Statehood leaders have been especially burdened with this particular duality. On the one hand, they tried to convince islanders that permanent political unification with the United States is feasible despite differences in vernaculars. At the same time, these leaders tried to convince members of Congress that Puerto Ricans wanted to become an integral part of the American family in the broadest sense of the term. This may explain why the PNP leadership decided against resurrecting Moreno Rodríguez's 1990 language bill that declared Spanish the first language and English the second official language. Congress could interpret such a law as saying that islanders considered themselves Puerto Ricans first and Americans second. Convincing Puerto Ricans of one thing and reassuring Congress of another is not an easy task. Not surprisingly, many statehood opponents have accused the PNP of employing Janus-faced arguments—saying one thing in San Juan and something else in Washington.

For New Progressives a major concern was how to word the 1993 language law. If they pushed English too far the Populares could claim that Novoprogresistas were reintroducing Americanization. Given the distribution of the Puerto Rican electorate, such an insinuation could spell disaster for the PNP either in the forthcoming elections or even in the status plebiscite itself. Yet, the party had to send its "message" to Washington. In an attempt to achieve some sort of equilibrium, the PNP decided to restore the status quo ante and symbolically reaffirm the official equality of the two languages.

The 1993 Status Plebiscite

The decision to proceed with a status plebiscite was controversial, even within the PNP. Various factions were vying for control of the party: one headed by Governor Rosselló, one by Resident Commissioner Romero-Barceló, and another was spearheaded by the Federación de Alcaldes— the Mayors' Federation (Meléndez 1998: 22). Some of the most vocal apprehensions about a plebiscite were voiced by the Federación de Alcaldes. This organization, consisting of PNP municipal executives, felt that a plebiscite should be postponed until internal divisions within the party were ameliorated (Archilla 1993: 3). Their concerns were pushed to the side by the party's leadership.

While the Puerto Rican legislature discussed a status plebiscite, Congress did likewise. The House's Subcommittee on Insular and International Affairs took up the matter early in the summer of 1993. In the course of the ensuing congressional debates, PIP leader Fernando Martín reminded Washington that statehood was a permanent status—a precedent established by the Civil War (U.S. House 1993: 80). He added that Puerto Rico had a long-standing independence movement that persevered despite fundamental changes in insular society and decades of persecution. The point was not the existing strength of the independence movement but the possibility that one day it *could* represent the median voter. As a case in point he brought up the situation in Quebec (U.S. House 1993: 81). Martín pointed out: "So long as Puerto Rico continues to be a nation and thinks of itself as a nation, the political manifestation of that nationality will always be at a given moment the claim for sovereignty, self-government and the right of self-determination" (U.S. House 1993: 81).

Representatives from the Partido Nuevo Progresista sought to brighten this gloomy scenario. They pointed to the fact that a pro-statehood party was popularly elected. Senator Kenneth McClintock-Hernández proudly exclaimed before Congress: "Puerto Rico, as you are aware, will be voting on its political future next November 14. My written testimony expounds on the fairness of this process and includes a copy of the plebiscite law in Puerto Rico's newest official language" (U.S. House 1993: 127). Senator McClintock-Hernández wanted to remind federal lawmakers that a plebiscite was in the works, and he reemphasized the role of English as one of the island's official languages.

Over the years Puerto Ricans enjoyed a certain degree of cultural autonomy, which was represented by the Spanish language and the island's separate teams in international sporting events and beauty contests. Statehood leaders had long claimed that these practices could continue even after the island's admission into the union. Statehood activist Miriam Ramírez de Ferrer wanted Congress to spell out these fine points. "These are not extraneous details. They are the core issues dictating the choice. A vote by the people of Puerto Rico without an understanding of the meaning and consequences of their choice would be worse than meaningless. It would be mischievous with a lack of commitment by the Congress" (U.S. House 1993: 162). Congress ultimately decided against sponsoring a federal status referendum, nor did it spell out the necessary conditions for any status option.

The Aftermath of Congressional Hearings

Lacking congressional approval, the Puerto Rican government proceeded with a local plebiscite. The Rosselló administration was confident it could obtain a statehood plurality or even a clear majority favoring permanent union (Martínez 1993e: 24). Some of this optimism was partially founded on the popularity of Governor Pedro Rosselló in his first year in office ("Satisfactoria" 1993: 4). Without a consensus from all three parties, the ruling PNP drafted the plebiscite bill and defined each of the three traditional options of independence, a continued commonwealth status, or statehood. The bill's characterization of statehood alluded to the island's right to maintain its cultural identity following its admission into the union based on the federal constitution's Tenth Amendment (Martínez 1993d: 6).

This definition was chastised and challenged by an opposition that pointed to the words of New York Senator Daniel Patrick Moynihan and his conclusion that, historically, Congress disfavored cultural autonomy for statehood aspirants with large non–English-speaking communities (García San Inocencio 1993: 47). Assuming that statehood attained a plebiscitary majority, Congress would have the final say over what linguistic prerequisites, if any, would be imposed. However, public opinion polls taken in the summer of 1993 showed that this was less than assured, given that support for the commonwealth option was slightly ahead of its competitors ("No hay mayoría" 1993: 4).

A few members of Congress became thoroughly entwined in the Puerto Rican status discussions. Two Democratic lawmakers, Pennsylvania Representative Austin Murphy and Illinois Senator Paul Simon, came out and publicly endorsed Puerto Rican statehood (Mulero 1993d: 12; 1993e: 8). Yet the most talked about congressmen during the 1993 plebiscite campaign were two Republican House members—Toby Roth of Wisconsin and Gerald Solomon of New York. Roth and Solomon were known English language supporters and they were concerned with the picture of statehood the PNP was painting. Roth and Solomon wanted the public to be aware of their view that admission into the union included linguistic restrictions or requirements favoring English over other languages (Benítez 1998: 123–26).

A fascinating account of the events leading up to the 1993 status plebiscite, from the PPD's perspective, was published by former education secretary Celeste Benítez. PPD leader Miguel Hernández Agosto asked her to direct the pro-commonwealth campaign in the forthcoming plebiscite (Benítez 1998: 60–61). She recalled that the Partido Popular Democrático was well aware of Roth's and Solomon's stance on the federal language policy. Taking advantage of what appeared to be a golden opportunity, the PPD contacted Representative Roth's office and informed the Wisconsin legislator of the PNP's public statements (Benítez 1998: 123–24). Although he did not endorse the commonwealth cause, Roth decided to appear on PPD-sponsored television advertisements attacking the pro-statehood camp. The collaboration of Puerto Rican Popular Democrats with mainland Republicans is another example that politics do make for strange bedfellows.

Representative Roth spelled out congressional linguistic precedents for statehood applicants (Luciano 1993c: 10). Island voters should be aware that if they voted for statehood Puerto Rico would be required to establish English as the official language (Mulero 1993a: 26). Adding to his message's impact, Congressman Roth delivered his announcement in English and subtitles were added in Spanish (Benítez 1998: 126). Puerto Ricans frequently hear individual words and certain terms in English on islandwide television and radio broadcasts, but rarely do they ever hear entire speeches delivered in the American vernacular. Roth's comments represented his personal views; they were not sanctioned by either the Senate or the House of Representatives. However, the fact that a mainland politician was adding directly to the language debate became a concern for the pro-statehood forces. Gerald Solomon joined Roth by pointing to the linguistic barriers for Puerto Rico, the elimination of the Commonwealth's special tax exemptions upon statehood, and the financial burden Puerto Rico would inflict on the federal treasury (Mulero 1993b: 23).

As the status plebiscite campaign progressed, the group English First jumped into the fray. Days before the plebiscite was held, this association took out advertisements in Puerto Rican newspapers stating that acquisition of English was a de facto statehood requirement ("Aviso" 1993: 49). Ironically, English First published these advertisements in Spanish!

Resident Commissioner Carlos Romero-Barceló took on Congressman Solomon. As a member of the House of Representatives, Romero-Barceló was firm but diplomatic in his criticisms of this New York lawmaker (Mulero 1993c: 13). Somewhat stronger language was used by former governor and PNP founder Luis A. Ferré, who lashed out at Solomon, arguing that Puerto Rico's bilingualism should be recognized as a strength and not a liability (Mulero 1993e: 11). Harsher words were reserved for Congressman Roth since he appeared in a PPD-sponsored ad. In an attempt to discredit Roth, statehood supporters labeled the Wisconsin lawmaker an extremist and an ultra-right winger, and in terms of guilt by association readers were reminded that Roth came from the same state as the infamous Senator Joseph McCarthy (Dávila Colón 1993: 65). Groups such as English First were simply dismissed as extremist and nonrepresentative of the mainstream of American political thought.

The Plebiscite's Aftermath

Commonwealth won the 1993 status plebiscite with 48.6 percent of the popular vote. Statehood was backed by 46.3 percent, and independence was endorsed by 4.4 percent of the public (Comisión Estatal de Elecciones 1993b: 2). These results paralleled Puerto Rico's general elections since the mid-1960s, whereby no political party could count on majority support. Rosselló used these results to reexamine his party's strategy and gear up for another plebiscite.

Perhaps as interesting as the plebiscite results was the introduction of American individuals and groups into a Puerto Rican process usually ignored on the mainland. With the exception of periods of political violence, Puerto Rico remains on the outermost periphery of American political debates. The reader should not have the impression that American politicians were descending on the island like plagues of locusts; their visits were well documented, but few. Still, their involvement in 1993 echoed in the following years. Among the most passionate arguments were not issues of finances and the economic impact of a status change but controversies surrounding cultural compatibility and the precise role of the English language in American public policy. The more that pro-statehood forces tried to tout their loyalty to the United States by parading the 1993 bilingualism act, the more some in Congress became suspicious. There is no concrete evidence proving causality between the PPD-backed language law from 1991 and the increase in mainland interest in Puerto Rican language policies.

Out of office the PPD was able to use the language issue to its tactical advantage. The PPD's Nested Game delivered it a substantial long-term benefit. The PPD was without a doubt a weaker organization in 1993 than in 1991. At the same time, the commonwealth status was arguably in stronger shape in late 1993 than it had been two years earlier. Its added strength came from diminishing support for statehood in Washington. Once one pro-commonwealth government passed a unilingual law, it became clear that a future Puerto Rican government could do it again.

As Benítez (1998: 125) pointed out, both Roth and Solomon represented districts close to the Canadian border and they were well aware of the linguistic tug of war between the French-speaking province of Quebec and the Canadian federal government. Puerto Rico's 1991 language law may have reminded them of Québécois nationalism and Quebec's famous language law—Bill 101. Could Puerto Rico represent for the United States what Quebec was for Canada? The concern in Congress over statehood and culturolinguistic compatibility would force the PNP to go even further in promoting the English language in Puerto Rico.

11

Creating a Bilingual Citizenry

Following the 1993 plebiscite, Pedro Rosselló prepared for another status vote. He felt obliged to provide Congress with evidence that Puerto Ricans were leaning toward statehood. He also had to demonstrate that his administration was willing to *promote* the English language. That task became more difficult with a Republican majority in Congress and with the appearance of autonomists and separatists in Congress openly displaying Puerto Rico's cultural distinctiveness. Rosselló had to move beyond official bilingualism in order to convince Washington. He had to promote the English language in the public school system, a move that risked antagonizing the island's teachers' unions and exposed the PNP to charges that it was reinstituting Americanization. Puerto Rican autonomists, separatists, American conservatives, and English-language advocates joined forces in frustrating Rosselló's Nested Games strategy.

Revisiting the Status Dilemma

Less than two weeks after the 1993 plebiscite vote, Republican Congressman Don Young of Alaska called for the island's formal incorporation (Mulero 1993f: 4). In 1900 the U.S. Supreme Court held that the 1898 Treaty of Paris converted this Caribbean island into an American *possession* but not into an integral *part* of the country.[1] Puerto Rico established the precedent whereby territories would be distinguished as either *incorporated* or *unincorporated*.[2] Incorporated territories were slated for statehood, while the eventual fate of their unincorporated counterparts was left to congressional whims.

Congressman Young wanted to initiate a process of decolonization whereby islanders could select from the following options: independence, free association, or statehood. Both independence and statehood were well-known options. Free association jurisdictions such as the Marshall Islands and the Federated States of Micronesia had greater autonomy than the existing commonwealth arrangement but fell short of full sovereignty.

Under Young's proposal, one warmly received by the PNP, commonwealth would be eliminated as a viable status choice (Martínez 1993f: 4).

Some of the strongest opposition to the PNP's objectives in the halls of Congress came from the more conservative elements of the Republican Party. Consequently this faction became the target of the PNP's political efforts (Meléndez 1998: 247–48). Appeasing the Republicans meant adapting or ejecting long-standing policies and practices. For example, Puerto Ricans were accustomed to a large public sector. Parties counted on these jobs to provide their supporters with patronage. But U.S. conservatives were unlikely to look kindly upon such a bloated system. The remedy was Rosselló's privatization plan (Meléndez 1998: 255–56). The most controversial of these proposals was the summer 1998 sale of the Puerto Rico Telephone Company. Ostensibly Rosselló wanted to improve government efficiency, but at their core these changes were designed to appeal to a more conservative Congress.

According to PIP leader Rubén Berríos Martínez, many in Congress were thankful that statehood was defeated in the 1993 plebiscite. Before a congressional hearing he said: "To the United States, Puerto Rico poses a problem not of individual rights, but of collective rights of a people, of a right of a distinct nationality to govern itself in its separate and distinct homeland" (U.S. House 1995: 51). Never one to forgo the opportunity to alarm Congress, Berríos Martínez, in the Charles Dickens tradition, portrayed himself as the "Ghost of Christmas yet to come." Political instability in Quebec, Ireland, Bosnia, and Chechnya were harbingers of what Puerto Rico might become for the United States (U.S. House 1995: 52). These cases indicated that "as long as Puerto Ricans are Puerto Ricans with their distinct identity and language, Congress as a body cannot seriously consider statehood" (U.S. House 1995: 53).

Héctor Luis Acevedo, San Juan's mayor and the PPD's 1996 candidate for governor, also expressed his opinions before the same body. Mayor Acevedo also claimed Congress had an obligation to formally recognize Puerto Rico's cultural distinctiveness (U.S. House 1995: 41). Yet he took a softer tone than Berríos Martínez. Mayor Acevedo exclaimed that Puerto Ricans' pride in their heritage in no way hampered their reverence for a close relationship with the United States (U.S. House 1995: 41).

Congress revisited the status quandary in March of the following year. Again Rosselló insisted that states had the authority to establish their own language policies (U.S. House 1996: 31). Yet the PNP did not address how Congress itself would operate were the island a state. Congressional deliberations are currently conducted in English. San Juan's PPD mayor decided to test congressional reaction to speeches in Spanish. Héctor Luis Acevedo addressed the House Subcommittee on Native American and Insular Affairs, saying: "Hoy vengo a hablarles de nuestra nación"— Today I come to speak to you about our nation (U.S. House 1996: 32). Months earlier, Acevedo had addressed Congress in English. Carlos Romero-Barceló, the island's nonvoting delegate in Congress, fielded Acevedo questions in English while the mayor responded in Spanish (U.S. House 1996: 45). Subsequently Berríos Martínez, a separatist leader extolled for the eloquence of his diction in English, also addressed the subcommittee in Spanish:

> Es necesario además, que el Congreso entienda que mientras la nuestra constituye una nacionalidad diferente a la americana, el pueblo de Puerto Rico tendrá el derecho inalienable para la libre determinación e independencia. (U.S. House 1996: 50)

> [Furthermore, it is necessary that Congress understand that while ours constitutes a different nationality from the American, the people of Puerto Rico will have the inalienable right to free determination and independence.]

Those representing the PPD and PIP continued speaking in Spanish. Resident Commissioner Romero-Barceló maintained his composure until PPD Senator Antonio J. Fas Alzamora spoke. Fas Alzamora greeted the committee in English; thereafter, he proceeded in Spanish (U.S. House 1996: 74). Romero-Barceló could no long suppress his consternation, whereupon he interrogated Fas Alzamora *in Spanish* (U.S. House 1996: 84). What started as a bilingual dialogue became a fiery exchange between two Spanish speakers in the middle of a congressional hearing. Perhaps the "Ghost of Christmas yet to come" had just arrived.

Months after this hearing, Congressman Randy Cunningham and Senator Richard Shelby proposed a bill that would declare English the sole language of the federal government. Observers in Puerto Rico were aware that such a measure would devastate support for statehood on the island. Romero-Barceló downplayed the impact of this bill by emphasizing that it only applied to the federal government and not the individual states or the territories (Mulero 1996a: 7). Most English-language proponents also opposed Don Young's federal plebiscite bill (Mulero 1996b: 8). Outside Congress, California Governor Pete Wilson insisted English should become the official language of a future Puerto Rican state (Mulero 1996e: 5). Conservative activist Patrick Buchanan asserted that the island's Spanish language and its enduring independence movement were insurmountable impediments to its full incorporation into the union (Mulero 1996d: 10).

The Solomon Factor

Throughout these debates Gerald Solomon remained an unwavering supporter of boosting the American vernacular's status in federal law. This New York Republican congressman opposed the Young bill because it did not specify, among other things, the island's official language under statehood (Mulero 1996f: 4). Puerto Rican statehood could complicate efforts to declare English the official language of the United States and might even lay the groundwork for official bilingualism. The model of bilingualism many Americans envisioned was Canadian. To Québécois nationalists the Canadian confederation was an unequal partnership. In response they induced the Révolution Tranquille—the Quiet Revolution—a more militant and separatist strain of nationalism (Levine 1990: chap. 3). The epicenter of the English-French language tempest was Montreal (Laponce 1980: 155).

Solomon represented New York State's twenty-second congressional district. Its northern fringes in Essex County run close to the Canadian border and the linguistic fault lines of Montreal. Solomon's familiarity with language controversies in Canada may have tinted his view of U.S.-Puerto Rican relations. His district was also a relatively short distance from New York City—the locus of the largest Puerto Rican enclave outside of the Caribbean. Deliberations over the status question became an opportunity to revisit the language issue. As the chairman of the House Rules Committee, Solomon had the power to bring the federal status bill to a grinding halt.

Former governor Rafael Hernández Colón did not see Solomon as someone prejudiced against Puerto Ricans but as a lawmaker who was looking out for the long-term interests of his people.

Solomon was here. He was in Vieques as a member of the armed forces. He got to know us. He knows how we are. He has many Puerto Rican friends. He has nothing against us Puerto Ricans. What he wants is to be assured [of] the linguistic unity of his nation. And he knows that we speak Spanish and he also knows that there is a growing well-dispersed population in the United States of Spanish-speaking people and also other languages. And all that presents him with problems of national cohesion for the United States. And that is the problem Gerald Solomon addresses.[3] (Hernández Colón 1998b)

Another Republican congressman sharing Solomon's concerns over language and statehood was Dana Rohrabacker from California (Mulero 1998b: 8). Unlike Solomon, Rohrabacker encouraged Puerto Rican independence (Mulero 1996g: 6). Not all House Republicans concurred. While Speaker Newt Gingrich supported declaring English the official language he also favored the Young bill (Mulero 1996c: 8). Some speculated that Gingrich perceived the statehood issue as a way to increase Republican support among Latino voters. President Clinton endorsed holding a federal status plebiscite, but he opposed establishing English as the country's official language (Galib 1992: 28). His administration supported "statehood in Spanish" and argued that linguistic diversity should not impede political union (Mulero 1997a: 4).

It has been suggested that Solomon's calls to make English the official federal language and to insist that a future Puerto Rican state declare English its official language irreparably damaged the status bill's chances for passage in 1996 (Meléndez 1998: 250). Adding to the fray were English-language advocacy groups. On election day in 1996, the group U.S. English published a full-page advertisement in Puerto Rico claiming that "Statehood and English are inseparable. La estadidad y el inglés son inseparables" ("One nation" 1996: 45). Notwithstanding the restoration of official bilingualism, many on the mainland were not convinced of Puerto Rico's commitment to a cultural and linguistic rapprochement with the United States. The PNP had to reevaluate its languages policies and whether to engage in a Nested Game.

Language Policy in the Public School System

In the next round of budget talks the island's Education Department asked for additional funds for, among other things, converting several schools into bilingual educational centers (Millán 1996a: 20). The territorial government also considered establishing magnet schools throughout the island that would teach entirely in English (Millán 1996b: 18). Images of the old Americanization policy resurfaced. None of the pro-statehood administrations in the commonwealth era had instituted any fundamental changes to educational language policy (Muntaner 1990: 205–15). Carlos Chardón, education secretary under the pro-statehood Romero-Barceló administration, stated:

The problem is that we've had 100 years to learn English. And the issue of
English is no longer a pedagogical issue. I would call it a political issue.
But more importantly, it's an issue of will. We've had no government
in the history of Puerto Rico, outside those initial governors of Puerto
Rico, who have really made an effort to teach English in Puerto Rico.
That includes me as a former secretary. The statehood party has a very
poor record, almost as poor as the Popular Democratic Party. (Chardón
1998)

In 1996 the Partido Nuevo Progresista reconsidered that inaction. Historically the party wanted to avoid a showdown with the two major teachers' unions—the larger Asociación de Maestros de Puerto Rico and the
smaller, but more militant, Federación de Maestros de Puerto Rico. After
all, the AMPR led the movement against teaching in English. Furthermore,
promoting English opened the door for the opposition to label New Progressives cultural assimilationists, just as promoting unilingualism in 1991
opened the PPD to attacks that it was toying with separatism.

But in 1996 the PNP was less influenced by potential conflicts with
teachers or winning future elections. Their target was Congress, particularly conservative Republicans. The PNP gambled that a commitment to cultural accommodation with the mainland would translate into an increased
likelihood of statehood's approval in Washington (Meléndez 1998: 258).
Restoration of official bilingualism in 1993 was a return to the status quo
ante and consistent with public opinion polls. Due to the potential electoral
fallout the PNP withheld outlining details of its new language strategy until
after the 1996 elections.

Bilingual Citizens/Cuidadanos Bilingües

Following his 1996 reelection, Pedro Rosselló and Education Secretary
Víctor Fajardo drew up plans to revamp the public school system with
an eye to increasing the visibility of English language instruction. As
a justification for emphasizing the English language, Secretary Fajardo
pointed to the Official Languages Act of 1993 ("A enseñar" 1997: 20).
Both English and Spanish were co-equal and official languages of the
Puerto Rican government—a point not overlooked in the Education Department's report, *Project for the Development of a Bilingual Citizen*
(Department of Education 1997: 5 and 14). Within the Education Department Juan Rodríguez González, special assistant to the secretary on
academic affairs, was the person primarily responsible for outlining the
administration's bilingual citizenry project. He said: "[b]eing these two

our official languages we have a situation seen year after year. Students are not . . . reaching standards that we as educators have set for them. In '93 English is made official again in Puerto Rico. A process of strong education reform also begins with this development. And within the educational reform process there has been curricular reform" (Rodríguez González 1998).[4]

Regardless of partisan leanings, most Puerto Ricans recognize that learning English is a crucial part of the school's curriculum. This includes independence supporters. "In the end, besides supporting the satisfactory usage of our language all Puerto Ricans believe that the greatest possible number of people [should] sufficiently understand English in order to take advantage of English as the great world language" (Martín 1998).[5] Separatists see learning English primarily as a means to facilitate interactions with the rest of the world, including the United States, rather than a contrivance to bring the island into the American federation.

Critics of the Rosselló-Fajardo language and education reforms pointed out that in order to improve the teaching of English the government had to first improve the teaching of Spanish. Students with difficulties in certain subjects would only see their problems compounded if they had to study these subjects in an unfamiliar language. Additionally, most Puerto Rican students rarely have the opportunity to practice the English they learn in school.

> Look, the boys and girls do not know math in Spanish. How are they going to know it in English? First one has to master their mother tongue in order to then master, in our case, English. . . . Here boys and girls do not practice English. Here boys and girls finish a bachelor's degree and do not know how to express themselves in English. They cannot sustain a conversation in English. (López Galarza 1998)[6]

Officials from Fajardo's offices acknowledged that in order to improve the teaching of English the government was obliged simultaneously to reemphasize the vernacular. As the government's report indicated, "The native language and the second language are complementary rather than mutually exclusive" (Department of Education 1997: 11). Rodríguez González claimed that fortifying Spanish was part and parcel of the government's effort to improve language education and help create a bilingual citizenry.

> Well, many of the studies consulted clearly point out that to master a second language first you must master your mother tongue. And that

is where we started. The public policy of the Project for the Development of the Bilingual Citizen endeavors, over all, to fortify
the teaching of Spanish so that the student can learn English well.
(Rodríguez González 1998)[7]

Fajardo proposed using English as a medium of instruction starting
in the 1997–1998 school year (Rodríguez, M. 1997: 6). He contemplated
a gradualist strategy introducing English-language texts in such courses
as mathematics, chemistry, and biology. "We are recommending them
to the teachers and schools that use reference books—mathematics and
in the sciences—since the terminology in science upon translation many
times loses its essence and there are some terms and some words that are
not translatable" (Rodríguez González 1998).[8] To go along with this new
policy, officials at the Education Department planned to produce special
teaching guides for the new English-language textbooks (Valdivia 1997a:
10).

Puerto Rico's Education Department has always faced a major problem, a finite supply of teachers specifically trained as English-language
specialists. Their highly prized skills make these university graduates
valuable to a private sector willing to remunerate their services beyond
what the school system can offer. Additionally, unfettered travel between
the island and the U.S. mainland opens the way for many highly skilled
bilinguals to seek more lucrative job opportunities stateside. To alleviate
this situation, the Rosselló administration proposed creating a scholarship program for students aspiring to become English teachers and
wanted to establish more aggressive recruiting practices at the island's
universities (Department of Education 1997: 21–22).

Another idea under consideration was to hire specialized teachers for
kindergarten and the first three grades of elementary school (Ghigliotty
1997a: 36). These grades became the focus of government attention (Valdivia 1997c: 6). Recall that the loudest student protests against Americanization came from high schoolers. Young children were less likely to
oppose government policies than their older siblings. One of the most
divisive proposals was the plan to employ mainland teachers. Exchange
programs were being negotiated with Pennsylvania, Connecticut, and
Massachusetts (Millán 1997c: 22). Secretary Fajardo tried to reassure
teachers that no Puerto Ricans would lose their positions due to this or
any other aspect of the bilingual policy (Varela 1997a: 20). His assurances
did not allay everyone's fears. After all, these proposals represented the
most dramatic educational reforms in half a century.

Predictably the Rosselló-Fajardo reforms sparked a furor among intellectuals, teachers' unions, and statehood opponents (Delgado Cintrón 1997: 67). The Federación de Maestros immediately pronounced its opposition to these proposals (Millán 1997a: 10). The Federación and the Asociación de Maestros announced that their memberships were ready to oppose both the expanded use of English in the classroom and the introduction of mainland teachers (Valdivia 1997b: 16). Students at the University of Puerto Rico organized a protest against Governor Rosselló that took place while he delivered a speech on campus (Ghigliotty 1997c: 8). Plastered on their placards and signs was the letter ñ—a frequently employed symbol of Spanish-language advocates. Stationed between n and o, this letter of the alphabet exemplifies Spanish's distinctiveness vis-à-vis English and by implication Puerto Rico's uniqueness vis-à-vis the United States.

Popular Democratic politicians also joined in the condemnation. They had no objections to improving the teaching of English, per se, but they rejected a policy aimed at influencing the congressional deliberations on the island's status (Ghigliotty 1997b: 12). "It is simply an instrument of the party in power to create the impression in the United States that this Rosselló administration is moving Puerto Rico toward cultural assimilation with the United States" (Benítez 1998b).[9] PPD Senator Antonio Fas Alzamora went so far as to suggest that these policies were possibly illegal and in violation of the 1990 Education Reform Act (García, P. 1997: 26). As far as Fas Alzamora was concerned, there was no problem with inviting American teachers to the island as long as their role was limited to training Puerto Ricans (Rivera Renta 1997: 24). Fajardo and Rosselló denied these charges (Hernández Beltrán 1997: 18; Millán 1997b: 10). The Education Department said: "no one should fear that becoming a bilingual person will affect learners' cultural identity" (Department of Education 1997: 15). Statehood activist Miriam Ramírez de Ferrer said that cultural Americanization would be a long-term result of these educational reforms. However, she saw nothing wrong with this outcome (Penchi 1997: 14).

The PNP's Nested Game

Pedro Rosselló stated that the co-officiality of English coupled with the intensification of English-language instruction in public schools should improve Puerto Rico's prospects for statehood (Mulero 1997c: 14). Given the ideological distribution of the Puerto Rican electorate, it was politically questionable for Rosselló to move in such a direction. Just as he attacked his opponents as extremists in 1991 for passing the López Galarza language bill, Pedro Rosselló was now vulnerable to charges of promoting assimilationist policies. Perhaps Rosselló thought that there was a change in the electorate—a swing favoring statehood. Clearly this was not the case. A public opinion poll published in 1997 revealed that the commonwealth status had the support of 43 percent of the electorate, statehood was backed by 39 percent, and independence was favored by only 4 percent ("Sin preferencia" 1997: 4). The same newspaper subsequently published another survey, and by then support for the status quo rose to 45 percent while statehood fell to 36 percent ("No se quiere" 1997: 4).

Regardless of the pedagogical justifications behind them, these education and language initiatives were politically hazardous. Employing standard Downsian notions, one would have to label the PNP's language policies as irrational. Still, like the PPD's language policies in the early 1990s, the PNP's initiatives were certainly rational when one understands that the party was not trying to maximize an electoral payoff. The PNP in 1997 was engaged in a Nested Game.

Returning to the model of nationalist politics outlined in chapter 8 (equation 8.2), we should ask why the equilibrium between electoral and nationalist payoffs changed so much for the Rosselló administration in 1996–1997. Governor Rosselló felt that Congress was ready to tackle the status question. Puerto Rico and the United States were approaching the centennial of the Spanish-American War and this anniversary animated Congress to try to resolve an embarrassing situation. With the Chinese repatriation of Hong Kong from Britain, Puerto Rico became the world's most populous colonial dependency. This put the United States in an uncomfortable position and the PNP was ready to take advantage.

Congress and Language Reform

It soon became clear that organizations such as English First would continue to oppose Puerto Rican statehood unless Congress imposed specific linguistic requirements on the island (Mulero 1997b: 28). These reforms did not impress Congressman Gerald Solomon, who not only insisted upon mandating English as the language of instruction under statehood but also that the island's electorate needed to express its desire for full incorporation by a "Super-Majority" (Mulero 1997d: 8). As congressional debate continued, Solomon persevered with his plans to add an English language amendment to the Young bill (Mulero 1997e: 8).

Secretary Fajardo said that regardless of events in Washington he would proceed with his reforms (Colombani 1997: 37). Showing his determination, Víctor Fajardo announced plans to sign new teacher exchange accords (Varela 1997b: 14). This was still not enough to persuade Gerald Solomon to drop his objections (Mulero 1997g: 16). How would the Puerto Rican government respond if Solomon's linguistic amendment to the status bill were approved? Rosselló announced that he would not back down even if Congress approved the Solomon amendment (Ghigliotty 1997d: 7).

Besides Gerald Solomon, the Puerto Rican government had to contend with conservative groups such as the Heritage Foundation that publicly opposed the Young bill and the whole notion of Puerto Rican statehood (Mulero 1997h: 38). Others such as U.S. English said that statehood was possible but only after a long process of cultural integration (Mulero 1997i: 12). English First worried that linguistic differences could foretell a political divorce or separation some time in the future (Mulero 1998a: 14). Resident Commissioner Romero-Barceló countered: "In a similarly intimidating fashion they try to raise havoc with the linguistic issue by arguing that there is no room for a Spanish-speaking State, failing to mention, once again, that the official languages of the Government of Puerto Rico and the languages of instruction in school are both Spanish and English" (*Congressional Record* 1998a: H693).

At this point the 105th Congress was in session and Romero-Barceló was now one of four Puerto Ricans in the House of Representatives. In addition to the resident commissioner there were three from mainland districts: José Serrano and Nydia Velásquez of New York, and Luis Gutiérrez of Illinois. José Serrano, representing the South Bronx, was first elected to the House in 1990. He was the longest-serving Puerto Rican in Congress. Officially Serrano took no position on the island's status question, except to say that he endorsed self-determination and favored a federally backed plebiscite. Along with Gutiérrez and Velásquez he supported allowing ethnic Puerto Ricans living on the U.S. mainland to vote on the island's status deliberations. Serrano did, however, criticize the commonwealth arrangement as a colonial status (Mulero 1997f: 6). As a result of such comments and his close collaboration with Romero-Barceló on the Young bill, some suggested that his sympathies bent toward statehood. Velásquez and Gutiérrez had different perspectives.

Despite representing a district centered in Brooklyn, Congresswoman Velásquez had a past affiliation with the PPD. Many assumed that she favored the commonwealth status. Chicago-based Congressman Luis Guti-

érrez made comments suggesting that he favored the island's independence from the United States. While Romero-Barceló tried to convince
his House colleagues that Puerto Ricans wanted to move closer to the
United States, Velásquez and Gutiérrez led a counteroffensive. Gutiérrez
emphasized that:

> Puerto Rico has spoken Spanish for over 500 years. When I get to
> Puerto Rico and see my parents, we speak in Spanish. When I go
> to a courtroom in Puerto Rico, it is in Spanish. When I register a
> deed, it is in Spanish. When a police officer pulls somebody over
> for going a little too quickly, the citation is in Spanish, and the
> subsequent sentencing, I assure my colleagues, is in Spanish, and
> you better have a lawyer that can speak Spanish. (*Congressional
> Record* 1998b: H803)

Both Gutiérrez and Velásquez insisted that any federal plebiscite bill had
to explicitly recognize Puerto Rico's right to maintain Spanish as an official language regardless of the island's status (*Congressional Record*
1998b: 803).

Outside of these Puerto Rican lawmakers, others in Congress worried
about the role of Spanish and the island's status. Bob Goodlate noted the
role language played in the statehood petitions of Louisiana and Oklahoma. Referring to the Young bill, this representative from Virginia said:
"Make no mistake, H.R. 856 will create an American Quebec. If Puerto
Rico gains statehood under this bill, it is likely to declare Spanish as the
official language, which could then force the U.S. Government to make
Spanish the quasi-official language to accommodate the needs of Puerto Ricans" (*Congressional Record* 1998b: H799). Another legislator
expressing major concerns and fears about Puerto Rican statehood was
John Duncan of Tennessee:

> However, in spite of all the many good things there are about Puer-
> to Rico and its people, I do not believe Puerto Rico should become
> a State at this time. First, and foremost to me, the American people
> do not support this expansion. . . . Second, according to this Con-
> gressional Research Service, Tennessee would potentially be one of
> the six or seven States to lose a House Member. . . . Third, the GAO
> and others have estimated this could cost American taxpayers $3
> to 5 billion a year in added costs to the Federal Government. . . .
> Fourth . . . I think all U.S. citizens need to be truly, honestly, fluent in

English. We need a unifying national language. Look at the problems Canada has now with many in French-speaking Quebec wanting to split Canada in the middle. English is and should be our national language, even if some do not like it. . . . Fifth and finally, some say only a little over half of Puerto Ricans want to become a State of the United States if they are given a truly free choice with fair definitions. I do not believe we should add any State unless an extremely high percentage, at least 75 percent or even more, want to become citizens. We certainly do not need to add a State where almost half of the people do not want to. (*Congressional Record* 1998a: H695)

As the debate progressed, Congressman Gerald Solomon reiterated his traditional insistence that the Congress should specify linguistic requirements under statehood. As this point the representative from New York State put it succinctly: "Admitting a State requires the assimilation of a territory within the Union of States, and language differences are the number one barrier to actual assimilation. The bill before us today contains the most vacuous statement on language policy that I have ever seen" (*Congressional Record* 1998b: H777).

Carlos Romero-Barceló reminded House members that English was one of the island's official languages and that the Rosselló administration was committed to promoting English in public schools (*Congressional Record* 1998b: H802). Robert Underwood—Guam's delegate to the House of Representatives—and Nancy Pelosi of California also underscored Romero-Barceló's point about the current government's language policies (*Congressional Record* 1998b: H799 and H805). Rhode Island Congressman Patrick Kennedy noted that while some in Congress wanted to impose linguistic requirements on statehood applicants, Puerto Rican servicemen drafted in U.S. wars were never required to be fluent in English (*Congressional Record* 1998b: H809).

To statehood opponents in Congress, the Rosselló administration's language policies were simply not enough to allay their anxieties. To them Puerto Rico represented a potentially destabilizing factor to the integrity of the American federation. Congressman Steve Horn of California commented:

But Puerto Rico should never have been a territory. . . . We should have left Puerto Rico independent. We did not. And we need not continue that error forever. . . . The niceness of the people and their heroism, we should honor. But we should not be getting ourselves entangled in situations that will be another Quebec, no matter how much we teach the English language. (*Congressional Record* 1998b: H785)

Underscoring Puerto Rico's cultural distinctiveness, Congressman Gutiérrez of Illinois took advantage of the ongoing debate and proceeded to deliver his remarks in Spanish. Unlike the speeches by Puerto Rican Senator Fas Alzamora and Mayor Héctor Luis Acevedo, this one was not delivered in committee but on the floor of the House itself. In a light reprimand the House leadership reminded Gutiérrez that languages other than English could not be transcribed (*Congressional Record* 1998b: H22). Gutiérrez gave his colleagues a taste of how things could be.

The 1998 Status Plebiscite

In the end the House passed the Young bill by one vote. Party discipline broke down but most supporters were Democrats and most opposed were Republicans (Mulero 1998c: 4). Senate Majority Leader Trent Lott announced that he was in no hurry to pass the Young bill and it was unlikely that the upper chamber had the time to debate and vote on the measure (Rodríguez, M. 1998a: 6). North Carolina Senator Jesse Helms fully agreed with Lott (Mulero 1998d: 14). Larry Craig of Idaho, Senate sponsor of the status bill, contended that at a minimum the issue should be debated and discussions over language should be postponed (Mulero 1998d: 34). In the end, the Senate let the 1998 federal status bill wither on the vine, and with that Washington washed its hands of the Puerto Rican status quandary, at least for 1998.

Within a few weeks the ruling Partido Nuevo Progresista began debating another local status vote without congressional approval (Estrada 1998a: 4). On July 25, 1998—the centennial of Puerto Rico's invasion by the United States and the forty-sixth anniversary of the founding of the Commonwealth—Governor Pedro Rosselló announced his intention to hold a plebiscite vote later that year (Estrada 1998b: 4). The date selected was Sunday, December 13 (Estrada 1998c: 6). New Progressives remembered their 1993 defeat and they decided to make a few changes to the 1998 ballot. In the first place, there were four options instead of three—independence, commonwealth, statehood, and "free association" (Rodríguez, M. 1998b: 4). The last option, lying somewhere between outright independence and the status quo, was included to divide commonwealth supporters and help generate a statehood plurality (Rodríguez, M. 1998c: 7). Next, the ballot options would appear in four untitled vertical columns. According to the PNP, voters would be obliged to read each alternative carefully (Rodríguez, M. 1998b: 4). Like the 1993 plebiscite process the PNP defined each option. PPD supporters strenuously opposed the commonwealth definition, and the ballot option underscored that the Estado Libre Asociado remained under the federal constitution's territorial clause. Lastly, voters were given a fifth option: *ninguna de las anteriores*—none of the above.

The PPD tried unsuccessfully to have the status plebiscite thrown out in court. Some thought that the government would postpone the plebiscite due to the devastation wrought by Hurricane Georges in September 1998. Rosselló refused to allow any hindrance, whether a natural disaster or the telephone company strikers, to delay the status vote. Nor did Rosselló heed the advice of some entrepreneurs to delay the December 13 vote due to its potential interference with Christmas holiday sales. Failing to postpone the vote, some Populares suggested supporting the fifth ballot option (Ghigliotty 1998a: 20). *None of the above* became the commonwealth party's officially endorsed preference for the 1998 plebiscite (Dávila, J. 1998: 4).

For Populares the euphoria experienced with the 1998 plebiscite results was déjà vu. Their nominee for 1998—*none of the above*—won the plebiscite with 50.4 percent, compared to 46.7 percent for statehood (Ghigliotty 1998b: 4). Independence was favored by only 2.6 percent of the electorate, Free Association was supported by 0.3 percent. The first ballot option—the status quo—was backed by less than one-tenth of one percent. The PNP argued that the fifth column did not count; thus, statehood won with over 90 percent of the vote (Estrada 1998d: 6). Few accepted this argument; most mainland media outlets declared the commonwealth cause the winner (Navarro 1998: A12). The results embarrassed both the PNP and PIP (Rodríguez, M. 1998d: 20). However, the Popular Democrats did not leave the plebiscite process unscathed. Congress had yet to agree to any significant increase in the degree of autonomy exercised by the Commonwealth, and as far as federal lawmakers were concerned the island was still subject to the constitution's territorial clause. A century after the U.S. invasion, the precise outline of the island's relationship to the mainland remained unclear.

12

The Struggle Continues

Long after it was officially abandoned, the federal government's Americanization project still resonates in the popular psyche in Puerto Rico. That half-century episode became a critical determinant in the evolution of Puerto Rican identity. *Puertorriqueñidad* is more than just language. Many elements have been objectified into this society's ethno-national pantheon. But the special place held by language on that cultural altar is due, in large measure, to a regime-directed course of action. Paradoxically, those implementing this directive believed not only in the inherent superiority of American sociocultural norms but also in their beneficence. Convinced of the divine inspiration of their mission, Washington's legates in the tropics only wanted what they perceived to be in the best interests of its forcefully adopted colony. In their eyes the inhabitants of "Porto Rico" would profit from the blessings of American rule. Thanks to Americanization, the distinctions between "us" and "them" became only clearer.

After more than a hundred years of American rule the vast majority of Puerto Ricans are still Spanish speakers. Furthermore, only a relatively small portion of the island's inhabitants can speak English fluently. Puerto Ricans remain proud of their language and their cultural distinctiveness. This applies not only to those living on the island but is also a common sentiment found among ethnic Puerto Ricans residing on the U.S. mainland. Despite the fact that more recent generations of U.S.-based Puerto Ricans are no longer Spanish dominant, they still hold the idiom in high regard and deem it a valued symbol of cultural pride. In light of these events we can understand why many considered the old bilingual law from 1902 anachronistic. After all, official bilingualism was enacted by the new regime for the benefit of monolingual American bureaucrats. It was only in the early 1990s that cultural forces and political opportunities converged. While official unilingualism lasted less than two years, its echo still resonates.

Concurrently, lawmakers faced the impact of economic dependency on the United States and the desire of most islanders to maintain strong ties with the mainland. In the absence of government-sponsored initiatives to promote language shift, animosity toward the United States diminished. Coupled with a vigorous American economic presence and the pivotal role played by federal funds in the insular economy, partisan preferences shifted away from separatism and toward greater links with the United States. Early in the commonwealth era separatists constituted the official opposition. By the late 1960s statehood supporters won control of the governorship for the first time. Since then annexationists and autonomists represent the vast majority of the insular electorate. The average voter shifted toward the metropolitan "center" on economic matters while swinging toward the "periphery" on question of culture. Parties ignoring the status question soon found themselves out of office.

In the 1980s, Representative Héctor López Galarza was aware of these realities, as were the leaders of his Partido Popular Democrático. He served in the legislature when his own party rejected various language proposals. Whether these language measures were bent on implementing substantive changes in educational policy or purely symbolic, the end result was the same. Political realities kept the party's leader, Governor Rafael Hernández Colón, from endorsing such unilingual measures. Conditions changed in the early 1990s, and the PPD leadership reassessed the potential payoffs associated with declaring Spanish the island's sole official language.

Employing standard theories from political science, one would have to conclude that the PPD's leadership was irrational. This was not simply a case of miscalculation or error. Members of the party's inner circle were well aware of electoral preferences. Indeed, until the early 1990s their behavior in the legislature was consistent with mainstream notions of political behavior. Moreover, the incumbent Popular Democrats were all too aware that most of the public had no desire to eliminate English as an official language. Every time an autonomist legislator announced the submission of a unilingual bill, pro-statehood lawmakers quickly attacked the proposal as a first step toward eventual independence. Logic dictated that candidates avoid policies that could be categorized as too nationalistic or quasiseparatist, for fear of losing the support of most voters. Regardless of such conventional wisdom, the Populares persisted and instituted official unilingualism as government policy.

Later in the 1990s their rivals engaged in much of the same "irrational" behavior. Novoprogresistas promoted English in the public school system to a degree not seen since the days of Americanization. Language reform in the school system followed the reinstatement of English as one of the island's official languages. To many, these initiatives were signs that the island's government was encouraging language shift, leaving the PNP vulnerable to allegations that it was promoting extremist and even anti–Puerto Rican policies. When it came to the language issue we see two contending administrations in Puerto Rico violating a fundamental tenet in politics. Brazenly they appeared to move toward the ideological fringes and away from the median voter.

The evidence presented indicates that these leaders were far from irrational. To the contrary, they were engaged in a very precise and carefully designed set of policies with clear agendas in mind. Simply put, these party leaders were concerned less with winning the following elections and more with improving the conditions for their preferred status option. In this context culture was more than just a sentiment or the sum total of a group's social norms. Various political actors brandished culture, in the form of competing language statutes and policies, as political weaponry. Once the language debate hit the hallways of Congress, mainland organizations joined the scuffle.

As a supporter of the status quo, Hernández Colón and the PPD's leadership gambled that a law elevating the symbolic stature of Spanish would diminish support for statehood in Congress. Independentistas made the same basic assumption. On the other side of the coin, the PNP under Pedro Rosselló aspired to have Puerto Rico admitted as the country's fifty-first state. With that goal in mind, this party reinstituted official bilingualism. When it became apparent that this symbolic gesture was insufficient to quell congressional doubts, the Rosselló administration embarked on a new educational policy bent on fortifying the role of the English language in the public school system. Puerto Rican politics are focused on more than just winning elections; they are obsessed with the status question. With American firms and the U.S. federal government controlling vast portions of the Puerto Rican economy, local politicians are limited in how they can use economics as a tool in the status game. Culture, on the other hand, is a tool within their easy reach.

Why did policy makers in this Caribbean territory focus on Congress rather than the island's electorate? The U.S. Constitution gives the federal legislature plenary authority over the union's territorial possessions. Washington may keep Puerto Rico as a commonwealth and in its current form if it so chooses. It could concede the Estado Libre Asociado greater autonomy, grant it independence, or admit Puerto Rico into the federation. Voters may put politicians into office, but Congress ultimately decides the territory's fate. Even without effective congressional representation, strategists in Puerto Rico attempted to influence decisions made in Washington. Such a tactic would only work if the American people and their elected representatives held strong convictions about the language-identity connection and how a Spanish-speaking jurisdiction would affect national unity.

Of the two sets of policies—unilingualism under the PPD or bilingualism under the PNP—which had the greater impact on Congress? Pro-statehood administrations were elected in 1992 and reelected in 1996. Governor Pedro Rosselló used these opportunities to restore official bilingualism and initiate a new pro-English directive in the public school system. As the elected head of the Puerto Rican government, Rosselló used congressional hearings to remind Washington of these undertakings. During these two terms, the pro-commonwealth camp was out of power and facing financial difficulties. Under less than ideal conditions the PPD defended its status alternative in two plebiscites.

In both 1993 and 1998 Congress failed to pass either a federally backed referendum or plebiscite. Without official support, its endorsement, or a guarantee that Congress would even pay attention to the plebiscite results, the Rosselló administration pressed ahead with local plebiscites. Inside the Beltway the biggest hang-ups by far were over statehood rather than the other two status alternatives. Each time the issue of statehood arose, language and culture resurfaced as major concerns. Adding to the woes of the statehood movement were reports from the Congressional Budget Office indicating that this status alternative would cost the federal coffers much more per year. But in the final analysis, the island already receives billions of dollars in federal assistance as an American commonwealth. When we keep in mind the size of the U.S. federal budget, Puerto Rican statehood represents a drop in the bucket. What is more troubling in the United States is how Puerto Rico would affect national cohesion.

Federal lawmakers were reminded of the 1991 unilingual act and Puerto Rico's cultural nationalism. To drive the point home, both separatist and autonomist delegates insisted on delivering remarks in Spanish before congressional committees. By the mid-1990s it was not only island-based politicians reminding Congress of the 1991 unilingual law but also lobbyists and spokespersons from various mainland groups committed to establishing English as the country's sole official language.

Social conservatives led the mainland assault on Puerto Rican statehood. For them this territory represented a future American Quebec. As some observers of Canadian politics noted, the Parti Québécois penned the province's famous "Charter of the French Language" the same year the country celebrated the 110th anniversary of confederation. Years of political union and a brutal repression in the midtwentieth century failed to dissolve nationalist sentiments in Basque and Catalan regions of Spain. Popular support for statehood today could not guarantee that Puerto Ricans might not prefer independence tomorrow. Since the Civil War it has been clear that most Americans consider statehood a permanent status alternative. Issues of national unity had to be weighed.

Based on congressional reactions to both sets of language policies, it is clear that the Populares were more effective at scaring Congress than were the Novoprogresistas at allaying congressional anxieties. That one act, a simple unilingual statute, may have done more to impede the Puerto Rican statehood movement in Congress than any other single activity. Still, apprehension toward statehood does not build up support for either of the two remaining status options. Washington has yet to show any willingness to significantly augment the Commonwealth's autonomy or support independence.

How could such a simple strategy work so effectively? It was based on attacking the statehood movement at its most vulnerable point—the customarily unspoken nexus between the English language and American cultural identity. The ancestors of most Americans spoke other languages, but the experience of speaking another vernacular belongs in the folkloric past. The people of the United States are proud of their language and dread the consequences associated with permanent non-English-speaking enclaves. Whether anyone likes it or not, when Congress thinks about linguistic diversity and political status the case that usually tops the list is Canada.

It would be a different story were we focusing on a tiny community. For example, the fact that there was a group of people speaking Hawaiian did not stop that state from joining the union. But we are not talking about a tiny cluster, either in absolute terms or as a proportion of the total population. Puerto Ricans number in the millions. Spanish speakers are not a linguistic minority in Puerto Rico, as is the case with Hawaiian speakers in their homeland. Add to this millions of Spanish-speaking Latinos already residing on the U.S. mainland. Regardless, many in the United States fear being labeled racist or xenophobic should they publicly air their views on this subject.

Two interesting parallels immediately show themselves in the complex relationship between Puerto Ricans and Americans. Puerto Ricans want cultural sovereignty while maintaining strong economic ties with the United States. It appears that most Americans prefer linguistic homogeneity while maintaining a reputation for cultural diversity and tolerance. Thus, it is possible that Congress is also playing a kind of Nested Game when it comes to Puerto Rico. It entertains debate on statehood all the while knowing that it will not seriously contemplate political amalgamation with this territory. Lacking strong support for independence, this leaves Puerto Ricans living in a perpetual state of colonialism.

Beyond the confines of Puerto Rico and the United States, this study may be useful to those looking at nationalism and ethnic mobilization in other settings. Critics have long labeled nationalist sentiments as irrational emotions. Part of the problem may lie in the personal prejudices and biases of many scholars of nationalism. Also, scholars often lose sight of the fact that nationalist movements and parties are not just geared toward holding office but are committed to constitutional reform. When discussing nationalist movements and ethnic politics, we must weigh attempts to maximize votes with efforts to generate a nationalist dividend. Under the right conditions, it is logical for political actors to enact policies even if they endanger electoral success. Politics, especially in nationalist settings, is no game for the timid.

Appendix 1. Official Languages Act of 1902

§ 51. Official Languages

In every department of the statutory government, in every court on this island and in all public offices, the English and Spanish languages will be employed indistinctively; and when necessary, translations and oral interpretations from one language to another will be made, to permit the interested parties to understand any procedure or communication in said languages. February 21, 1902, p. 83, sec. 1; Const. art. I, sec. 1, eff. July 25, 1952.

History

Codification

The term "Insular Government" was substituted with "Statutory Government," in accordance with the [Commonwealth] Constitution.

Prior Law

General Orders No. 192, Chief of Staff of the Army, Office of the Adjunct-General, Washington, D.C., September 30, 1898, as it appears published in the Puerto Rico Gazette, No. 23, January 27, 1899, provided: "By direction of the Secretary of War, all documents executed in English and offered for registration in Cuba and Porto Rico, when accompanied by translation of the same into Spanish, shall, when recorded, have the same force and effect as if executed in Spanish."[1]

District Court of the United States

Before the District Court of the United States for Puerto Rico all pleadings and procedures will be carried out in English, in accordance with Art. 42 of the Puerto Rican Federal Relations Act, that appears among the Historical Documents, pp. 207 *et seq.*

Counter References

Statutes, discrepancies between the Spanish and English texts, see the Civil Code, 1930, Art. 13, Sec. 13 of Title 31.

Languages used in pleadings, see Rule 8.5 of the Civil Procedure of 1979, App. III of Title 32.

Annotations

1. Registry of Goods. The Language Law of 1902, Sect. 51 to 55 of this title, from the time it took effect, authorized the presentation in Property Registries [of] documents or titles written in English for their recording, without the same being accompanied by the corresponding translations into Castilian. *RCA Communications v. Registrador,* 1956, 79 D.P.R. 77.

General Order No. 192 of December 30, 1898, inasmuch as it required documents executed in English and presented for recording be accompanied by the corresponding translation in Castilian, was repealed by the Language Law of 1902. Id.

2. Judicial Procedures. The language to be used in judicial proceedings in the courts of the Commonwealth of Puerto Rico is Spanish, and the provision in this section that "the English and Spanish languages will be used indistinguishably" only has administrative reach and does not confer a right, neither for the accused nor his attorney, to choose the language in which the proceeding should be aired. *Pueblo v. Tribunal Superior,* 1965, 92 D.P.R. 596.

§ 52. Interpreters and Translators

All departments, as well as the courts and the heads of public offices will use, whenever necessary, competent interpreters and translators to carry out the provisions of Sect. 51 to 55 of this title. February 21, 1902, p. 83, Sec. 2, eff. July 1, 1902.

§ 53. Public and Private Documents

No public or private document will be repealed, written in any of the languages mentioned in Sec. 51 of this title, on account of that in which it is expressed. February 21, 1902, p. 83, Sect. 3, eff. July 1, 1902.

§ 54. Document, Definition of

As used in Sec. 51 to 55 of this title the word "document" will be understood to make references and include manuscripts, typed and printed documents and combinations of any or all of the forms of stated writings. February 21, 1902, p. 83, Sect. 4, eff. July 1, 1902.

§ 55. Municipalities; Municipal and Police Courts

Nothing contained in Sect. 51 to 55 of this title will apply to the offices of any municipality or the municipal or police courts or subordinate offices of the aforementioned. February 21, 1902, p. 83, Sec. 5, eff. July 1, 1902.

History

References in the Text

The Law of May 15, 1950, No. 432, p. 1127, creating one municipal court with tribunals in all Puerto Rico, revoked the municipal courts referred to in this section. The Law of July 24, 1952, No. 11, p. 31, eff. July 25, 1952, repealed said law that created a District Court with jurisdiction over matters that previously fell to the Municipal Court.

The police courts were abolished after June 30, 1902, by the Criminal Procedure Code, 1902, Art. 14.

Appendix 2. The Berríos Martínez Language Bill

March 11, 1976 (S.B. 1763)

Referred to the Education, Government and Civil Law Commissions

To declare Spanish the official language of Puerto Rico and to require its use in scholastic, professional, commercial, industrial and other activities.

Statement of Purpose

In 1949, the Secretary of Education, Mr. Mariano Villaronga, responding to the demands of Puerto Rican public opinion, decreed by way of an administrative order that teaching would be carried out in the national language, Spanish, at all levels of the public school system. The measure constituted a significant step forward in the country's educational policy, but it did not resolve in a definitive way the so-called "language problem" that vexed Puerto Ricans since the first years of U.S. colonial domination over Puerto Rico. As known, the new master invested English with the status of official language and the language of instruction with the affirmed and established purpose of rapidly instigating the process of "Americaniz[ing]" the Puerto Rican people and destroy[ing] their national cohesion.

To evaluate the total grievous scope of this measure, it is essential that we clarify some concepts. In the first place we should point out that in 1898, the year of the military occupation of our land, the Puerto Rican people already possessed all the constitutive elements of a nation: territory, population, long historic past, institutions, religion, *language,* customs and characteristic traditions, norms of ethical conduct, hierarchy of values, national consciousness and feelings. Within that connection, none of these elements could be considered "in abstracto," nor any less autonomous or replaceable by another foreign to the cohesion and living unity of the whole, without these being ruined or, at least, seen as seriously threatened. As a result, the imposition of English on our people would inevitably operate as a solvent of our national consciousness.

In the second place, we should be clear as to what language is in general and what his mother tongue signifies to each man. On [the topic of]

language the following eminent Italo-German philosopher, theologian and psychologist, Romano Guardini, in his work *The World and the Person*, Pp. 203–204 says:

> man by his nature is in a dialogue. His mental life is ordained by a communication. . . . mental life is carried on essentially in language. Language is not only the means by which we communicate conclusions, but mental life and activity are carried on in the process of speech. Though it is not a pre-verbal act of the mind which only later, as a result of some decision or for some particular purpose, is formulated in words, but it takes place from the first moment in the form of interior speech. Language is not a system of signs by means of which two nomads exchange ideas *but it is the very realm of consciousness in which every man lives.*[1]

If this can be preached about language in general and its function in the inward and spiritual life of man, what can be said about the language [we] heard from the crib and have spoken since we uttered our first words: the language that has been "the field of senses" in which our ancestors and progenitors lived and in which we ourselves live; that language that shaped our thinking, our sentiments, our sensibilities and our values and, at the same time, has been shaped by them! Can we fully realize what it has meant to the essential life of each Puerto Rican and our national community, the prolonged attempt to substitute this language—"ark of our tradition," according to Unamuno—for another foreign language that forcibly committed us to a continual [and] total internal readaptation?

Our language, Puerto Rico's Spanish, has served us and it serves to give expression to our particular manner of being, to attain awareness of ourselves, for creative literary expression, to rescue ourselves from time, space and death; it is a true instrument of personal and collective liberation.

The philosopher and linguist Stenzel said of this objective:

> It is said that in reference to a nation the language's importance does not have to be overestimated, and that a people become a nation by their historic destiny, by their luck and their misfortune, by common memory, by action and will. *But all that is made real by the people only by way of language; only by virtue of their language does history become their own patrimony, patrimony that always must find [itself] anew by the cultivation of its language. The spiritual decadence of a people always goes hand-in-hand with this.*

And the illustrious philologist Karl Vossler, adds more categorically:

When the national sentiment has been stripped of all refuges, language becomes the spiritual fortress from which one day, when times are propitious it comes out to reconquer its position. *The man who rejects or abandons this final refuge and point of departure of his national sentiments, has no honor, he is dead for the social community in which he received his first language experience.*

We ponder both texts with reference to the linguistic situation that we wish to correct in order to avoid its dire consequences. Various scientific studies have denoted the interference of English in our Spanish: the unnecessary borrowings, literal translations, grammatical constructions extraneous to the nature of our language, the impoverishment of expressive nuances, the scanty agility and ease of expression.

It is evident that the administrative decree of 1949 has not prevented the harmful effects of teaching English and there are still many private schools, and some university faculties that lecture in English. Moreover, the study of English occupies a privileged position in the school curriculum and is attended to with special care and abundant resources, unlike the attention that Spanish receives, a fact that can be proved with the simple comparison of class hours, number of supervisors, equipment and facilities that are granted to the professional improvement of teachers of both languages. Likewise, for many years some sought to convert pupils into bilingual men alleging political, economic and cultural reasons. It is important to remember here what the distinguished pedagogue, grammarian and academic of the Spanish language Dr. Samuel Gili Gaya said about bilingualism:

"Historic experience—he says—allows one to affirm that bilingual environments are unfavorable to artists of the word because bilingualism, by jointly submerging the spirits of two systems that do not interconnect with another, wounds all artistic activities of the word at their roots. Many bilinguals call attention to themselves due to the poor expressive resources with which they use their mother tongue: meager vocabulary and few nuances, repetition of the same grammatical formulas, lack of verbal agility. Their parlance, even if not precisely incorrect, gives the impression of being corseted, of being paralyzed in its movements; it appears more learned than native." And this occurs "because inside the bilingual man there is a constant effort to adjust two expressive systems that do not interconnect with one another; and that which is differentiated, characteristic, particular, idiomatic in this endeavor dies and the colorless forms of

a standardized saying endure. *The more both languages approach one another the more they impoverish one another. The bilingual man is a hinterland soul that no longer knows how to live apart from the borderland gibberish and is hardly inclined to discover new horizons inland his own spirit."*
(See Samuel Gili Gaya, *The Bilingual Man*, Rev., I.C.P.R.)

It is false, we add, that the bilingual man is more cultured than the monolingual: moreover culture is [the] perception of nuances.

On various occasions the Puerto Rican legislature attempted to legislate over these matters so important to the life, culture and national consciousness of our people. The House of Representatives headed by De Diego attempted it; Sen. Rafael Arjona Siaca also attempted it when he led Senate Bill 51. Both attempts were blocked: the first by the Executive Council and the second by the direct intervention of U.S. Presidents Franklin D. Roosevelt and Harry S. Truman[.] [These] facts verifying the political nature and intent of teaching in English with meridian clarity [and] its design to "Americanize" Puerto Ricans were scientifically confirmed by the doctoral thesis of professor Dr. Aida N. de Montilla.

At this time there is no law of greater transcendental importance for the destiny of our people than that which declares Spanish the only official language of Puerto Rico, establishes the teaching in Spanish in the entire public and private school system and mandates the use of Spanish in certain professional, commercial, industrial and other kinds of activities.

Be it decreed by the Legislative Assembly of Puerto Rico:

Article 1. This law will be known officially as "The Language Law of Puerto Rico."

Article 2. Official Language

a. Spanish is the official language of Puerto Rico and should be used in all functions, activities and pursuits of the Government of Puerto Rico, its corporations, and the municipalities.

b. In all public offices the necessary facilities to render services to people who do not know how to speak or write in Spanish will be provided.

Article 3. Public Schools

a. The Spanish language will be used to teach all subjects in all elementary and secondary public schools.

b. All instructional materials used in said schools will be written in Spanish.

c. In cases of clear need the Secretary of Education may authorize the use of materials written in languages other than Spanish and when doing so will immediately notify the Governor, the Legislative Assembly and the public, conveying the reasons his decision was founded on.

d. Sections (a) and (b) of this article will not apply to the teaching of languages other than Spanish.

e. The Secretary of Education may exempt those classes or schools whose students received all their previous education in a language other than Spanish from complying with this article.

Article 4. Private Schools

a. The provisions in Article 1 will apply to all private elementary and secondary schools.

b. The Department of Education will not accredit any school that does not comply with the provisions in this article.

Article 5. University of Puerto Rico

a. The Spanish language will be used to teach all subjects, except languages other than Spanish, in all campuses, colleges and other units of the University of Puerto Rico.

b. All teaching materials used in the University of Puerto Rico, except for those referring to the teaching of languages other than Spanish, will be written in Spanish.

c. In cases of clear need the Council on Higher Education may authorize the directors of campuses, colleges and other university units to dispense with the fulfillment of clauses (a) and (b) of this article by means of regulations to this end.

d. The Council on Higher Education will take the necessary measures to assure the compliance of the stipulations in this article. To these ends it will require semestral reports from the directors of all university units.

Article 6. Private Universities and Colleges

a. The provisions in Article 4 will apply to all private universities and post-secondary colleges accredited by the Council on Higher Education.

b. The Council on Higher Education may withdraw the accreditation of any university or college not complying with the provisions in this article.

Article 7. Property Registries

a. The Spanish language will be used in all matters and operations of property registration.

b. Property Recorders will return any document drafted exclusively in a language other than Spanish without carrying out any procedure on it.

Article 8. Courts of Justice

a. The Spanish language will be used exclusively in all courts of justice.

b. The use of translators will be permitted in civil and criminal cases when a witness does not know Spanish or when the accused in a criminal case does not know Spanish.

c. In civil cases the translators' honorarium will be paid by the party using them, in criminal cases they will be paid from public funds.

Article 9. Quasi-judicial and Quasi-legislative Entities

a. The Spanish language will be used exclusively in all quasi-judicial and quasi-legislative entities.

b. The use of translators will be permitted in said entities when witnesses, person giving evidence or the parties do not know Spanish.

c. The parties using them will pay the translators' honorarium.

Article 10. Prescriptions and Medical Certificates; Clinical and Radiological Laboratory Reports

a. All prescriptions, reports, and recorded certificates signed by a physician for use in Puerto Rico will be written in Spanish.

b. No pharmacist will fill out a prescription that is not written in Spanish.

c. All clinical and radiological laboratory certificates and reports to be used in Puerto Rico will be written in Spanish.

Article 11. Medicines

a. All instructions and all explanations on the contents of all medicines sold in Puerto Rico will be written in Spanish.

b. No pharmacy or other establishment will sell any medicine that does not comply with clause (a) in this article.

Article 12. Public Establishments

a. All advertisements or instructions posted or distributed in any establishment dedicated to the sale of public articles or services will be written in Spanish.

b. All food and drink menus used in restaurants, soda fountains, taverns and similar establishments will be written in Spanish.

c. All announcements and instructions posted or distributed in any nocturnal center, cinema, theater and similar establishment will be written in Spanish.

d. All announcements and instructions posted or distributed in any hotel, inn, guesthouse and similar establishments will be written in Spanish.

e. Commonwealth entities charged with the surveillance, inspection and approval of the establishments mentioned in this article will deny their authorization for non compliance with this article.

Article 13. Corporations, Banks, and Insurance Agencies

a. All reports, applications, stocks and other documents of corporations registered with the Commonwealth, including banks, financial enterprises and insurance agencies, directed to their stockholders residing in Puerto Rico or any entity of the Commonwealth will be written in Spanish.

b. All forms, applications, reports and other documents used by banks, financial enterprises or any enterprise dedicated to similar services, for the use of their clients or the public in general, will be written in Spanish.

c. All applications, policies, reports and other documents of any insurance agency [used] for conducting business in Puerto Rico and for the use of their clients will be written in Spanish.

d. Commonwealth entities charged with the surveillance, inspection and approval of the establishments mentioned in this article will deny their authorization for non compliance with this article.

Article 14. Duties of the Attorney General

a. The Attorney General will oversee the compliance of this law and for this purpose may submit to the courts of justice any petition or actions deemed necessary or convenient.

Article 15. Translations

a. Nothing contained in this law concerning any written material will encumber the addition of a translation in another language along with the text in Spanish so long as the translation [is not][2] emphasized more than the original version in Spanish.

Article 16. Freedom of the Press

a. Nothing contained in this law will apply to information published in newspapers and magazines, or transmitted by radio and television nor in any way will be understood to be a restriction on freedom of the press.

Article 17. Legal Effect

a. This law will begin to take effect one year after its enactment except for Articles 3 and 4 (public and private schools), 5 and 6 (University of Puerto Rico and private universities), and Article 9 (Medicines) which will take effect two years after its enactment.

Article 18. Repealing Clause

a. The law of February 21, 1902, entitled "A Law with Respect to the Language to be used in the Departments, Courts and Offices of the Insular Government" is repealed.

b. All law and portions of law in conflict with the regulations in the present status are repealed.

Appendix 3: The Peña Clos Language Bill

January 15, 1982 (S.B. 411)

Referred to the Education Commission

To add a second paragraph to Article 1 of Law No. 4 of July 24, 1952, that establishes in Puerto Rico a free, public and non-sectarian education, in order to provide that all education in primary and secondary public schools in the country be in the Spanish language and that among the assignments comprising the school curriculum that English be included as an additional language.

Statement of Purpose

Currently the language arts, that are: speaking, listening, reading and writing, have become indispensable functions for all individuals due to the need for efficient communication demanded by rapid social and economic changes.

The development of the language arts has always been the school's responsibility. To these ends this measure is directed towards providing that education in all primary and secondary public schools of the country be in the Spanish language, with the intent of conserving our vernacular language and to develop basic skills throughout all these years of study for each Puerto Rican.

It is vitally important to prioritize the teaching of Spanish. Student knowledge of the vernacular language will help them enormously in their work in other courses and will facilitate the learning of English as a second language.

This Legislative Assembly considers it fitting to legislate with the ends pointed to previously recognizing that the effective use of our vernacular language, Spanish, is a basic need for all Puerto Ricans.

Be it decreed by the Legislative Assembly of Puerto Rico:

Section 1. A second paragraph to Article 1 of Law No. 4 of July 24, 1952, will be added, so that it may read as follows:

"Article 1. There will be in Puerto Rico a public education system which will be entirely free and non-sectarian. *All education in primary and secondary public schools of the country will be in the Spanish language. Among the subjects that comprise the curriculum of said schools will be included English as an additional language.*"

Section 2. This law will take effect on the date of its approval.

Appendix 4: The Peña Clos and Fas Alzamora Language Bill

April 15, 1986 (S.B. 857)

Referred to the Education and State Government Commissions

To establish Spanish as the official language of Puerto Rico to be used in all departments, agencies, offices, and courts of the Commonwealth of Puerto Rico and to repeal the law of February 21, 1902, that established English and Spanish as official languages of Puerto Rico.

Statement of Purpose

Since the discovery and colonization of the island of Puerto Rico in the XV century, Spanish has been the vernacular language of Puerto Ricans and is still the language used by all Puerto Ricans. Upon the change in sovereignty in 1898, by means of Spain's cession of Puerto Rico to the United States, a military government was established on the island that left the juridico-governmental structure practically unaltered until the enactment of the Organic Act of 1900, known as the "Foraker Act." Under the former federal law our Legislative Assembly passed the law of February 21, 1902, establishing English and Spanish as official languages of Puerto Rico.

In 1952 the Constitution of the Commonwealth of Puerto Rico was enacted and in this way our people attained the political power to govern themselves consistent with the majoritarian will of those governed. That followed from Sections 1 and 2 of Article 1 of said Constitution that read as follows:

Section 1. The Commonwealth of Puerto Rico is hereby constituted. Its political power emanates from the people and shall be exercised in accordance with their will, within the terms of the compact agreed upon between the people of Puerto Rico and the United States of America.

Section 2. The government of the Commonwealth of Puerto Rico shall be republican in form and its legislative, judicial and executive branches as established by this Constitution shall be equally subordinate to the sovereignty of the people of Puerto Rico.[1]

The people of Puerto Rico possessing the political power to declare Spanish as the official language and there being no provision in the Constitution or in federal laws that limit it, it is desirable and convenient that said power be exercised declaring Spanish as the official language of Puerto Rico.

In addition to the aforementioned, it is appropriate to point out other spiritual and practical considerations that fortify the suitability of having Spanish declared the official language of the island.

To this effect, below we cite the words of the ex-governor and leader of Puerto Rico, Mr. Luis Muñoz Marín, on the occasion of the inauguration of the Puerto Rican Academy of the Spanish Language on April 1, 1955, in the Ateneo Puertorriqueño.

Language is the spirit's breath. For generations the language of a people has been of that people and of the people where they stemmed from. It is a process of the most intimate interaction and concordance between word and spirit. Thus, the people breathe upon speaking their language, they do not translate and thus on the whole, they do not have to translate themselves in their manner of being and feeling in order to speak. To add one language to another enriches the understanding of a people; but the partial substitution of the vernacular by a second language, by invasion or inertia, disorganized and unintentional to one, inconsistent with another, deprives that community's individuals of a great deal of their subtle liberty to be sincerely themselves.

Finally we would like to point out that by resolving the case *The People of Puerto Rico v. Superior Court of Puerto Rico*, 92 D.P.R. 596, our Supreme Court expressed itself in the following manner through their chief justice, the Honorable Luis Negrón Fernández, "It is a fact not subject to historic rectification that the medium of expression, the language of the Puerto Rican people [an] integral part of our origin and our Hispanic culture—has been and continues to be Spanish."

Be it decreed by the Legislative Assembly of Puerto Rico:

Article 1. The Spanish language is declared and established the official language to be used in all departments, agencies, instrumentalities, dependencies and offices of the executive, legislative and judicial branches of the Commonwealth of Puerto Rico, and when necessary, written translations and oral interpretations will be made to and from the English language in accordance with adopted regulations.

Article 2. All civil servants in charge of such departments, agencies, instrumentalities, dependencies and offices are authorized and ordered to promulgate those regulations they deem necessary and appropriate, in order to provide those facilities, resources and personnel necessary to comply with the provisions in this law. All regulations should comply with the provisions of law No. 122 of June 30, 1958, as amended, known as the 1958 Law on Regulations.

Article 3. The law of February 21, 1902, is repealed.

Article 4. This law will begin to take effect immediately after its enactment.

Appendix 5: Official Language Act of 1991

Law No. 4—Approved April 5, 1991 (H.B. 417)

To declare and establish that Spanish will be the official language of Puerto Rico to be used in all departments, municipalities or other political subdivisions, agencies, public corporations, offices and government dependencies of the executive, legislative and judicial branches of the Commonwealth of Puerto Rico and to repeal the law of February 21, 1902, "Law with Respect to the Language to be used in the Departments, Courts and Offices of the Insular Government."

Statement of Purpose

When the United States acquired Puerto Rico and the Philippines as a result of the Spanish-American War, the new rulers attempted to substitute the institutions of these peoples with U.S. institutions. The imposition of English as an official language was the cornerstone of this policy of cultural assimilation.

In the Philippines, where the use of Spanish was never generalized among the native populace and as a result nor did it become the mother tongue of the majority of Filipinos, the North American rulers in 1900 ordered that English would become the only official language as of January 1, 1906. That date was later postponed until January 1, 1911, and finally until January 1, 1913.

In Puerto Rico, a homogeneous society in its culture and language, the new rulers decreed, with the same intent of cultural assimilation, the indistinctive use of Spanish and English in the departments, offices and courts of the insular government. In the first years of this century, the president of the United States was accustomed to appointing civil servants that only spoke English to the highest positions of the island government. Additionally it was ordered that English would be the medium of instruction in the country's schools and that Spanish would be taught as a subject. The 1902 language legislation is reflective of a time gone by.

Resistance to both measures was firm and persistent. Early on the voices of Luis Muñoz Rivera, Eugenio María de Hostos, José de Diego, Luis Llorens Torres and other vigorous defenders protested.

After many failed efforts of the old Chamber of Delegates, arising in 1913, and the Legislative Assembly later on, this goal to provide that Spanish become the medium of instruction was reached when Luis Muñoz Marín became the first governor elected by the direct vote of all Puerto Ricans. The 1902 law, that in reality did not fulfill the aim its proponents pursued since it did not establish any official language but was limited to allowing the indistinctive use of the two languages coexisting in our surroundings, on the other hand lost what could remain as a reason for being once the government of Puerto Rico ceased to be in the hands of U.S. administrators that did not know Spanish. As it was always out of tune with Puerto Rican circumstances, the February 21, 1902, law that is repealed by this act, became an inconsequential expression in 1965 when our Supreme Court deprived its compulsory character in Puerto Rican judicial procedures.

The rationale for the legislation adopted today is to abolish an anachronism and reaffirm our historic condition as a Spanish-speaking people, freely united with the U.S. people. By virtue of the strong economic and ideological ties that bind us to that nation, the people of Puerto Rico are committed to fully mastering English as a second language, but are not willing to surrender their language, nor their culture, nor the fundamental prerogative to conclude that their government communicate in the people's vernacular: the Spanish language.

Be it decreed by the Legislative Assembly of Puerto Rico:

Article 1. Spanish is declared and established as the official language of Puerto Rico to be used in all departments, municipalities or other political subdivisions, agencies and governmental dependencies of the executive, legislative and judicial branches of the Commonwealth of Puerto Rico.

Article 2. All executive civil servants of the various departments, municipalities or other political subdivisions, agencies, public corporations, offices and governmental dependencies of the executive, legislative and judicial branches of the Commonwealth of Puerto Rico are authorized and ordered to promulgate all regulations deemed necessary and fitting, in order to provide the installations, resources and personnel necessary to faithfully comply with the provisions of this law, ordering that in cases of executive branch dependencies interested in using the exception authorized in Article 3 of this law, will require beforehand the express authorization of the governor. All regulations promulgated under the provisions of this law should comply with the requirements of law No. 170 of August 12, 1988, known as the "Law of Uniform Administrative Procedures of the Commonwealth of Puerto Rico." When necessary written translations and oral interpretations will be made, from and to the English language, in such a way that the interested parties may understand all procedures or communications in the language that most suits them, conforming to the previously adopted regulations alluded to.

Article 3. With exceptions, the three branches of the government may use in their transactions and documents, and in the same way maintain files or parts of them, in another language when convenient, necessary or indispensable, and in compliance with the norms established by rule or regulation. Executive branch dependencies, agencies and public interested in using the exception provided in this article should request previous authorization from the governor and the rule or regulation promulgated to these effects should be approved by him in order to be valid. The provisions in this law do not limit in any way the constitutional rights of any person on the basis of their vernacular or the language they use as a medium of expression.

Article 4. The law of February 21, 1902, "A Law with Respect to the Language to be used in the Departments, Courts and Offices of the Insular Government" is repealed.

Article 5. The provisions in this law will not impinge on the effect of laws containing dispositions expressly regulating the use of languages, nor will be interpreted to diminish the teaching of English as a second language in the schools or educational institutions of the public educational system of the Commonwealth of Puerto Rico.

Article 6. Documents granted or expedited prior to the date this law takes effect will not be subject to its provisions.

Article 7. This law will begin to take effect immediately after its enactment.

Appendix 6: The Moreno Rodríguez Language Bill

September 14, 1990 (H.B. 1115)

Referred to the Education and Culture Commission

To establish Spanish as the first official language and English as the second official language to be used by the Executive, Legislative, and Judicial branches of the Government of Puerto Rico, likewise its agencies and instrumentalities and to repeal the Official Languages Law from February 21, 1902.

Statement of Purpose

Since the time of Spanish colonization and even after the presence of the United States in Puerto Rico, our people have felt a great pride and an enormous responsibility to preserve our Spanish language as the most esteemed element of our cultural heritage. The population of Puerto Rico is, at ninety-eight (98) percent, Spanish speaking. The defenders of all political and cultural tendencies have publicly proclaimed that "the Spanish language is not negotiable."

Regardless of this decisive reality, Puerto Rico is a country of approximately 3.6 million inhabitants that all hold American citizenship since the year 1917. The U.S. Nation, whose citizenship we hold, though it has no official language, carries out its government transactions in the English language and this is the language currently used by the Government of Puerto Rico in its relations with the federal government and its dependencies, with other states of the union, likewise in its international relations. And so the need and practicality of using English as a second official language is recognized, likewise to assure its improved teaching and learning in our schools.

Despite the coexistence in Puerto Rico of the Hispanic, Afro-Antillean and Anglo-Saxon cultures, we Puerto Ricans speak and cultivate a Spanish language of great quality and purity, as attested to by our rich literature and folklore, along with the critiques of noted linguists and contemporary literati.

Spoken languages as much as official languages should be seen as manifestations of the spirit, whose intent is to communicate our sentiments, emotions, transmit our culture, make possible the process of socialization, likewise to transmit information and leave behind historic evidence of our legacy. Never should they be seen nor used as instruments of disunion, discord and bitterness. In this sense Puerto Rico has an eloquent tradition.

In the harmonious coexistence in Puerto Rico of the two great cultures of this hemisphere, with their respective linguistic manifestations lies the transnational role of Puerto Rico as a point of convergence and understanding of the Hispanic and Anglo-Saxon cultures. Puerto Rico should not renounce, and least of all voluntarily, the eminent historic role that destiny has provided it in America's future.

Puerto Rico should reaffirm that its vernacular language Spanish has bestowed it with pride and prestige; and recognize the coexistence, already official, of English as our second official language.

Puerto Ricans should have access to and take advantage of all available opportunities to improve their skills and capabilities in handling languages.

In the daily performance of official government functions is generally where our people learn the technical and distinctive aspects of English in their respective professions and disciplines.

By not including English as an official language, we would be eliminating one of the principal sources and opportunities to acquire proficiency in the management of said language. This inclusion is not in conflict with the importance, nor with the appreciation for our vernacular language.

Be it decreed by the Legislative Assembly of Puerto Rico:

Article 1. Spanish is hereby declared the first official language and English as the second official language to be used in all departments, political subdivisions, agencies, offices and governmental dependencies of the Executive, Legislative, and Judicial branches of the Government of Puerto Rico.

Article 2. The official language to be used in the first instance will be determined by the nature of the matter likewise the originating and consigned agency, except for that which is established for judicial proceedings in Article 5.

Article 3. When necessary written translations and oral interpretations will be made from the Spanish language to the English language and vice versa when the particular situation warrants and merits it in such a way that the interested parties can comprehend any procedure or communication in their own language.

Article 4. The languages to be used in school instruction will be those established in the corresponding Education Law.

Article 5. The language to be used in judicial proceedings in the courts of the Commonwealth of Puerto Rico will be Spanish, as resolved in the case *People v. Superior Court*, 1965, 92 DPR 596.

Article 6. When deemed necessary agencies of the Government of Puerto Rico are empowered to contract competent translators to carry out the work indicated in Article 3.

Article 7. All regulations promulgated under the provisions of this Law should comply with Law No. 112 of June 30, 1958, as amended known as the "Law on Regulations of 1958."

Article 8. The Law of Official Languages of February 21, 1902, known as the "Law of Official Languages," is hereby repealed.

Article 9. This law will take effect immediately upon its enactment.

Appendix 7: Official Languages Act of 1993

Law No. I—Approved January 28, 1993 (H.B. I)

A law to establish that Spanish and English shall be the official languages of the Government of Puerto Rico, and that both may be used interchangeably; and to repeal Law Number 4 of April 5, 1991.

Statement of Purpose

In 1898 it was established, under General Order Number 192 of the Chief of Staff of the Army, Office of the Adjutant General, in Washington, D.C., that the official language to be utilized in the Government of Puerto Rico would be English. On February 21, 1902, a law was enacted that authorized the interchangeable use of the Spanish and English languages in the Government of Puerto Rico. Eighty-nine years later, Law Number 4 of April 5, 1991 declared Spanish to be the official language of Puerto Rico for use in transacting the official business of all departments, municipalities and other political subdivisions, agencies, public corporations, offices and governmental dependencies of the Executive, Legislative and Judicial Branches of the Commonwealth of Puerto Rico. According to the preamble of that law, its purpose is to reaffirm our historical status as a Spanish-speaking people, while simultaneously manifesting a commitment to acquire a full mastery of English as a second language, without surrendering either our native tongue nor our culture.

The preamble to the Constitution of the Commonwealth of Puerto Rico declares, among other things, that "We consider to be determining factors in our lives, United States citizenship . . . [and] the coexistence in Puerto Rico of the two great cultures of the American hemisphere. . . ." In addition, the People of Puerto Rico have repeatedly manifested, throughout the entire 20th century, their desire to maintain and to strengthen their ties with the United States of America. The political, economic and social progress of the People of Puerto Rico are intimately linked to the proposition that both Spanish and English be official languages within their jurisdiction.

Law Number 4 of April 5, 1991, has not fulfilled the expectations of today's Puerto Rico, which aspires to active participation in the development initiatives of the Caribbean Basin, Latin America, North America, and the international community. Practical means are required to facilitate the Government of Puerto Rico's continued effective communication with its own constituents and with the world at large. Today, English constitutes the language most frequently utilized to conduct international communications. For historical reasons, our people have been utilizing Spanish and English interchangeably for more than nine decades, without this signifying that we have suppressed or abandoned our vernacular, the Spanish language, or surrendered either our language or our culture. On the contrary, our citizens find themselves in a privileged position, for having been exposed to, and having had the opportunity to learn and to speak, two important languages. As they have in the past, Spanish and English can co-exist in harmony and in conformity with the needs of the Puerto Rican people, without one diminishing the value of the other.

Nothing contained in this law signifies any linguistic retrogression or a cultural imposition upon the People of Puerto Rico. Any reference to a cultural assimilation motive is obsolete. The purpose of this measure is to remedy the adverse effects and the practical inconveniences resulting from Law Number 4 of April 5, 1991, by declaring and establishing that Spanish and English shall be the official languages for use interchangeably in all of the departments, municipalities and other political subdivisions, agencies, offices and governmental dependencies of the Executive, Legislative and Judicial Branches of the Commonwealth of Puerto Rico. In this manner, justice is served and an approximately century-old reality existent in our society is validated.

In order to dispel all doubt about the legislative intention of this measure, we reiterate the following:

1. This measure permits English to be utilized anew within the Government of Puerto Rico. For most purposes, the use of English to effect government business was prohibited here in 1991, when legislation was enacted to establish Spanish as the sole official language. Until then, English had also been an official language in Puerto Rico. In summary, with the approval of this measure, we restore—without eliminating or adding anything—the legal situation that existed in Puerto Rico prior to the adoption of the 1991 statute.

2. Throughout this measure, the Legislative Assembly in no way endeavors to establish by legislative fiat any sort of generalized bilingualism, contrary to the reality of Puerto Rican daily life. We go no further than to recognize another reality: that Puerto Rico's relationship with the United States, ever-closer from a political and economic standpoint, along with

the aspiration to perpetuate that relationship expressed at the ballot box by the voters of the two principal parties—which together account for more than 90 percent of the electorate, multiplies the instances in which it is necessary that our government receive and reply to communications in English and conduct official affairs in that language. To prohibit the use of English, by pure legislative fiat, as was done in 1991, unnecessarily and unjustifiably hampers and renders more costly the functioning of our government.

3. No aspect of this measure lends credence to or confirms the unfounded speculation that, by approving it, the Legislative Assembly would open the doors to the possible utilization of any language other than Spanish as a medium for instruction in the public schools. This bill neither repeals, or alters, nor amend Article 1.02 of the Education Department Organic Act—Law Number 68 of August 28, 1991—which, in its pertinent passage, establishes "that education will be imparted in the vernacular language, Spanish. English will be taught as a second language." We reaffirm here the public policy to that effect.

4. No aspect of this bill lends credence to the unfounded speculation that, by approving it, the Legislative Assembly would be authorizing or validating the use of any language other than Spanish in the judicial proceedings of the courts of the Commonwealth of Puerto Rico. The judicial language question was resolved by our Supreme Court in the case of *People vs. Superior Court* (1965) and what was therein established undergoes no change whatsoever with the approval of this measure. Neither does it alter Civil Procedure Rule 8.5 to the effect that "allegations, petitions and motions must be formulated in Spanish" in the Courts of Puerto Rico.

Be it decreed by the Legislative Assembly of Puerto Rico:

Article 1. It is established the Spanish and English shall be the official languages of Puerto Rico. Both may be utilized, interchangeably, in all departments, municipalities and other political subdivisions, agencies, public corporations, offices and governmental dependencies of the Executive, Legislative and Judicial Branches of the Commonwealth of Puerto Rico, subject to the provisions of this law, or the dispositions of special legislation.

Article 2. When necessary, oral or written translations and interpretations shall be made, from one language to the other, to permit interested parties to comprehend proceedings or communications in both languages.

Article 3. The departments, municipalities and other political subdivisions, agencies, public corporations, offices and governmental dependencies of the Executive, Legislative and Judicial Branches of the Commonwealth of Puerto Rico shall, when necessary, employ competent interpreters and translators in order to implement the dispositions of this law.

Article 4. It shall be impermissible to nullify any public or private document on the grounds that it is drafted in either one or the other of the official languages of Puerto Rico, subject to the provisions of this law, or the dispositions of special legislation.

Article 5. The departments, instrumentalities and public corporations, municipalities or other political subdivisions, agencies, offices and dependencies of the Government of Puerto Rico may utilize in their transactions languages other than the official languages when that becomes convenient or necessary.

Article 6. The Legislative Assembly and the Judicial Branch will adopt, if necessary, the regulatory dispositions that each deems appropriate and convenient, to implement in their respective internal operations the public policy established in this law.

Article 7. The dispositions of this law in no way limit any of the constitutional rights of any person due to the language that may be such person's vernacular or medium of expression.

Article 8. Law Number 4 of April 5, 1991 is hereby repealed in its entirety.

Article 9. If any part, section, paragraph or clause of this law is declared unconstitutional by a court competent to exercise jurisdiction over the matter, the sentence issued to that effect will neither affect nor invalidate the remainder of this law, but rather will be limited to the part, section, paragraph or clause declared unconstitutional.

Article 10. This law shall take effect immediately upon its enactment.

Notes

1. Culture, Identity, and Policy

1. Eighteen individuals were interviewed for this project: seventeen in Puerto Rico and one (Governor Dukakis) on the U.S. mainland. Most of the interviewees in Puerto Rico spoke in Spanish. However, former education secretary Chardón and former house speaker Jarabo decided to give their interviews in English.

2. Spanish and Puertorriqueñidad

1. Many in the Spanish-speaking world identify themselves with two family names—their father's surname followed by their mother's maiden name. A hyphen might be written between the two names (e.g., Maldonado-Denis) or not (e.g., Trías Monge). Individuals can be identified by their father's surname alone (e.g., Maldonado or Trías) but should not be acknowledged by their mother's family name alone.

2. However, there are societies where language regimes develop as "constellations" of multiple languages rather than one particular idiom (Laitin 1997: 279).

3. Puerto Rico has been politically organized under three civilian governments while under American rule: the Foraker Act of 1900, the Jones Act of 1917, and the 1952 Commonwealth Constitution. The first two organic laws were acts of Congress; the 1952 constitution, while drafted by Puerto Ricans, was amended and given final approved by Congress. Under the Foraker and Jones acts the island's governors, like all presidential appointees, were confirmed by the U.S. Senate. Most appointments were political favors doled out to individuals who usually knew little about Puerto Rico prior to becoming the island's governor (Maldonado-Denis 1972: 77). Puerto Rico's education commissioners in the first half of the 1900s, in contrast to the other territories, were also presidential appointees (Barreto 1998: 95).

4. Although a territory, Puerto Rico exercises limited autonomy in a few areas. When it comes to international beauty contests, Puerto Rico sends a separate delegation from the United States as if it were a separate country. The same applies to sports; Puerto Rico participates under its own banner under the auspices of the Puerto Rico Olympic Committee.

5. Original: "Los puertorriqueños hablamos español a toda hora, en todos los lugares, en todos los espacios, y pensamos en español. Y creo que a pesar de que hemos tenido una influencia norteamericana tan grande hemos logrado prevalecer en términos del idioma más que cualquier otro estado de Sudamérica" (Rivera Ramírez 1998).

6. Original: "Por lo tanto, hablar de Puerto Rico, por ejemplo, sin hablar de los Estados Unidos, sin hablar de ciudadanía americana, sin hablar de todos los demás

elementos que mundialmente han afectado a los Estados Unidos, y por consecuencia Puerto Rico, es prácticamente dislocar la verdadera historia de Puerto Rico" (Cintrón García 1998).

7. Linguistic identity is used by elites to identify and galvanize the collective when it suits their interests. A case in point is Creole resistance in colonial Mexico. Here local elites fought the Crown's policy of teaching Spanish to indigenous communities for fear of losing their role as bilingual intermediaries between the Mexican masses and the Spanish state (Heath 1972: 42–50).

8. Likewise, nineteenth-century Basque nationalists celebrated *Euskera*—the Basque language—although few urbanites spoke it (Heiberg 1982: 358). The founder of modern Basque nationalism, Sabino de Arana y Goiri, who did not learn the Basque language until his teens, was nonetheless responsible for coining the word *Euzkadi*—the Basque homeland—from the word *Euskera*, the Basque language (Clark 1979: 41–42).

9. In the first half of the twentieth century, Puerto Rican elites found it in their best interests to initiate ethnogenesis and articulate Puerto Rican vis-à-vis American cultural traits. They also made the strategic, if not contradictory, decision to actively partake in the New Deal programs in the 1930s and 1940s. Elite dependency on federal benefits channeled nationalism in an autonomist rather than a separatist direction (Urrutia 1993).

10. The Foraker Act created a bicameral legislature. Members of the House of Delegates were elected. In contrast, the Executive Council consisted of presidential appointees: the territorial cabinet plus five additional appointees (Ramírez Lavandero 1988: 64–66). Thus, under the Foraker Act, Americans dominated both the executive branch of the local government and one of the two legislative chambers. Interestingly, while the separation of powers principle was jealously guarded on the U.S. mainland, it was not considered vital for Puerto Rico.

11. Original: "Como se sabe la ley original que hacía el español y el inglés idiomas oficiales de principios de siglo evidentemente respondía a una realidad muy evidente. Era que las principales figuras del gobierno de Puerto Rico bajo la ley Foraker eran americanos y no sabían hablar el español. Y por lo tanto era evidente que el inglés, en aquel momento, tenía que ser uno de los idiomas oficiales de Puerto Rico. Porque si no la administración colonial norteamericana no hubiera podido funcionar" (Martín 1998).

12. One of the issues addressed by the territory's highest court in this divorce case was a discrepancy between the English and Spanish texts of the island's Civil Code. Despite the equality accorded the two languages under the 1902 language law, Justice Wolf wrote: "There can be no doubt that the English text, which was signed by the Governor, is the law which must govern" (*Cruz v. Domínguez*, 8 D.P.R. 551, 555–60 [1905]).

13. Original: "Yo creo que no hay nación en el mundo que haya sobrevivido ese intento sistemático y masivo de transculturación, de desarraigar al pueblo de

su raíz. Por lo tanto, la ley del 91 yo la ví como un auxilio a las luchas hereóicas de un pueblo que logró superar esa etapa" (Noriega Rodríguez 1998).

3.The Power of English

1. The only gubernatorial election held under the Jones Act was in 1948. Yet Muñoz was not the island's first Puerto Rican governor. That distinction befell Jesús T. Piñero, who was appointed governor by President Truman in 1946.

2. Original: "Puerto Rico no es bilingüe y los datos del censo lo prueban. . . . Aquí una pequeña porción de la población maneja con soltura y con facilidad el inglés. La mayor parte de los puertorriqueños somos unilingües; somos hispanoparlantes. Pero ciertamente una de las grandes aspiraciones educativas de Puerto Rico es la de enseñar bien el inglés" (Benítez 1998b).

3. As a territory, Puerto Rico cannot control immigration. That responsibility is strictly federal.

4. When assessing the impact of immigration, one must also account for the large number of undocumented Dominicans residing in Puerto Rico (Rivera-Batiz and Santiago 1996: 115).

5. Studies confirm that the Cuban community overwhelmingly supports Puerto Rico's pro-statehood movement (Cobas and Duany 1995: 107–8).

6. Rivera-Batiz and Santiago (1996: 116–17) confirmed that as a group Cubans in Puerto Rico enjoy a privileged economic position. Interestingly, their analysis refuted the equally prevalent idea that Dominicans occupied an inferior economic standing vis-à-vis Puerto Ricans.

7. Among those unable to speak Spanish—less than two percent of Puerto Rico's total population—only 22.54 percent speak English easily (U.S. Dept. of Commerce 1993b: 70).

8. Arlene Dávila's (1997) study detailed how U.S. multinational firms in Puerto Rico sponsor local festivals. In the quest for profits, these companies exalt the island's culture; they do not promote a corporate version of Americanization. Interestingly, the Puerto Rican culture these companies frequently sponsor emanates from the popular sectors, the culture of the subalterns and the masses, rather than the official sanctioned "Hispanophile" culture endorsed by the government-run Instituto de Cultura Puertorriqueña (ICP, Puerto Rican Institute of Culture).

9. Original: "prevalece la idea errónea de que las escuelas privadas, por ser privadas, son mejores" (Benítez 1998b).

10. Original: "Los mayores ingresos económicos usualmente están ligados a una escolaridad más alta de manera que el estudiante tiene ya, por provenir de este tipo de hogar, un estímulo en el hogar para aprender bien el inglés, para sobresalir en la escuela, etcetera. Lamentablemente muchos estudiantes de las escuelas públicas, porque provienen de otro tipo de hogar, no tienen esos estímulos en el hogar que los ayudan hacer mejor trabajo en la escuela que a los que provienen de hogares de otras circunstancias" (Benítez 1998b).

11. Original: "Porque lo más increíble es que aquí siempre ha habido políticos que no quieren que los pobres de este país aprenden inglés. Que no quieren que se incentive más la enseñanza del inglés en Puerto Rico porque tienen temor de que eso acerque más a Puerto Rico a la anexión con los Estados Unidos. Sin embargo casi todos los políticos de aquí, primero envían sus hijos a estudiar en escuelas privadas en Puerto Rico donde la enseñanza primaria es en inglés" (Rodríguez Negrón 1998).

12. Puerto Rican dependency on the United States led Carlos Romero-Barceló (1978) to argue that statehood was most beneficial for the island's poor. As Meléndez (1993a: 210–11) suggested, the economic plight of the poor would not change under statehood, per se, but rather welfare checks would increase. Statehood advocates suggest that economic dependency on the United States, coupled with its century-long links, make independence an unrealistic option (Grosfoguel et al. 1997: 10).

13. A consequence of constant migration is the frequent use of English terms in Puerto Rican Spanish (Del Rosario 1969). Fusing languages—while common among those straddling cultural borders—is often negatively stigmatized, as is the case with mainland Puerto Rican Spanish (Zentella 1990: 90). Nonetheless, language mixing is treated as something ordinary and routine by many Puerto Ricans (Urciuoli 1991: 299).

4. The Politics of Status

1. While we use the term *model* throughout this work, scholars such as Snidal (1985) would contend that our analysis of language policy in Puerto Rico is more akin to game theory as metaphor, rather than a truly rigorous and formal model.

2. Interestingly, many annexationists have stated that remaining a colony is unacceptable and if statehood were not attainable they would endorse independence (Meléndez 1993a: 11).

3. In contrast to the PIP, other separatist parties refused to discount revolutionary tactics. Two prime examples are the Partido Nacionalista (Nationalist Party) of the 1930s under the leadership of Pedro Albizu Campos (Bothwell 1979a: 600) and the Partido Socialista Puertorriqueño (PSP—Puerto Rican Socialist Party) of the 1970s led by Juan Mari Bras (1984: 203).

4. Governor Rosselló recently shocked many by openly admitting that the commonwealth government had long persecuted Puerto Rican separatists and called for the "end of an embarrassing chapter in Puerto Rico's history" (Estrada 1999: 4). For many this statement was a moral victory and tantamount to a confession (Nieves 1999: 8). In contrast, FBI officials claimed that they had nothing to apologize for and denied keeping tabs on individuals based on their ideological convictions (Colombani 1999: 14).

5. Measures of electoral support are based on the percentage of votes obtained by the parties' gubernatorial candidates. The two electorally active separatist parties in this period were the Partido Independentista Puertorriqueño (1952–1996)

and the Partido Socialista Puertorriqueño (1976 and 1980). The Partido Popular Democrático (1952–1996) and the Partido del Pueblo (1968 and 1972) were the two autonomist parties. Both the PIP and PPD antedate the establishment of the Commonwealth. Four annexationist, or pro-statehood, parties were tallied: the Partido Estadista Puertorriqueño (1952), the Partido Socialista (1952), the Partido Estadista Republicano (1956–1968) and the Partido Nuevo Progresista (1968–1996). Socialists in the 1940s and early 1950s, in contrast to late twentieth-century Puerto Rican socialists, endorsed statehood (Bothwell 1979a: 647). The two nonstatus parties were the Partido Acción Cristiana (1960 and 1964) and the Partido Renovación Puertorriqueña (1984).

6. The year 1968 also marked a major milestone in Puerto Rican politics. The PIP boycotted the 1967 status plebiscite as did the PER leader Miguel Angel García Méndez. In response to the PER boycott, Luis A. Ferré asked the group Estadistas Unidos (United Statehooders) to support annexation in this special election. Following the plebiscite, Ferré founded the PNP (Bayrón 1989: 246). At the same time, PPD Governor Roberto Sánchez Vilella broke ranks with his party and he formed his own, the Partido del Pueblo (People's Party). Sánchez Vilella weakened the PPD sufficiently to hand the PNP its first gubernatorial victory in 1968.

5. Reviving the Language Debate

1. Original: "yo toda mi vida he sido soberanista. Yo he creído en la libertad de mi pueblo—en la estadidad o la independencia. En lo que no puedo creer es en la colonia y esto es una colonia" (Peña Clos 1998).

2. Original: "Bueno, yo siempre he creído en que los niños aprenden más y mejor en el idioma que maman de la teta de su madre, la que se hable en su hogar" (Peña Clos 1998).

3. *Meyers v. Nebraska,* 262 U.S. 390 (1923). The U.S. Supreme Court invalidated a Nebraska law that forbade the use of any language of instruction other than English in both private and public schools (Stone et al. 1986: 840).

4. Original: "De hecho, se habían presentado otros proyectos. Y yo, para mí, tengo la impresión de que otros proyectos no progresaron al punto de convertirse en ley por algún tipo de renuencia política en el sentido de que no se entendiera que era un paso, un tanto, nacionalista. Y eso se le atribuyó a temores dentro del partido de gobierno de entonces que es al partido al cual pertenezco. De hecho, es curioso que uno de los autores de un proyecto de ley estableciendo el español como idioma [oficial] es el actual Senador Sergio Peña Clos. Y que a ese proyecto no se le dió curso fundamentalmente por temores políticos que venían de la más alta dirección del partido—o sea, del propio gobernador Rafael Hernández Colón" (Hernández Agosto 1998).

5. Original: "Desde el cuarenta y pico hasta el noventiuno, en que se aprobó la ley a la cual usted se refiere, pues, húbo un número de proyectos que se presentaban en la Asamblea Legislativa para hacer el idioma español el único oficial. Ningunos

de esos proyectos prosperó porque se entendía que era mejor—más conveniente políticamente para el gobierno que estuviera en el poder—el no tocar el tema" (Hernández Colón 1998b).

6. The former French colony of Louisiana became the first state admitted into the union where language was a serious issue (Barreto 1998: 57). Congress obliged this state to establish English as its official language and the medium of legislative and judicial proceedings (Serrano and Gorrín 1979: 524). Louisiana could keep its French-based legal system as long as it was administered in English (Moynihan 1993: 74).

6. The Official Language Act of 1991

1. Original: "No es una ley del Partido Popular. Esto debe estar claro. Esto es una preocupación que yo tengo desde que yo era profesor de escuela superior a principios de la década del 70" (López Galarza 1998).

2. Original: "Y el español es la lengua oficial de los puertorriqueños porque yo concibo que lengua oficial es aquella en que el gobierno se comunica con su gente. . . . Aún Rosselló no se atreve a dar un discurso en inglés en Puerto Rico (López Galarza 1998).

3. Original: "Entonces el 27 de marzo de 1989 yo radiqué un proyecto que es el Proyecto de la Cámara número 417. . . . Se queda un tiempo allí, pero yo dije: no, mira, perdóname, yo no voy a hacer lo que se ha hecho en ocasiones anteriores. Que se vienen a radicar proyectos de ley que tengan que ver con el idioma para engavetarlos. Y entonces yo decidí que ibamos a echar para adelante este proyecto de ley porque yo presidí en la Cámara de Representantes la Comisión de Educación y Cultura. . . . Cuando lo fui hacer lo consulté con el presidente de la Cámara y entonces decidimos hablar con el gobernador" (López Galarza 1998).

4. Original: "Nosotros creemos, y yo soy fiel creyente, en la necesidad de que se mejore la enseñanza del inglés en Puerto Rico. Y no solamente que se enseñe [el inglés] sino que se enseñe el francés y otras lenguas" (López Galarza 1998).

5. Original: "hasta mis asesores me decían: eso no te conviene políticamente" (López Galarza 1998).

6. Surveys consistently demonstrate that separatism is supported by 6 to 9 percent of the electorate. Yet, recent plebiscite results set independence support under 5 percent. Some speculate that there are *independentistas* who dread a possible statehood victory and vote instead for the commonwealth option. These closet separatists may have been partly responsible for the commonwealth's plebiscite victories in the 1990s.

7. Original: "Por lo tanto, romper con la ley del 1902 era fundamentalmente aventurar a Puerto Rico en un proceso de nacionalización, de separación sociológica de los Estados Unidos, con la intención de luego poder lograr la separación política que eventualmente iba en contra de los intereses de la mayoría de este pueblo. . . . Por lo tanto, esa ley del 1991 no era solamente una ley de idiomas. Era . . . parte de un escenario que se venía construyendo por el entonces gobernador Hernández Colón y su gobierno para poco a poco ir estableciendo los

cimientos de unos cambios en la estructura de Puerto Rico, para ir socialmente desrelacionando o separando a los puertorriqueños de los norteamericanos" (Cintrón García 1998).

8. Original: "Yo francamente creo que fue una agenda cuidadosamente desarrollada para distanciar a Puerto Rico de la influencia norteamericana. No me cabe la menor duda de eso" (Rodríguez Negrón 1998).

9. Original: "Primero, estaba creando una imagen equivocada de Puerto Rico en el Congreso de los Estados Unidos—dando la impresión de que este pueblo ... quisiera alejarse de los Estados Unidos cuando este pueblo lo que ha querido siempre ha sido una vinculación más estrecha con los Estados Unidos, bien a través de un Estado Libre Asociado o a través de la Estadidad" (Rexach Benítez 1998).

10. Original: "Con la celebración del quinto centenario del descubrimiento de América y de Puerto Rico como que el país fue desarrollando un orgullo por lo propio—un poco distinto a lo que habíamos tenido en los años anteriores" (Hernández Agosto 1998).

7. Rational Politics

1. A political actor indifferent to alternatives x and y (xI_iy) and y and z (yI_iz) will harbor no partiality between choices x and z: xI_iz (Shepsle and Bonchek 1997: 25–26).

2. Let us use an example from economics to highlight a cardinal utility calculus. Assume that we have one hundred dollars to invest and our investment choices are limited to buying lottery tickets or opening a savings account. If we win the lottery we win one million dollars. With a 5 percent interest rate an individual would earn five dollars by depositing the one hundred dollars into a savings account. What prevents most people from pouring their life savings into the lottery? The answer is *probability*. One's chances of being struck by lightning are statistically greater than those associated with winning many lotteries.

Let us say that the probability of earning savings' interest is 100 percent ($p = 1.00$). Our odds of winning the lottery is only a tiny fraction of one percent, let us say that $p = 0.00000001$. By multiplying our lottery payoff times the probability of it occurring we obtain an expected utility of only 0.01. Our interest payoff of five dollars is multiplied by its probability of occurring, in this case one hundred percent. We obtain an expected utility of 5. Thus, our expected utility from opening a savings account (EU = 5) is greater than our expected utility from investing in lottery tickets (EU = .01).

8. Culture, Policy, and Nested Games

1. Original: "había un compromiso de parte de nosotros de que se iba a derogar esa ley. Es más, lo advertimos desde el 1991 cuando se aprobó la ley" (Rexach Benítez 1998).

2. Original: "Yo nunca creí que esa ley fuera necesaria. Y no creía que era necesaria porque era como decir el sol sale por el este y se pone por el oeste. La realidad

socioeconómica subyacente es que Puerto Rico es un país de cultura hispana—un país hispanoparlante" (Benítez 1998b).

3. Original: "Yo debo decir con franqueza que fue más bien algo dirigido por la dirección del Partido Popular . . . más que un reclamo del pueblo. . . . Claro, después cuando se planteó la situación se convierte en un *issue* en el pueblo. Porque entonces la gente despierta. . . . La gente entonces empieza a preocuparse y hablar del idioma. Pero como es natural es el idioma nuestro. Es el vernáculo. Pues, a los únicos que les molesta es aquellas personas que plantean otras ideologías políticas ajenas a las idiosincrasias del puertorriqueño" (Alicea Vázquez 1998).

4. Original: "Francamente el liderato político del Partido Popular no hizo un esfuerzo concertado ni serio por contrarrestar esa propaganda del Partido Nuevo Progresista. Y aquella ley del español entonces se vió envuelta en una controversia política que le hizo daño al Partido Popular" (Benítez 1998b).

5. Original: "Luego, puede haber sido perjudicial desde el punto de vista partidista. Pero creo que en aquel momento no se produjo dándole peso al impacto político—ni beneficioso ni perjudicial" (Hernández Agosto 1998).

6. Original: "Sí, desde el punto [de vista] político partidista realmente el proyecto era estúpido porque no le proporcionaba al Partido Popular, que lo promovió, una ventaja política. Al contrario, ocasionaba un daño político porque en Puerto Rico mucho más del 70 porciento de la gente quiere la unión permanente con Estados Unidos" (Rexach Benítez 1998).

7. Original: "Rafael Hernández Colón vió también esa ley como una manera de bregar con la cuestión del status" (López Galarza 1998).

8. Original: "Yo creo que uno de los obstáculos a la estadidad precisamente es el idioma. . . . yo creo que Estados Unidos no aceptaría un estado cuya lengua oficial y cuya lengua materna fuera el español. . . . Que haya multiplicidades de culturas en Estados Unidos las hay. Pero hay en Estados Unidos un sentido todavía de unidad nacional y esa unidad nacional se la da el inglés aunque se hablen otros idiomas" (López Galarza 1998).

9. Original: "Bueno, cuando no se aprobó legislación en el Congreso, entonces sentimos nosotros la necesidad de dar algunos pasos acá para clarificar aquello que queríamos clarificar conjuntamente con el Congreso. Y uno de los asuntos que queríamos clarificar era el tema de la identidad puertorriqueña. Por eso podemos decir llegó el momento de hacer un acto de afirmación lingüística, de afirmación del español como afirmación de nuestra identidad, como afirmación de nuestro ser. Pero al mismo tiempo con unas intenciones de lingüística como tales con el propósito de que en el pais se fortaleciera y se enriqueciera y se mejorara el uso de la lengua propia el cual había venido empobreciendose de manera marcada por muchos años. Y dimos el paso" (Hernández Colón 1998b).

10. Original: "Yo sabía que ellos iban a alegar eso. Pero eso a mi no me preocupaba. Yo sabía donde yo estaba parado claramente. A mi la política demagógica de ellos nunca me ha creado preocupación al grado de moverme a la inacción. La

tomo en consideración, pues, para mantener las cosas clara ante el pueblo. Pero no me paralice" (Hernández Colón 1998b).

11. Original: "Pero esa declaración de lo obvio, de lo evidente, en Puerto Rico constituía en términos políticos también una declaración difícil de digerir y de masticar para un Congreso de Estados Unidos" (García San Inocencio 1998).

12. Original: "Ciertamente nosotros veíamos esa dimensión como una dimensión importante; no cabe duda" (Martín 1998).

13. Original: "No, no, el que en Estados Unidos percibiera la diferencia y que esto estimulara al debate sobre el rol del idioma en Puerto Rico—los obstáculos a la estadidad y el carácter latinoamericano de los puertorriqueños—hasta el punto que un gobierno de Puerto Rico, aún colonial, puede decir que el español es la lengua oficial de Puerto Rico—un poco apoyaba nuestra tesis de que es de recordarle a los norteamericanos que—a los que no lo saben—Puerto Rico es una nación diferente a los Estados Unidos, que tiene un idioma diferente, y que la mayor parte de la gente en Puerto Rico no entiende el inglés" (Martín 1998).

14. Let us say that k equals one—the traditional Downsian assumption. One multiplied by the electoral payoff (PO_{ei}) equals the electoral payoff.

Payoff where k is equal to 1

$$PO_i = kPO_{ei} + (1-k)PO_{pi}$$
$$PO_i = (1)PO_{ei} + (1-1)PO_{pi}$$
$$PO_i = PO_{ei} + (0)PO_{pi}$$
$$PO_i = PO_{ei} + 0$$
$$PO_i = PO_{ei}$$

However, if the individual assessed k at 0, the parliamentary arena would become the true focus of the actor's payoff strategy.

15. Downs's model is based on the assumption that political actors look toward the next election. Today's actions will directly affect the outcome of future events; thus, they are playing an *iterated game*. But, if the issue is very important actors engage in a one-shot or single-shot game. Tsebelis (1990: 171) noted, "the stakes are very high, so they cannot be traded off against other issues or promises about future behavior."

10. Restoring Official Bilingualism

1. Original: "proyectar a Puerto Rico como algo asimilable ante los ojos de los Estados Unidos" (García San Inocencio 1998).

2. Original: "O sea, yo creo que la decisión . . . del Gobernador Rosselló fue la misma de Rafael pero a la inversa. O sea, fue demostrarle a los Estados Unidos, *mira*, aquí no solamente rechazaron lo que dijo Rafael, de que no queremos separarnos de ustedes, sino que viene un partido estadista de forma abrumadora controlando Cámara y Senado y casi todos los municipios. . . . Y ahora yo te voy a decir que tengo el mandato del pueblo para nuevamente restituir los dos idiomas" (Rivera Ramírez 1998).

3. Original: "Bueno, en el Congreso se tiene que haber visto como un paso en la

dirección correcta. O sea, que estamos eliminando una cosa que no representaba el sentir del pueblo puertorriqueño" (Rexach Benítez 1998).

4. Original: "Nos ayudó mucho ante los ojos del Congreso de los Estados Unidos y nos ayudó mucho aquí en Puerto Rico. Porque obviamente aquella nos proporcióno un *issue* electoral muy, pero muy poderoso contra el Partido Popular" (Rexach Benítez 1998).

5. Original: "la aprobación de la ley del idioma que se hace bajo la administración Rosselló es para decirle: *mire*, hemos cambiado el curso de separación que llevaba el Partido Popular Democrático por . . . un curso de unión a los Estados Unidos. Nosotros defendemos la estadidad y hacemos el inglés idioma oficial. Eliminamos de ante mano un problema que podría existir para Puerto Rico de ser admitido a la Unión" (Hernández Agosto 1998).

6. Original: "Bueno, la ley del 93 obviamente responde al cambio en el balance de poder en Puerto Rico y . . . reconocía el PNP que la ley del 91 les metía un dedo en el ojo, que lo primero que hicieron al llegar fue revocarla. Claro, la revocación por parte del PNP, que era predecible y que es desde el punto de vista de ellos perfectamente comprensible, tiene siempre el problema y el defecto del ridículo. Porque eso de usted hacer en su país idioma oficial a un idioma que la mayor parte de la gente no entiende siempre tiene algo de ridículo" (Martín 1998).

7. Aurelio Méndez also served in the first territorial legislature under U.S. rule, representing the district of Aguadilla (Bayrón 1989: 116). His pro-statehood Partido Republicano Puertorriqueño advocated using English as the language of instruction in the public school system (Bothwell 1979a: 261 and 278). Ironically, some of the annexationists under American rule were separatists while the island was under Spain's sovereignty (Quintero 1986: 32; Meléndez 1993a: 1). Indeed, Aurelio Méndez was a member of the revolutionary council during the Grito de Lares uprising against the Spanish Crown in 1868 (Figueroa 1979: 302).

8. Original: "quien va a imponer las condiciones es el Congreso americano" (Méndez Soto 1998).

9. Original: "Yo creo que estos movimientos de cambio, por ejemplo en el 91 para la lengua española solamente por Rafael Hernández Colón y más tarde Pedro Rosselló para las dos lenguas, son movimientos de líderes para conseguir lo que ellos tienen en su mente como fórmula final para Puerto Rico" (Méndez Soto 1998).

11. Creating a Bilingual Citizenry

1. *Downes v. Bidwell*, 182 U.S. 241.

2. For more on incorporated versus unincorporated territories, consult Rivera Ramos (1996) and Torruella (1985).

3. Original: "Solomon estuo aquí. Estuvo en Vieques como miembro de las fuerzas armadas. Nos conoció. Sabe como somos. Tiene montones de amigos puertorriqueños. El no tiene nada en contra de nosotros los puertorriqueños. El

lo que quiere es asegurar la unidad lingüística de su nación. Y él sabe que nosotros hablamos español y sabe también que hay, pues, una población bien distribuída en los Estados Unidos, creciente, de gente de habla hispana y también de otras lenguas. Y todo eso le plantea unos problemas de cohesión nacional a los Estados Unidos. Y ese es el problema al cual se dirigía Gerald Solomon" (Hernández Colón 1998b).

4. Original: "Al ser estos dos idiomas nuestros idiomas oficiales tenemos un fenómeno que se ve año tras año. Los estudiantes no están . . . alcanzando unos estándardes que nosotros como educadores tenemos para ellos. En el 93 se hace oficial el inglés en Puerto Rico nuevamente. Comienza también con todo este proceso el proceso de reforma educativa fuerte. Y dentro del proceso de reforma educativa ha habido reforma curricular" (Rodríguez González 1998).

5. Original: "Después de todo, todos los puertorriqueños favorecemos además del manejo adecuado de nuestro idioma que en Puerto Rico el mayor número de gente posible domine el inglés lo suficiente para aprovecharse del inglés como el gran idioma del mundo" (Martín 1998).

6. Original: "Mira, los muchachos no saben matemáticas en español. ¿Cómo lo van a saber en inglés? Primero hay que dominar la lengua materna para después dominar aquí, en el caso nuestro, el inglés. . . . Aquí los muchachos no practican el inglés. Aquí los muchachos terminan un bachillerato y no saben expresarse en inglés. No pueden sostener una conversación en inglés" (López Galarza 1998).

7. Original: "Muchos de los estudios que se consultaron, pues, claramente señalan que para tú poder dominar un segundo idioma primero tienes que dominar tu lengua materna. Y por allí fue que nosotros empezamos. La política pública del proyecto para el desarrolo del ciudadano bilingüe pretende, sobre todo, que se fortalezca la enseñanza del español para que el estudiante pueda aprender buen inglés" (Rodríguez González 1998).

8. Original: "Estamos recommendado a los maestros y a las escuelas que utilizan libros de referencia—matemáticas y ciencias—ya que la terminología de ciencia al traducirse muchas veces pierde la esencia y hay algunos términos y algún vocablo que no es traducible" (Rodríguez González 1998).

9. Original: "Es sencillamente un instrumento del partido en poder para crear la impresión en los Estados Unidos de que esta administración de Rosselló está moviendo a Puerto Rico hacia una asimilación cultural con los Estados Unidos" (Benítez 1998b).

Appendix 1: The Official Languages Act of 1902

Author's note: Translation of 1 L.P.R.A. §§ 51–55 by Barreto.

1. Excerpt taken from the English text of General Order No. 192 (U.S. Dept. of Army 1900: 11).

Appendix 2: The Berríos Martínez Language Bill

Author's note: Translated by Barreto. Emphasis in original. The Spanish text of this bill was reprinted in the journal of the Puerto Rico Bar Association (*Revista* 1993: 105–12).

1. Excerpt taken from Stella Lange's translation (Guardini 1965: 130).

2. It appears that there was a typographical error and the word "no" was missing in the bill's text. Without this word the entire meaning of Article 15 is reversed, which clearly runs counter to the intent of this bill's *independentista* author. This omission was found in both the reprint in the Puerto Rico Bar Association's journal (*Revista* 1993: 112) and a copy of the bill obtained at the Puerto Rico Senate Archives.

Appendix 3: The Peña Clos Language Bill

Author's note: Translated by Barreto. A copy of the bill was provided by the Puerto Rico Senate Archives.

Appendix 4: The Peña Clos and Fas Alzamora Language Bill

Author's note: Translated by Barreto. A copy of the bill was provided by the Puerto Rico Senate Archives.

1. The English translation of these two sections of Puerto Rico's constitution was taken from Ramírez Lavandero (1988: 195).

Appendix 5: Official Language Act of 1991

Author's note: Translated by Barreto. The Spanish text of this bill was reprinted in the journal of the Puerto Rico Bar Association (*Revista* 1993: 441–43).

Appendix 6: The Moreno Rodríguez Language Bill

Author's note: Translated by Barreto. The Spanish text of this bill was reprinted in the journal of the Puerto Rico Bar Association (*Revista* 1993: 117–19).

Appendix 7: Official Languages Act of 1993

Author's note: *Congressional Record* (1993: H329–30).

Bibliography

"¡A defender tu español!" 1993. *El Nuevo Día,* San Juan, P.R. (January 22): 18.

"A enseñar más en inglés." 1997. *El Nuevo Día,* San Juan, P.R. (April 22): 20.

Acosta, Ivonne. 1987. *La Mordaza: Puerto Rico, 1948–1957* (The Gag order: Puerto Rico, 1948–1957). Río Piedras, P.R.: Editorial Edil.

———. 1991. "Hacia una historia de la persecusión política en Puerto Rico." *Homines* 15, no. 2 and 16, no. 1 (October): 142–51.

Adames, Celimar. 1990. "Reafirma su apoyo al español." *El Mundo,* San Juan, P.R. (September 22): 10.

Agosto Cintrón, Nélida. 1996. *Religión y cambio social en Puerto Rico (1898–1940)* (Religion and social change in Puerto Rico [1898–1940]). Río Piedras, P.R.: Ediciones Huracán.

Aitchison, Jean. 1991. *Language Change: Progress or Decay?* 2d ed. Cambridge: Cambridge University Press.

"Al frente la opción estadista." 1990. *El Mundo,* San Juan, P.R. (July 23): 3.

Algren de Gutiérrez, Edith. 1987. *The Movement Against Teaching English in Schools of Puerto Rico.* Lanham, Maryland: University Press of America.

Alicea Vázquez, Rafael. 1998. Interview. Lares, P.R., July 21.

Alvar, Manuel. 1982. "Español e inglés: Actitudes lingüísticas en Puerto Rico." *Revista de Filología Española* 62, no. 1–2 (January): 1–38.

Anderson, Benedict. 1983. *Imagined Communities: Reflections on the Origin and Spread of Nationalism.* London: Verso Editions.

Anderson, Robert. 1965. *Party Politics in Puerto Rico.* Stanford: Stanford University Press.

———. 1983. "Political Parties and the Politics of Status." *Caribbean Studies* 21, no. 1–2: 1–43.

Andreu Cuevas, Leila A. 1990. "Ismael Fernández coincide con el PIP." *El Mundo,* San Juan, P.R. (September 5): 8.

Archilla Rivera, Milvia Y. 1993. "Dividido el PNP por celebración plebiscito en 1993." *Claridad,* San Juan, P.R. (March 19–25): 3.

Arington, Michele. 1991. "English-Only Laws and Direct Legislation: The Battle in the States Over Language Minority Rights." *Journal of Law and Politics* 7, no. 2 (winter): 325–52.

"Avanza el Nuevo ELA." 1990. *El Mundo,* San Juan, P.R. (September 26): 1.

"¡Aviso electoral!" 1993. *El Nuevo Día,* San Juan, P.R. (November 11): 49.

Baron, Dennis. 1990. *The English-Only Question: An Official Language for Americans?* New Haven: Yale University Press.

Barreto, Amílcar A. 1991. "The Debate Over Puerto Rican Statehood: Language and the 'Super Majority.'" *Homines* 15, no. 2 and 16, no. 1 (January): 135–41.

————. 1995. "Nationalism and Linguistic Security in Contemporary Puerto Rico." *Canadian Review of Studies in Nationalism* 22, no. 1–2: 67–74.

————. 1998. *Language, Elites, and the State: Nationalism in Puerto Rico and Quebec.* Westport, Conn.: Praeger.

Barreto, Amílcar A., and D. Munroe Eagles. 2000. "Modelos ecológicos de apoyo partidista en Puerto Rico, 1980–1992." *Revista de Ciencias Sociales* 9: 135–65.

Barth, Fredrik. 1969. Introduction to *Ethnic Groups and Boundaries: The Social Organization of Culture Difference,* ed. Fredrik Barth. Boston: Little, Brown and Company.

Batty, Susan E., and Vesna Danilovic. 1997. "Gorbachev's Strategy of Political Centrism: A Game-Theoretic Interpretation." *Journal of Theoretical Politics* 9, no. 1 (February): 89–106.

Baumgarter, Juana. 1993. "Nuestro vernáculo es el español, ¿Okey?" Editorial. *El Nuevo Día,* San Juan, P.R. (January 21): 69.

Bauzá, Nydia. 1993. "'Inaceptable' un plebiscito sin consenso." *El Nuevo Día,* San Juan, P.R. (April 5): 19.

————. 1996. "Revive la pugna del idioma oficial." *El Nuevo Día,* San Juan, P.R. (October 29): 20.

Bayrón Toro, Fernando. 1989. *Elecciones y partidos políticos de Puerto Rico* (Puerto Rico's elections and political parties). 4th ed. Mayagüez, P.R.: Editorial Isla.

Beirne, Charles J. 1976. *El problema de la «Americanización» en las escuelas católicas de Puerto Rico* (The "Americanization" problem in Puerto Rico's Catholic schools). Río Piedras, P.R.: Editorial Universitaria.

Benítez, Celeste. 1976. "El Estado Libre Asociado ayer y hoy." Editorial. *El Mundo,* San Juan, P.R. (March 25): 7A.

————. 1998a. *El día en que Puerto Rico habló* (The day that Puerto Rico spoke). Río Piedras, P.R.: Editorial Cultural.

————. 1998b. Interview. Río Piedras, P.R., July 16.

Bentham, Jeremy. 1988 [1781]. *The Principles of Morals and Legislation.* Amherst, New York: Prometheus Books.

Berríos, Nelson G. 1988a. "Washington, reacio al cambio." *El Nuevo Día,* San Juan, P.R. (October 31): 8.

————. 1988b. "Bush gesta un plebiscito para la isla." *El Nuevo Día,* San Juan, P.R. (December 24): 4.

————. 1989. "Gran desconfianza de la oposición." *El Nuevo Día,* San Juan, P.R. (January 3): 6.

Berríos Martínez, Rubén. 1990. "Congreso y status." Editorial. *El Nuevo Día,* San Juan, P.R. (August 20): 59.

Blondel, Jean. 1990. Types of Party Systems. In *The West European Party System,* ed. Peter Mair. New York: Oxford University Press.

Bosque Pérez, Ramón. 1997. Carpetas y persecusión política en Puerto Rico: la dimensión federal. In *Las Carpetas: Persecución política y derechos civiles en Puerto Rico—Ensayos y documentos* (The files: Political persecution and civil rights in Puerto Rico—Essays and documents), ed. Ramón Bosque Pérez and José Javier Colón Morera. Río Piedras, P.R.: Centro para la Investigación y Promoción de los Derechos Civiles.

Bothwell González, Reece B. 1979a. *Puerto Rico: Cien años de lucha política— Programas y manifiestos, 1869–1952* (Puerto Rico: One hundred years of political struggle—Platforms and manifestos, 1869-1952). Vol. I-1. Río Piedras, P.R.: Editorial Universitaria.

———. 1979b. *Puerto Rico: Cien años de lucha política—Programas y manifiestos, 1869–1952* (Puerto Rico: One hundred years of political struggle— Platforms and manifestos, 1869-1952). Vol. I-2. Río Piedras, P.R.: Editorial Universitaria.

Brau, Salvador. 1978 [1904]. *Historia de Puerto Rico* (History of Puerto Rico). Barcelona: Editorial Vosgos.

"Bush's Address to Congress: President's Budget Proposals: Few Specifics, No New Taxes." 1989. *Congressional Quarterly Weekly Report* 47, no. 6 (February 11): 276–79.

Cabán, Luis A. 1990a. "Reconoce al español como obstáculo." *El Mundo*, San Juan, P.R. (September 8): 8.

———. 1990b. "Advierten que el proyecto del idioma podría malinterpretarse." *El Mundo*, San Juan, P.R. (September 15): 10.

Cabán, Pedro. 1993. Redefining Puerto Rico's Political Status. In *Colonial Dilemma: Critical Perspectives on Contemporary Puerto Rico*, ed. Edwin Meléndez and Edgardo Meléndez. Boston: South End Press.

Candelas, Laura. 1990a. "RHC apoya el español como idioma oficial." *El Nuevo Día*, San Juan, P.R. (August 16): 12.

———. 1990b. "Urge Peña Clos aplazar el debate del español." *El Nuevo Día*, San Juan, P.R. (August 24): 8.

Carroll, Henry K. 1975 [1899]. *Report on the Island of Porto Rico; Its Population, Civil Government, Productions, Roads, Tariff, and Currency*. New York: Arno Press.

Castro Pereda, Rafael. 1982a. "Peña Clos: la Corte Federal debe desaparecer." *El Nuevo Día*, San Juan, P.R. (January 22): 10.

———. 1982b. "Salen en defensa de la enseñanza en inglés." *El Nuevo Día*, San Juan, P.R. (January 24): 28.

Castrodad, José A. 1982. "Peña Clos, 'Una papa caliente para la Pava.'" *El Nuevo Día*, San Juan, P.R. (January 27): 18.

Chardón, Carlos. 1998. Interview. Santurce, P.R., June 23.

Chilcote, Ronald H. 1994. *Theories of Comparative Politics: The Search for a Paradigm Reconsidered*. 2d ed. Boulder, Colo.: Westview.

Cintrón García, Angel. 1998. Interview. San Juan, P.R., July 22.

Citrin, Jack. 1990. "Language Politics and American Identity." *The Public Interest* 99: 96–109.

Clark, Robert P. 1979. *The Basques: The Franco Years and Beyond.* Reno: University of Nevada Press.

Cobas, José, and Jorge Duany. 1995. *Los cubanos en Puerto Rico: Economía étnica e identidad cultural* (Cubans in Puerto Rico: Ethnic economy and cultural identity). Río Piedras, P.R.: Editorial de la Universidad de Puerto Rico.

Colberg Ramírez, Severo. 1990. "El español: idioma oficial." Editorial. *El Mundo,* San Juan, P.R. (September 3): 27.

Colombani, Juanita. 1997. "'Ciudadanos bilingües' para el regreso escolar." *El Nuevo Día,* San Juan, P.R. (July 31): 37.

———. 1999. "FBI no pedirá disculpas." *El Nuevo Día,* San Juan, P.R. (December 17): 14.

Colomer, Josep M. 1990. "The Utility of Bilingualism: A Contribution to a Rational Choice Model of Language." *Rationality and Society* 2, no. 3: 310–34.

Colón Martínez, Noel. 1990. "Primero en español." Editorial. *El Mundo,* San Juan, P.R. (September 2): 46.

Colón Morera, José J. 1993. Economic constraints and political choices: U.S. congressional deliberations on the status of Puerto Rico, 1989–1991. Ph.D. diss., Boston University.

———. 1997. Consenso, represión y descolonización. In *Las Carpetas: Persecución política y derechos civiles en Puerto Rico—Ensayos y documentos* (The files: Political persecution and civil rights in Puerto Rico—Essays and documents), ed. Ramón Bosque Pérez and José Javier Colón Morera. Río Piedras, P.R.: Centro para la Investigación y Promoción de los Derechos Civiles.

Comisión Estatal de Elecciones. 1993a. *Resultados Finales—Elecciones Generales, 3 de noviembre de 1992* (Final results—General elections, November 3, 1992). San Juan, P.R.: Comisión Estatal de Elecciones.

———. 1993b. *Resultado de escrutinio por municipio para el plebiscito sobre el status político de Puerto Rico—14 de noviembre de 1993* (Ballot results by municipality for the plebiscite on the political status of Puerto Rico—November 14, 1993). San Juan, P.R.: Comisión Estatal de Elecciones.

———. 1996. *Resultados del escrutinio de las elecciones generales de 1996* (Ballot results for the 1996 general elections). San Juan, P.R.: Comisión Estatal de Elecciones.

Comptroller General. 1980. *Report to the Congress of the United States—Experiences of Past Territories Can Assist Puerto Rico Status Deliberations* (GGD-80-26). Washington, D.C.: U.S. Government Printing Office.

———. 1981. *Report to the Congress of the United States—Puerto Rico's Political Future: A Divisive Issue with Many Dimensions* (GGD-8148). Washington, D.C.: U.S. Government Printing Office.

Congressional Record. 1991. 137, no. 51 (April 9). Washington, D.C.: U.S. Government Printing Office.

———. 1993. 139, no. 12 (February 2). Washington, D.C.: U.S. Government Printing Office.

———. 1998a. 144, no. 19 (March 3). Washington, D.C.: U.S. Government Printing Office.

———. 1998b. 144, no. 20 (March 4). Washington, D.C.: U.S. Government Printing Office.

Connor, Walker. 1994. *Ethnonationalism: The Quest for Understanding.* Princeton: Princeton University Press.

Cordero, Gerardo. 1990. "Innecesario el proyecto del idioma español." *El Nuevo Día*, San Juan, P.R. (August 20): 12.

———. 1993. "Dirigirá Ramos una comisión de status." *El Nuevo Día*, San Juan, P.R. (January 3): 20.

Cornell, Barbara. 1991. "Júbilo boricua en EU por el español." *El Nuevo Día*, San Juan, P.R. (April 29): 8.

Corrada del Río, Baltazar. 1986. Puerto Rico: Its Dilemma and Its Destiny. In *The Political Status of Puerto Rico*, ed. Pamela S. Falk. Lexington, Mass.: Lexington Books.

Coss, Manuel E. 1991. "Alcaldes PNP no hablan inglés." *Claridad*, San Juan, P.R. (April 12–18): 5.

Covas Quevedo, Waldo D. 1991. "Orquestan la rebelión penepé." *El Nuevo Día*, San Juan, P.R. (April 6): 6.

Dávila, Arlene M. 1997. *Sponsored Identities: Cultural Politics in Puerto Rico.* Philadelphia: Temple University Press.

———. 1999. Local/Diasporic Taínos: Towards a Cultural Politics of Memory, Reality and Imagery. In *Taíno Revival: Critical Perspectives on Puerto Rican Identity and Cultural Politics*, ed. Gabriel Haslip-Viera. New York: Centro de Estudios Puertorriqueños, Hunter College, C.U.N.Y.

Dávila, Jesús. 1998. "Busca custodios a la quinta columna." *El Nuevo Día*, San Juan, P.R. (October 17): 4.

Dávila Colón, Luis R. 1993. "A 25 días." Editorial. *El Nuevo Día*, San Juan, P.R. (October 20): 65.

De Granda Gutiérrez, Germán. 1972. *Transculturación e interferencia lingüística en el Puerto Rico contemporáneo, 1898–1968* (Transculturation and linguistic interference in contemporary Puerto Rico, 1898–1968). Río Piedras, P.R.: Editorial Edil.

Delgado, José A. 1990. "Repercusión del debate lingüístico." *El Nuevo Día*, San Juan, P.R. (August 20): 12.

Delgado Cintrón, Carmelo. 1990. "Problemas jurídicos y constitucionales del idioma español en Puerto Rico—Estudio y Antología." *Revista del Colegio de Abogados de Puerto Rico* 50, no. 4 and 51, no. 1: 1–21.

———. 1991. "La declaración legislativa de la lengua española como el idioma oficial de Puerto Rico." *Revista Jurídica de la Universidad de Puerto Rico* 60, no. 2: 587–700.

———. 1993. "Historia de las luchas por el idioma español en Puerto Rico." *Revista del Colegio de Abogados de Puerto Rico* 54, no. 3–4 and 55, no. 1: 7–44.

———. 1997. "Actualidad de José de Diego." Editorial. *El Nuevo Día*, San Juan, P.R. (April 16): 67.

Del Rosario, Rubén. 1969. *La lengua de Puerto Rico: Ensayos* (The language of Puerto Rico: Essays). Río Piedras, P.R.: Editorial Cultural.

Department of Education. 1997. *Project for the Development of a Bilingual Citizen—"Shaping the Future Generation: Our Children First."* San Juan, P.R.

Downs, Anthony. 1957. *An Economic Theory of Democracy*. New York: Harper and Row.

Duany, Jorge. 1992. "Caribbean Migration to Puerto Rico: A Comparison of Cubans and Dominicans." *International Migration Review* 26, no. 1 (spring): 46–66.

———. 1999. Making Indians Out of Blacks: The Revitalization of Taíno Identity in Contemporary Puerto Rico. In *Taíno Revival: Critical Perspectives on Puerto Rican Identity and Cultural Politics*, ed. Gabriel Haslip-Viera. New York: Centro de Estudios Puertorriqueños, Hunter College, C.U.N.Y.

Dukakis, Michael. 1998. Interview. Boston, Mass., August 26.

"Dukakis Gets Puerto Rico Delegates as He and Gore Argue Nuclear Force." 1988. *New York Times* (April 14): D26.

Edwards, John. 1985. *Language, Society and Identity*. Oxford: Basil Blackwell, Ltd.

Enelow, James M., and Melvin J. Hinich. 1984. *The Spatial Theory of Voting: An Introduction*. Cambridge: Cambridge University Press.

Eriksen, Thomas H. 1993. *Ethnicity and Nationalism: Anthropological Perspectives*. London: Pluto Press.

Estrada Resto, Nilka. 1986. "Un disparate la eliminación del inglés." *El Nuevo Día*, San Juan, P.R. (January 17): 5.

———. 1991a. "De gala el idioma español." *El Nuevo Día*, San Juan, P.R. (April 6): 4.

———. 1991b. "Rosselló a la revancha." *El Nuevo Día*, San Juan, P.R. (April 6): 5.

———. 1991c. "Propone Rubén Berríos ampliar el referéndum." *El Nuevo Día*, San Juan, P.R. (April 8): 13.

———. 1993a. "Oposición a gritos en las avenidas capitalinas." *El Nuevo Día*, San Juan, P.R. (January 5): 5.

———. 1993b. "Amenaza al español." *El Nuevo Día*, San Juan, P.R. (January 8): 13.

———. 1993c. "Imputa intereses partidistas." *El Nuevo Día*, San Juan, P.R. (January 15): 8.

———. 1993d. "Repudio masivo a la derogación del español como idioma oficial." *El Nuevo Día*, San Juan, P.R. (January 21): 20.

———. 1998a. "Lanzado el PNP hacia el plebiscito." *El Nuevo Día*, San Juan, P.R. (April 27): 4–5.

———. 1998b. "Cita a plebiscito sin vínculo federal." *El Nuevo Día*, San Juan, P.R. (July 26): 4.

———. 1998c. "Separada la fecha." *El Nuevo Día*, San Juan, P.R. (July 30): 6.

———. 1998d. "Interpreta Rosselló la derrota a su manera." *El Nuevo Día*, San Juan, P.R. (December 14): 6–7.

———. 1999. "A pagar por las persecuciones." *El Nuevo Día*, San Juan, P.R. (December 15): 4.

Evans, Peter. 1979. *Dependent Development: The Alliance of Multinational, State, and Local Capital in Brazil*. Princeton: Princeton University Press.

Ferejohn, John. 1993. The Spatial Model and Elections. In *Information, Participation, and Choice: An Economic Theory of Democracy in Perspective*, ed. Bernard Grofman. Ann Arbor: University of Michigan Press.

Fernández, Ismael. 1982. "Darán rango constitucional al idioma español." *El Nuevo Día*, San Juan, P.R. (January 20): 8.

———. 1986. "Ataque contra el inglés." Editorial. *El Nuevo Día*, San Juan, P.R. (January 20): 41.

———. 1990. "A colgar el idioma inglés." Editorial. *El Nuevo Día*, San Juan, P.R. (August 27): 53.

———. 1993. "Innecesario el 'Spanish Only.'" Editorial. *El Nuevo Día*, San Juan, P.R. (January 11): 35.

———. 1997a. "El derecho de esos 650,000." Editorial. *El Nuevo Día*, San Juan, P.R. (May 12): 49.

———. 1997b. "Felicitaciones por el regreso." Editorial. *El Nuevo Día*, San Juan, P.R. (December 8): 49.

Fernández Colón, José. 1990. "Lenguaje caliente por el español." *El Mundo*, San Juan, P.R. (September 13): 19.

Ferrao, Angel. 1993. Nacionalismo, hispanismo y élite intelectual en el Puerto Rico de la década de 1930. In *Del nacionalismo al populismo: Cultura y política en Puerto Rico* (From nationalism to populism: Culture and politics in Puerto Rico), ed. Silvia Álvarez-Curbelo and María Elena Rodríguez-Castro. Río Piedras, P.R.: Ediciones Huracán.

Ferré, Luis A. 1991. "Premio a la perfidia." Editorial. *El Nuevo Día*, San Juan, P.R. (April 23): 45.

———. 1993. "Ponencia de Hon. Luis A. Ferré." *Revista del Colegio de Abogados de Puerto Rico* 54, no. 3–4 and 55, no. 1: 527–29.

Ferré Rangel, Luis A. 1991. "Dicta las exenciones al uso oficial del español." *El Nuevo Día*, San Juan, P.R. (April 23): 10.

Figueroa, Loida. 1979. *Breve historia de Puerto Rico* (Brief history of Puerto Rico). 6th rev. ed. Vol. 1. Río Piedras, P.R.: Editorial Edil.

Flores, Juan. 1993. *Divided Borders: Essays on Puerto Rican Identity.* Houston: Arte Público Press.

——. 2000. *From Bomba to Hip-Hop: Puerto Rican Culture and Latino Identity.* New York: Columbia University Press.

Frendreis, John, and Raymond Tatalovich. 1997. "Who Supports English-Only Language Laws? Evidence from the 1992 National Election Study." *Social Science Quarterly* 78: 354–68.

"Fustigan a Rosselló." 1990. *El Mundo,* San Juan, P.R. (October 17): 6A.

Galib Bras, Salomé. 1991a. "Represalia por el 'Spanish only.'" *El Nuevo Día,* San Juan, P.R. (March 15): 5.

——. 1991b. "'Indeseable' la estadidad." *El Nuevo Día,* San Juan, P.R. (March 18): 8.

——. 1991c. "'English Only' vs 'Spanish Only.'" *El Nuevo Día,* San Juan, P.R. (March 20): 5.

——. 1991d. "No dan por muerto el plebiscito." *El Nuevo Día,* San Juan, P.R. (March 25): 8.

——. 1991e. "Censura la Casa Blanca el 'Spanish Only.'" *El Nuevo Día,* San Juan, P.R. (April 3): 4.

——. 1991f. "Justifica RHC la entronización del español ante los congresistas." *El Nuevo Día,* San Juan, P.R. (April 11): 28.

——. 1992. "Amarra el idioma en casa y lo suelta en la Nación." *El Nuevo Día,* San Juan, P.R. (September 2): 28.

Gallisá, Carlos. 1991. "La nacionalidad no se pone a votación." Editorial. *Claridad,* San Juan, P.R. (April 12–18): 11.

García, Pepo. 1993. "Plantea elevarlo a rango constitucional." *El Nuevo Día,* San Juan, P.R. (January 6): 7.

——. 1997. "'Ilegal' la enseñanza en inglés." *El Nuevo Día,* San Juan, P.R. (May 6): 26.

García Martínez, Alfonso L. 1976. *Idioma y política: El papel desempeñado por los idiomas español e inglés en la relación política Puerto Rico–Estados Unidos* (Language and politics: The role played by the Spanish and English languages in the Puerto Rico–United States political relationship). San Juan, P.R.: Editorial Cordillera.

García Passalacqua, Juan M. 1990a. "La cuestión del idioma." Editorial. *El Nuevo Día,* San Juan, P.R. (August 23): 73.

——. 1990b. "La última verdad es no." Editorial. *El Nuevo Día,* San Juan, P.R. (October 25): 77.

García San Inocencio, Víctor. 1993. "Pandaemonium." Editorial. *El Nuevo Día,* San Juan, P.R. (August 2): 47.

——. 1998. Interview. San Juan, P.R., July 17.

Gautier Mayoral, Carmen, and Teresa Blanco Stahl. 1997. COINTELPRO en Puerto Rico: documentos secretos del FBI (1960–1971). In *Las Carpetas: Persecución política y derechos civiles en Puerto Rico—Ensayos y documentos*

(The files: Political persecution and civil rights in Puerto Rico—Essays and documents), ed. Ramón Bosque Pérez and José Javier Colón Morera. Río Piedras, P.R.: Centro para la Investigación y Promoción de los Derechos Civiles.

Gellner, Ernest. 1983. *Nations and Nationalism*. Ithaca, New York: Cornell University Press.

Ghigliotty, Julio. 1997a. "Refuerza Educación la enseñanza del inglés." *El Nuevo Día*, San Juan, P.R. (March 11): 36.

———. 1997b. "Tilda el PPD de política la propuesta Fajardo." *El Nuevo Día*, San Juan, P.R. (April 29): 12.

———. 1997c. "Propuesta a destiempo." *El Nuevo Día*, San Juan, P.R. (May 7): 8.

———. 1997d. "Cita a ciegas con el plan Young." *El Nuevo Día*, San Juan, P.R. (September 16): 7.

———. 1998a. "Promueve una quinta columna en la consulta." *El Nuevo Día*, San Juan, P.R. (October 9): 20.

———. 1998b. "Por amplia mayoría la quinta opción." *El Nuevo Día*, San Juan, P.R. (December 14): 4.

González, José L. 1980. *Puerto Rico: The Four Storeyed Country and Other Essays*, trans. Gerald Guinness. Princeton: Markus Wiener Publishing.

González, Manuel de J. 1991a. "Un asalto que perdieron los anexionistas." *Claridad*, San Juan, P.R. (February 8–14): 2.

———. 1991b. "Bajo presión el PPD con el idioma." *Claridad*, San Juan, P.R. (March 15–21): 2.

"Goza de aprobación la labor de Rosselló." 1993. *El Nuevo Día*, San Juan, P.R. (October 20): 6.

Green, Donald P., and Ian Shapiro. 1994. *Pathologies of Rational Choice Theory: A Critique of Applications in Political Science*. New Haven: Yale University Press.

Grosfoguel, Ramón. 1997. The Divorce of Nationalist Discourses from the Puerto Rican People: A Sociohistorical Perspective. In *Puerto Rican Jam: Rethinking Colonialism and Nationalism*, ed. Frances Negrón-Muntaner and Ramón Grosfoguel. Minneapolis: University of Minnesota Press.

Grosfoguel, Ramón, Frances Negrón-Muntaner, and Chloé S. Georas. 1997. Introduction—Beyond Nationalist and Colonialist Discourses: The Jaiba Politics of the Puerto Rican Ethno-Nation. In *Puerto Rican Jam: Rethinking Colonialism and Nationalism*, ed. Frances Negrón-Muntaner and Ramón Grosfoguel. Minneapolis: University of Minnesota Press.

Guardini, Romano. 1965. *The World and the Person*, trans. Stella Lange. Chicago: Henry Regnery.

Guerra, Lillian. 1998. *Popular Expression and National Identity in Puerto Rico: The Struggle for Self, Community, and Nation*. Gainesville: University Press of Florida.

"Gusta al estadoismo la pasión de Romero." 1997. *El Nuevo Día*, San Juan, P.R.

(August 12): 6.

Handler, Richard. 1988. *Nationalism and the Politics of Culture in Quebec.* Madison: University of Wisconsin Press.

Heath, Shirley B. 1972. *Telling Tongues: Language Policy in Mexico—Colony to Nation.* New York: Teacher's College Press, Columbia University.

Hechter, Michael. 1975. *Internal Colonialism: The Celtic Fringe in British National Development, 1536–1966.* Berkeley: University of California Press.

———. 1985. Internal Colonialism Revisited. In *New Nationalisms of the Developed West: Toward Explanation,* ed. Edward A. Tiryakian and Ronald Rogoswki. Boston: Allen and Unwin.

———. 1986. Rational Choice Theory and the Study of Race and Ethnic Relations. In *Theories of Race and Ethnic Relations,* ed. John Rex and David Mason. Cambridge: Cambridge University Press.

———. 1987. *Principles of Group Solidarity.* Berkeley: University of California Press.

Heiberg, Marianne. 1982. Urban Politics and Rural Culture: Basque Nationalism. In *The Politics of Territorial Identity: Studies in European Regionalism,* ed. Stein Rokkan and Derek W. Urwin. London: Sage Publications.

Hernández Agosto, Miguel. 1986. Why Statehood Would Be an Economic Disaster for Puerto Rico. In *The Political Status of Puerto Rico,* ed. Pamela S. Falk. Lexington, Mass.: Lexington Books.

———. 1998. Interview. Santurce, P.R., July 16.

Hernández Beltrán, Ruth. 1997. "Defiende Educación su plan de enseñar inglés." *El Nuevo Día,* San Juan, P.R. (May 15): 18.

Hernández Colón, Rafael. 1986. *La nueva tesis* (The new thesis). Río Piedras, P.R.: Editorial Edil.

———. 1990. "Plebiscito: una cuestión de puertorriqueñidad." Editorial. *El Nuevo Día,* San Juan, P.R. (August 25): 66.

———. 1991a. *Retos y luchas: 24 años de historia política puertorriqueña en los discursos de Rafael Hernández Colón* (Challenges and struggles: 24 years of Puerto Rican political history in the speeches of Rafael Hernández Colón). San Juan, P.R.: Rafael Hernández Colón.

———. 1991b. "An Open Letter to fellow citizens of the United States from the Governor of Puerto Rico." *New York Times* (April 9): A25.

———. 1993. "Mensaje del Gobernador Rafael Hernández Colón con motivo de la firma del proyecto de ley que declara el español como idioma oficial de Puerto Rico." *Revista del Colegio de Abogados de Puerto Rico* 54, no. 3–4 and 55, no. 1: 133–35.

———. 1996. "Reflexiones sobre la autodeterminación puertorriqueña (1989–1991)." *Revista Jurídica de la Universidad de Puerto Rico* 65, no. 3: 431–87.

———. 1998a. *La nación de siglo a siglo y otros ensayos* (The nation from century to century and other essays). Ponce, P.R.: Rafael Hernández Colón.

———. 1998b. Interview. Ponce, P.R., July 14.

Hobsbawm, Eric J. 1983. Introduction: Inventing Traditions. In *The Invention of Tradition*, ed. Eric J. Hobsbawm and Terence Ranger. Cambridge: Cambridge University Press.

———. 1990. *Nations and Nationalism Since 1780: Programme, Myth, Reality*. 2d ed. Cambridge: Cambridge University Press.

Hotelling, Harold. 1929. "Stability in Competition." *The Economic Journal* 39, no. 153: 41–57.

Ignatiev, Noel. 1995. *How the Irish Became White*. London: Routledge.

"'Inglés, No!' Puerto Ricans Shout." 1993. *New York Times* (January 25): A12.

Janda, Kenneth. 1993. Comparative Political Parties: Research and Theory. In *Political Science: The State of the Discipline—II*, ed. Ada W. Finifter. Washington, D.C.: American Political Science Association.

Janer, Zilkia. 1998. Colonial nationalism: The nation building literary field and subaltern intellectuals in Puerto Rico (1849–1952). Ph.D. diss., Duke University.

Jarabo Alvarez, José R. 1998. Interview. Río Piedras, P.R., July 8.

Jiménez Román, Miriam. 1999. The Indians are coming! The Indians are coming!: The Taíno and Puerto Rican Identity. In *Taíno Revival: Critical Perspectives on Puerto Rican Identity and Cultural Politics*, ed. Gabriel Haslip-Viera. New York: Centro de Estudios Puertorriqueños, Hunter College, C.U.N.Y.

"La 'emoción boricua' ayuda al ELA." 1997. *El Nuevo Día*, San Juan, P.R. (August 12): 5.

Laitin, David D. 1988. "Language Games." *Comparative Politics* 20, no. 3 (April): 289–302.

———. 1989. "Linguistic Revival: Politics and Culture in Catalonia." *Comparative Studies in Society and History* 31, no. 2 (April): 297–317.

———. 1993. "The Game Theory of Language Regimes." *International Political Science Review* 14, no. 3: 227–39.

———. 1997. "The Cultural Identities of a European State." *Politics and Society* 25, no. 3 (September): 277–302.

Langbein, Laura Irwin, and Allan J. Lichtman. 1978. *Ecological Inference*. Sage University Paper Series on Quantitative Applications in the Social Sciences, series no. 07-010. Beverly Hills, Calif.: Sage Publications.

Lao, Agustín. 1997. Islands at the Crossroads: Puerto Ricanness Traveling Between the Translocal Nation and the Global City. In *Puerto Rican Jam: Rethinking Colonialism and Nationalism*, ed. Frances Negrón-Muntaner and Ramón Grosfoguel. Minneapolis: University of Minnesota Press.

Laponce, Jean A. 1980. The City Centre as Conflictual Space in the Bilingual City: The Case of Montreal. In *Centre and Periphery*, ed. Jean Gottman. Beverly Hills, Calif.: Sage Publications.

———. 1984. "The French Language in Canada: Tensions Between Geography and Politics." *Political Geography Quarterly* 3, no. 2: 91–104.

———. 1987. *Languages and Their Territories*, trans. Anthony Martin-Sperry. Toronto: University of Toronto Press.

Leal, Gloria. 1991. "Voto unánime para Puerto Rico." *El Nuevo Día*, San Juan, P.R. (April 20): 4.

Leibowitz, Arnold H. 1989. *Defining Status: A Comprehensive Analysis of United States Territorial Relations*. Dordrecht, Netherlands: Martinus Nijhoff Publishers.

Levi, Margaret, and Michael Hechter. 1985. A Rational Choice Approach to the Rise and Decline of Ethnoregional Political Parties. In *New Nationalisms of the Developed West: Toward Explanation*, ed. Edward A. Tiryakian and Ronald Rogowski. Boston: Allen and Unwin.

Levine, Marc V. 1990. *The Reconquest of Montreal: Language Policy and Social Change in a Bilingual City*. Philadelphia: Temple University Press.

Licha, Silvia. 1982. "Peña Clos y el inglés." Editorial. *El Nuevo Día*, San Juan, P.R. (January 23): 27.

Lijphart, Arend. 1968. *The Politics of Accommodation: Pluralism and Democracy in the Netherlands*. Berkeley: University of California Press.

López Galarza, Héctor. 1998. Interview. Utuado, P.R., July 21.

López Laguerre, María M. 1997. *El bilingüismo en Puerto Rico: Actitudes socio-lingüísticas del maestro* (Bilingualism in Puerto Rico: Socio-linguistic attitudes of teachers). 2d ed. San Juan, P.R.: Editorial Espuela.

"Los jóvenes y la clase media con Rosselló." 1992. *El Nuevo Día*, San Juan, P.R. (September 1): 4.

"Los populares ya te quitaron el inglés." 1992. *El Nuevo Día*, San Juan, P.R. (November 1): 38.

Luciano, María J. 1989. "A las urnas las tres fórmulas políticas." *El Nuevo Día*, San Juan, P.R. (January 3): 4.

———. 1990a. "Polémica por el español como idioma oficial." *El Nuevo Día*, San Juan, P.R. (August 17): 10.

———. 1990b. "Toman el pulso a la oficialidad del español." *El Nuevo Día*, San Juan, P.R. (August 18): 22.

———. 1990c. "Jarabo endosa la enmienda." *El Nuevo Día*, San Juan, P.R. (August 23): 5.

———. 1990d. "Aviso de 'menosprecio' el proyecto de idioma." *El Nuevo Día*, San Juan, P.R. (September 8): 10.

———. 1990e. "Se le acaba el tiempo al español." *El Nuevo Día*, San Juan, P.R. (September 21): 6.

———. 1990f. "En ruta a la postergación el proyecto del idioma." *El Nuevo Día*, San Juan, P.R. (September 26): 12.

———. 1990g. "'Crisis institucional' con el proyecto del idioma." *El Nuevo Día*, San Juan, P.R. (October 19): 12.

———. 1990h. "Vota la Cámara la entronización del español." *El Nuevo Día*, San Juan, P.R. (October 23): 10.

———. 1990i. "Caldea la aprobación del español." *El Nuevo Día*, San Juan, P.R. (October 25): 4–5.

———. 1991a. "Aprueba el Senado como idioma oficial el español." *El Nuevo Día*, San Juan, P.R. (March 5): 19.

———. 1991b. "Advierte Romero sobre la 'verdad' del idioma." *El Nuevo Día*, San Juan, P.R. (April 18): 26.

———. 1992. "Obra inmediata y obra de paciencia de Rosselló." *El Nuevo Día*, San Juan, P.R. (November 15): 4–5.

———. 1993a. "Sin consenso la disputa idiomática." *El Nuevo Día*, San Juan, P.R. (January 14): 12.

———. 1993b. "Derrotadas en el Senado las enmiendas del PPD." *El Nuevo Día*, San Juan, P.R. (January 21): 19.

———. 1993c. "Candente el tema del idioma." *El Nuevo Día*, San Juan, P.R. (October 15): 10.

Maldonado-Denis, Manuel. 1972. *Puerto Rico: A Socio-Historic Interpretation*, trans. Elena Vialo. New York: Vintage Books.

Mallon, Florencia E. 1995. *Peasant and Nation: The Making of Postcolonial Mexico and Peru*. Berkeley: University of California Press.

Mari Bras, Juan. 1984. *El independentismo en Puerto Rico: Su pasado, su presente y su porvenir* (Independentism in Puerto Rico: Its past, present and future). Santo Domingo, Dominican Republic: Editorial CEPA.

Martín, Fernando. 1998. Interview. San Juan, P.R., July 17.

Martínez, Andrea. 1990. "'Fin' a la controversia." *El Nuevo Día*, San Juan, P.R. (August 29): 11.

———. 1991. "Exhortan a RHC a que vete el proyecto del español oficial." *El Nuevo Día*, San Juan, P.R. (March 13): 12.

———. 1993a. "Blindada la voluntad de fijar el inglés." *El Nuevo Día*, San Juan, P.R. (January 5): 4.

———. 1993b. "'Intento de asimilación.'" *El Nuevo Día*, San Juan, P.R. (January 20): 13.

———. 1993c. "'It's official.'" *El Nuevo Día*, San Juan, P.R. (January 29): 8.

———. 1993d. "Con nombre y apellido la anexión." *El Nuevo Día*, San Juan, P.R. (July 10): 6.

———. 1993e. "Hernández Colón vaticina un empate plebiscitario." *El Nuevo Día*, San Juan, P.R. (August 12): 24.

———. 1993f. "Saborea el PNP el proyecto Young." *El Nuevo Día*, San Juan, P.R. (November 24): 4.

Meléndez, Edgardo. 1991. "The Politics of Puerto Rico's Plebiscite." *Caribbean Studies* 24, no. 3–4: 117–50.

———. 1993a. *Movimiento anexionista en Puerto Rico* (Annexationist movement in Puerto Rico). Río Piedras, P.R.: Editorial de la Universidad de Puerto Rico.

———. 1993b. Colonialism, Citizenship, and Contemporary Statehood. In *Colo-*

nial Dilemma: Critical Perspectives on Contemporary Puerto Rico, ed. Edwin Meléndez and Edgardo Meléndez. Boston: South End Press.

———. 1995. "El estudio de los partidos políticos en Puerto Rico." *Revista de Ciencias Sociales* 30, 3–4 (May): 51–100.

———. 1998. *Partidos, política pública y status en Puerto Rico* (Parties, public policy and status in Puerto Rico). San Juan, P.R.: Ediciones Nueva Aurora.

Meléndez, Edwin, and Edgardo Meléndez. 1993. Introduction to *Colonial Dilemma: Critical Perspectives on Contemporary Puerto Rico*, ed. Edwin Meléndez and Edgardo Meléndez. Boston: South End Press.

Méndez Soto, Félix. 1998. Interview. Guaynabo, P.R., August 11.

Meyn, Marianne. 1983. *Lenguaje e identidad cultural: Un acercamiento teórico al caso de Puerto Rico* (Language and cultural identity: A theoretical approach to the case of Puerto Rico). Río Piedras, P.R.: Editorial Edil.

Michels, Robert. 1959 [1915]. *Political Parties: A Sociological Study of the Oligarchical Tendencies of Modern Democracy*. New York: Dover Publications.

"Miedo a la independencia." 1990. *El Mundo*, San Juan, P.R. (July 23): 5.

Mier Romeu, Mariano A., and Lisette Núñez. 1991. "Deniegan la dispensa sobre el español oficial." *El Nuevo Día*, San Juan, P.R. (April 26): 12.

Millán Pabón, Carmen. 1996a. "Compromiso político del PNP el bilingüismo." *El Nuevo Día*, San Juan, P.R. (August 23): 20.

———. 1996b. "Apuntan los partidos hacia la educación integral." *El Nuevo Día*, San Juan, P.R. (October 9): 18.

———. 1997a. "Sin masticar el inglés en otras asignaturas." *El Nuevo Día*, San Juan, P.R. (March 6): 10.

———. 1997b. "Mentís de Fajardo al uso del inglés con fines políticos." *El Nuevo Día*, San Juan, P.R. (May 2): 10.

———. 1997c. "Pactado el intercambio con maestros foráneos." *El Nuevo Día*, San Juan, P.R. (May 15): 22.

Miranda, Mickey. 1982. "Sentimiento nacionalista." Editorial. *El Nuevo Día*, San Juan, P.R. (January 29): 31.

Morales Carrión, Arturo. 1983. *Puerto Rico: A Political and Cultural History*. New York: W. W. Norton and Company.

Morris, Nancy. 1995. *Puerto Rico: Culture, Politics, and Identity*. Westport, Conn.: Praeger.

Moynihan, Daniel P. 1993. *Pandaemonium: Ethnicity in International Politics*. Oxford: Oxford University Press.

Mulero, Leonor. 1993a. "Roth justifica su participación en la campaña." *El Nuevo Día*, San Juan, P.R. (October 20): 26.

———. 1993b. "A refutar un congresista la campaña estadista." *El Nuevo Día*, San Juan, P.R. (October 26): 23.

———. 1993c. "Romero le refresca la memoria a un congresista." *El Nuevo Día*, San Juan, P.R. (October 29): 13.

———. 1993d. "Infunde aliento un congresista a la estadidad." *El Nuevo Día*, San Juan, P.R. (September 10): 12.

———. 1993e. "Simon 'vende' la estadidad." *El Nuevo Día*, San Juan, P.R. (November 5): 8.

———. 1993f. "Cierran el paso al estadolibrismo." *El Nuevo Día*, San Juan, P.R. (November 23): 4.

———. 1996a. "Atan el inglés a la estadidad." *El Nuevo Día*, San Juan, P.R. (July 24): 7.

———. 1996b. "Espaldarzo al 'English only.'" *El Nuevo Día*, San Juan, P.R. (July 25): 8.

———. 1996c. "A reclamar la estadidad con una mayoría simple." *El Nuevo Día*, San Juan, P.R. (August 15): 8.

———. 1996d. "Bofetada a la estadidad." *El Nuevo Día*, San Juan, P.R. (August 15): 10.

———. 1996e. "Insiste Wilson en el 'English only.'" *El Nuevo Día*, San Juan, P.R. (August 16): 5.

———. 1996f. "Sobre la mesa el Proyecto Young." *El Nuevo Día*, San Juan, P.R. (September 6): 4.

———. 1996g. "Supera un escollo el Proyecto Young." *El Nuevo Día*, San Juan, P.R. (September 19): 6.

———. 1997a. "Desarma la Casa Blanca la bomba del inglés." *El Nuevo Día*, San Juan, P.R. (March 20): 4–5.

———. 1997b. "En pugna el inglés y el Proyecto Young." *El Nuevo Día*, San Juan, P.R. (May 13): 28.

———. 1997c. "Rechazo a cláusula vitales del Proyecto Young." *El Nuevo Día*, San Juan, P.R. (May 15): 14.

———. 1997d. "Supermayoría además del inglés." *El Nuevo Día*, San Juan, P.R. (May 17): 8.

———. 1997e. "Aferrado Solomon al inglés." *El Nuevo Día*, San Juan, P.R. (May 28): 8.

———. 1997f. "'Inmoral' para José Serrano el ELA colonial." *El Nuevo Día*, San Juan, P.R. (September 13): 6.

———. 1997g. "Insiste Solomon en la estadidad con inglés." *El Nuevo Día*, San Juan, P.R. (October 23): 16.

———. 1997h. "Punzante darlo al estado 51." *El Nuevo Día*, San Juan, P.R. (November 6): 38.

———. 1997i. "'Obstáculos culturales' para la estadidad." *El Nuevo Día*, San Juan, P.R. (November 8): 12.

———. 1998a. "En pie la pugna por el idioma." *El Nuevo Día*, San Juan, P.R. (January 26): 14.

———. 1998b. "Sin reversa pese al inglés exclusivo." *El Nuevo Día*, San Juan, P.R. (February 27): 8.

———. 1998c. "Pocas ganas de atender el status." *El Nuevo Día*, San Juan, P.R. (March 6): 4.

———. 1998d. "Prioridad para el status." *El Nuevo Día*, San Juan, P.R. (March 11): 34.

———. 1998e. "Oposición de Helms al plebiscito." *El Nuevo Día*, San Juan, P.R. (July 22): 14.

Muntaner, Ada. 1990. The language question in Puerto Rico: 1898–1988. Ph.D. diss., State University of New York at Stony Brook.

Navarro, Mireya. 1998. "With a Vote for 'None of the Above,' Puerto Ricans Endorse Island's Status Quo." *New York Times* (December 14): A12.

Negrón de Montilla, Aida. 1975. *Americanization in Puerto Rico and the Public School System: 1900–1930*. Río Piedras, P.R.: Editorial Universitaria.

Negrón Muntaner, Frances. 1997. English Only Jamas but Spanish Only Cuidado: Language and Nationalism in Contemporary Puerto Rico. In *Puerto Rican Jam: Rethinking Colonialism and Nationalism*, ed. Frances Negrón-Muntaner and Ramón Grosfoguel. Minneapolis: University of Minnesota Press.

Negrón-Portillo, Mariano. 1997. Puerto Rico: Surviving Colonialism and Nationalism. In *Puerto Rican Jam: Rethinking Colonialism and Nationalism*, ed. Frances Negrón-Muntaner and Ramón Grosfoguel. Minneapolis: University of Minnesota Press.

Nelson, Anne. 1986. *Murder Under Two Flags: The U.S., Puerto Rico, and the Cerro Maravilla Cover-up*. New York: Ticknor and Fields.

Nieves Falcón, Luis, and Patricia Cintrón de Crespo. 1975. *Los maestros de instrucción pública de Puerto Rico: Perfiles sociológicos y profesionales* (Puerto Rico's public school teachers: Sociological and professional profiles). Río Piedras, P.R.: Editorial Universitaria.

Nieves Ramírez, Gladys. 1999. "Júbilo entre los 'encarpetados.'" *El Nuevo Día*, San Juan, P.R. (December 15): 8.

"No hay mayoría en el plebiscito." *El Nuevo Día*, San Juan, P.R. (August 23): 4.

"No se quiere cambio en el status político." 1997. *El Nuevo Día*, San Juan, P.R. (August 12): 4.

Noriega Rodríguez, David. 1998. Interview. Hato Rey, P.R., July 13.

Nozick, Robert. 1993. *The Nature of Rationality*. Princeton: Princeton University Press.

Núñez, Lisette, and Mariano A. Mier Romeu. 1991. "Onerosa la ley del español oficial." *El Nuevo Día*, San Juan, P.R. (April 16): 4.

Oboler, Suzanne. 1995. *Ethnic Labels, Latino Lives: Identity and the Politics of (Re) Presentation in the United States*. Minneapolis: University of Minnesota Press.

Olavarria, Bienvenido. 1986a. "Énfasis a la historia y al español." *El Nuevo Día*, San Juan, P.R. (January 5): 3.

———. 1986b. "Apoya Vélez experimentar con el inglés." *El Nuevo Día*, San Juan,

P.R. (January 15): 11.

Omi, Michael, and Howard Winant. 1994. *Racial Formation in the United States: From the 1960s to the 1990s.* 2d ed. New York: Routledge.

"One nation, one language." 1996. *El Nuevo Día,* San Juan, P.R. (November 5): 45.

Ordeshook, Peter C. 1986. *Game Theory and Political Theory: An Introduction.* Cambridge: Cambridge University Press.

Ortiz Tellechea, Ariel. 1986. "'Inconstitucional' el reglamento." *El Nuevo Día,* San Juan, P.R. (January 17): 5.

Osuna, Juan J. 1975 [1949]. *A History of Education in Puerto Rico.* New York: Arno Press.

Pabón, Milton. 1972. *La cultura política puertorriqueña* (Puerto Rican political culture). Río Piedras, P.R.: Editorial Xaguey.

Page, Scott E., Ken Kollman, and John H. Miller. 1993. Adaptive Parties and Spatial Voting Theory. In *Information, Participation, and Choice: An Economic Theory of Democracy in Perspective,* ed. Bernard Grofman. Ann Arbor: University of Michigan Press.

Pastrana Fuentes, Marcos. 1990. "Pide prioridad para proyecto de español." *Claridad,* San Juan, P.R. (October 26–November 1): 4.

Pedreira, Antonio S. 1978 [1934]. *Insularismo* (Insularism). Río Piedras, P.R.: Editorial Edil.

Peña Clos, Sergio. 1998. Interview. San Juan, P.R., July 6.

Penchi, Luis. 1986. "Peña Clos a favor." *El Nuevo Día,* San Juan, P.R. (January 19): 10.

———. 1989. "Le imponen el plebiscito a RHC, dice Romero." *El Nuevo Día,* San Juan, P.R. (January 14): 8.

———. 1990. "Sin el apoyo de Rivera el idioma." *El Nuevo Día,* San Juan, P.R. (September 2): 15.

———. 1993a. "Salvaguarda para el español." *El Nuevo Día,* San Juan, P.R. (January 11): 13.

———. 1993b. "Elogia gesta legislativa por la medida del idioma." *El Nuevo Día,* San Juan, P.R. (January 17): 18.

———. 1997. "Deseada la americanización." *El Nuevo Día,* San Juan, P.R. (April 29): 14.

Pérez, José J. 1993. "Gritan el repudio al proyecto del inglés." *El Nuevo Día,* San Juan, P.R. (January 25): 8.

Popkin, Samuel L. 1993. Information Shortcuts and the Reasoning Voter. In *Information, Participation, and Choice: An Economic Theory of Democracy in Perspective,* ed. Bernard Grofman. Ann Arbor: University of Michigan Press.

Pousada, Alicia. 1996. "Puerto Rico on the Horns of a Language Planning Dilemma." *TESOL Quarterly* 30, no. 3 (autumn): 499–510.

"Proyecto armonizaría polémica de idiomas." 1990. *El Mundo,* San Juan, P.R. (September 16): 18.

Quiñones Calderón, A. 1986. "Descarta la eliminación del inglés." *El Nuevo Día*, San Juan, P.R. (February 4): 3.

Quintero Rivera, Angel G. 1986. *Conflictos de clase y política en Puerto Rico* (Class and political conflicts in Puerto Rico). 5th ed. Río Piedras, P.R.: Ediciones Huracán.

———. 1993. La ideología populista y la institucionalización universitaria de las ciencias sociales. In *Del nacionalismo al populismo: Cultura y política en Puerto Rico* (From nationalism to populism: Culture and politics in Puerto Rico), ed. Silvia Álvarez-Curbelo and María Elena Rodríguez-Castro. Río Piedras, P.R.: Ediciones Huracán.

Ramírez Lavandero, Marcos, ed. 1988. *Documents on the Constitutional Relationship of Puerto Rico and the United States*. 3d ed. Washington, D.C.: Puerto Rico Federal Affairs Administration.

Ramos-Zayas, Ana Yolanda. 1997. La patria es valor y sacrificio: Nationalist ideologies, cultural authenticity, and community building among Puerto Ricans in Chicago. Ph.D. diss., Columbia University.

"Ratifican la lucha contra la ley del español." 1992. *El Nuevo Día*, San Juan, P.R. (October 4): 18.

"Reafirmarán el español." 1990. *El Mundo*, San Juan, P.R. (October 11): 3A.

Resnick, Melvin C. 1993. "ESL and Language Planning in Puerto Rican Education." *TESOL Quarterly* 27, no. 2 (summer): 259–75.

Revista del Colegio de Abogados de Puerto Rico. 1993. 54, no. 3–4 and 55, no. 1.

Rexach Benítez, Roberto F. 1998. Interview. San Juan, P.R., July 17.

"RHC rechaza el español como única lengua." 1986. *El Nuevo Día*, San Juan, P.R. (May 26): 16.

Rivera, Angel I. 1996. *Puerto Rico: Ficción y mitología en sus alternativas de status* (Puerto Rico: Fiction and mythology in its status alternatives). San Juan, P.R.: Ediciones Nueva Aurora.

Rivera, Angel I., Ana I. Seijo, and Jaime W. Colón. 1991. "La cultura política y la estabilidad del sistema de partidos de Puerto Rico." *Caribbean Studies* 24, no. 3–4: 175–220.

Rivera-Batiz, Francisco I., and Carlos E. Santiago. 1996. *Island Paradox: Puerto Rico in the 1990s*. New York: Russell Sage Foundation.

Rivera Ramírez, Alba. 1998. Interview. San Juan, P.R. August 4.

Rivera Ramos, Efrén. 1996. "The Legal Construction of American Colonialism: The Insular Cases (1901–1922)." *Revista Jurídica de la Universidad de Puerto Rico* 65, no. 2: 225–328.

Rivera Renta, José. 1997. "Favorce Fas Alzamora traer maestros de inglés." *El Nuevo Día*, San Juan, P.R. (May 19): 24.

Rodríguez, Magdalys. 1997. "Por el libro el inglés." *El Nuevo Día*, San Juan, P.R. (March 5): 6.

————. 1998a. "Anticipa Trent Lott que el Senado no actuará." *El Nuevo Día*, San Juan, P.R. (March 4): 6.

————. 1998b. "Fórmulas sin nombre en la papeleta." *El Nuevo Día*, San Juan, P.R. (August 12): 4.

————. 1998c. "Lista para la firma la consulta criolla." *El Nuevo Día*, San Juan, P.R. (August 14): 7.

————. 1998d. "Admite la fuga de pipiolos." *El Nuevo Día*, San Juan, P.R. (December 14): 20.

Rodríguez González, Juan J. 1998. Interview. Hato Rey, P.R., August 11.

Rodríguez Negrón, Enrique. 1998. Interview. San Juan, P.R., August 7.

Romero-Barceló, Carlos. 1978. *Statehood Is for the Poor*. San Juan, P.R.: Carlos Romero-Barceló.

————. 1986. Statehood for Puerto Rico. In *The Political Status of Puerto Rico*, ed. Pamela S. Falk. Lexington, Mass.: Lexington Books.

————. 1990. "¿Español solamente?" Editorial. *El Nuevo Día*, San Juan, P.R. (August 25): 67.

————. 1997. "Tras un ciudadano bilingüe." Editorial. *El Nuevo Día*, San Juan, P.R. (July 21): 37.

Roosens, Eugeen E. 1989. *Creating Ethnicity: The Process of Ethnogenesis*. Newbury Park, Calif.: Sage Publications.

Rosselló, Pedro. 1992. "El nuevo comienzo se puede." Editorial. *El Nuevo Día*, San Juan, P.R. (November 2): 55.

————. 1993. "Discurso del Hon. Pedro Rosselló Gobernador, en ocasión de la firma de la Ley No. 1 'Los dos idiomas oficiales.'" *Revista del Colegio de Abogados de Puerto Rico* 54, no. 3–4 and 55, no. 1: 145–48.

"Rosselló mantiene su ventaja pese al 'incidente.'" 1992. *El Nuevo Día*, San Juan, P.R. (October 25): 4–5.

Rudé, George. 1995. *Ideology and Popular Protest*. Chapel Hill: University of North Carolina Press.

Salas, Andrés. 1990. "Una nueva sociedad." Editorial. *El Mundo*, San Juan, P.R. (October 30): 9A.

Sánchez, L. Rubén. 1986. "La Federación de Maestros contra el inglés." *El Nuevo Día*, San Juan, P.R. (January 16): 5.

"Satisfactoria la imagen de Rosselló." 1993. *El Nuevo Día*, San Juan, P.R. (August 24): 4.

Scarano, Francisco A. 1996. "The Jíbaro Masquerade and the Subaltern Politics of Creole Identity Formation in Puerto Rico, 1745–1823." *American Historical Review* 101, no. 5 (December): 1398–1431.

Serrano Geyls, Raúl, and Carlos I. Gorrín Peralta. 1979. "Puerto Rico y la estadidad: Problemas constitucionales." *Revista del Colegio de Abogados de Puerto Rico* 40: 521–36.

"76% contra el español como idioma único." 1990. *El Nuevo Día*, San Juan, P.R.

(November 7): 5.

Shepsle, Kenneth A., and Mark S. Bonchek. 1997. *Analyzing Politics: Rationality, Behavior, and Institutions*. New York: W. W. Norton and Company.

"'Sí' a los dos idiomas." 1990. *El Mundo*, San Juan, P.R. (September 24): 1A.

"Sin preferencia definida el status." 1997. *El Nuevo Día*, San Juan, P.R. (May 22): 4–5.

Skelly, John T. 1990. "Obstáculo senatorial al plebiscito." *El Nuevo Día*, San Juan, P.R. (October 10): 4.

Smith, Anthony D. 1981. *The Ethnic Revival*. Cambridge: Cambridge University Press.

———. 1986. *The Ethnic Origin of Nations*. Oxford: Blackwell.

———. 1989. "The Origins of Nations." *Ethnic and Racial Studies* 12 (July): 340–67.

Smithies, Arthur. 1941. "Optimum Location in Spatial Competition." *Journal of Political Economy* 49, no. 3 (June): 423–39.

Snidal, Duncan. 1985. "The Game *Theory* of International Politics." *World Politics* 38, no. 1 (October 1985): 25–57.

"Sólo uno." 1992. *El Nuevo Día*, San Juan, P.R. (October 28): 37.

Steinberg, Stephen. 1981. *The Ethnic Myth: Race, Ethnicity and Class in America*. Boston: Beacon Press.

Stone, Geoffrey R., Louis M. Seidman, Cass R. Sunstein, and Mark V. Thushnet. 1986. *Constitutional Law*. Boston: Little, Brown and Company.

Suárez, Manuel. 1987. *Requiem on Cerro Maravilla: The Police Murders in Puerto Rico and the U.S. Government Coverup*. Maplewood, New Jersey: Waterfront Press.

———. 1988a. "Question of Statehood Is Dominating Puerto Rico's Party Vote." *New York Times* (March 18): D22.

———. 1988b. "In Puerto Rico Vote, Democrats Support Island's Status Quo." *New York Times* (March 22): D31.

Tatalovich, Raymond. 1995. "Voting on Official English Language Referenda in Five States: What Kind of Backlash Against Spanish-Speakers?" *Language Problems and Language Planning* 19, no. 1 (spring): 47–59.

Torres, Ismael. 1986. "Alarmada la Iglesia Católica." *El Nuevo Día*, San Juan, P.R. (January 21): 3.

———. 1990a. "Un solo idioma oficial en el país." *El Nuevo Día*, San Juan, P.R. (August 6): 16.

———. 1990b. "Firme apoyo al español." *El Mundo*, San Juan, P.R. (September 3): 14.

Torres Rivera, Alejandro. 1991. "Respaldo socialista al español." *El Nuevo Día*, San Juan, P.R. (April 19–25): 30.

Torruella, Juan R. 1985. *The Supreme Court and Puerto Rico: The Doctrine of Separate and Unequal.* Río Piedras, P.R.: Editorial de la Universidad de Puerto Rico.

Trías Monge, José. 1980. *Historia Constitucional de Puerto Rico* (Constitutional history of Puerto Rico). Vol. 1. Río Piedras, P.R.: Editorial de la Universidad de Puerto Rico.

———. 1982. *Historia Constitucional de Puerto Rico* (Constitutional history of Puerto Rico). Vol. 3. Río Piedras, P.R.: Editorial de la Universidad de Puerto Rico.

———. 1983. *Historia Constitucional de Puerto Rico* (Constitutional history of Puerto Rico). Vol. 4. Río Piedras, P.R.: Editorial de la Universidad de Puerto Rico.

———. 1997. *Puerto Rico: The Trials of the Oldest Colony in the World.* New Haven: Yale University Press.

"Tributo hispánico para Puerto Rico." 1991. *El Nuevo Día,* San Juan, P.R. (April 16): 5.

Tsebelis, George. 1990. *Nested Games: Rational Choice in Comparative Politics.* Berkeley: University of California Press.

United States Department of Commerce. 1963. *U.S. Census of Population: 1960.* Vol. 1, *Characteristics of the Population. Part 53, Puerto Rico.* Washington, D.C.: U.S. Government Printing Office.

———. 1973. *1970 Census of Population.* Vol. 1, *Characteristics of the Population. Part 53, Puerto Rico.* Washington, D.C.: U.S. Government Printing Office.

———. 1984. *1980 Census of Population.* Vol. 1, *Characteristics of the Population. Part 53, Puerto Rico* (PC80-1-D53). Washington, D.C.: U.S. Government Printing Office.

———. 1992. *1990 Census of Population: General Population Characteristics—Puerto Rico* (1990 CP-1-53). Washington, D.C.: U.S. Government Printing Office.

———. 1993a. *1990 Census of Population: Social and Economic Characteristics—Puerto Rico, Section 1 of 2* (1990 CP-2-53). Washington, D.C.: U.S. Government Printing Office.

———. 1993b. *1990 Census of Population and Housing: Summary Social, Economic, and Housing Characteristics—Puerto Rico* (1990 CPH-5-53). Washington, D.C.: U.S. Government Printing Office.

United States Department of the Army. 1900. *Military Orders having the Force of Law: Promulgated by the Commanding General Department of Porto Rico from October 18th, 1898, to April 30th, 1900.* Vol. 2, *Military Orders that were published in the Official Gazette of Porto Rico.* San Juan, P.R.

United States House of Representatives. 1993. *Puerto Rico Self-Determination Part I. Hearing Before the Subcommittee on Insular and International*

Affairs of the Committee on Natural Resources (103–36, pt. 1). July 13. Washington, D.C.: U.S. Government Printing Office.

———. 1995. *Puerto Rico Status Plebiscite. Joint Hearing Before the Subcommittee on Native American and Insular Affairs of the Committee on Resources and the Subcommittee on the Western Hemisphere of the Committee on International Relations* (104–56). October 17. Washington, D.C.: U.S. Government Printing Office.

———. 1996. *U.S.–Puerto Rico Political Status Act. Hearing Before the Subcommittee on Native American and Insular Affairs of the Committee on Resources* (104–87). March 23. Washington, D.C.: U.S. Government Printing Office.

United States Senate. 1989a. *Political Status of Puerto Rico. Hearing Before the Committee on Energy and Natural Resources* (S. Hrg. 101–98, pt. 1). June 1–2. Washington, D.C.: U.S. Government Printing Office.

———. 1989b. *Political Status of Puerto Rico. Hearing Before the Committee on Energy and Natural Resources* (S. Hrg. 101–98, pt. 2). June 16–17 and 19. Washington, D.C.: U.S. Government Printing Office.

———. 1989c. *Political Status of Puerto Rico. Hearing Before the Committee on Energy and Natural Resources* (S. Hrg. 101–98, pt. 3). July 11, 13–14. Washington, D.C.: U.S. Government Printing Office.

———. 1991. *Political Status of Puerto Rico. Hearing Before the Committee on Energy and Natural Resources* (S. Hrg. 102–3). January 30 and February 7. Washington, D.C.: U.S. Government Printing Office.

Urciuoli, Bonnie. 1991. "The Political Topography of Spanish and English: The View from a New York Puerto Rican Neighborhood." *American Ethnologist* 18, no. 1: 295–310.

———. 1994. "Acceptable Difference: The Cultural Evolution of the Model Ethnic American Citizen." *PoLAR: Political and Legal Anthropological Review* 17, no. 2 (November 1994): 19–35.

———. 1998. *Exposing Prejudice: Puerto Rican Experiences of Language, Race, and Class.* Boulder, Colo.: Westview.

Urrutia, Mayra R. 1993. Detrás de "La vitrina": Expectativas del Partido Popular Democrático y política exterior norteamericana, 1942–1954. In *Del nacionalismo al populismo: Cultura y política en Puerto Rico* (From nationalism to populism: Culture and politics in Puerto Rico), ed. Silvia Álvarez-Curbelo and María Elena Rodríguez-Castro. Río Piedras, P.R.: Ediciones Huracán.

Urwin, Derek W. 1982. Territorial Structures and Political Development in the United Kingdom. In *The Politics of Territorial Identity: Studies in European Regionalism,* ed. Stein Rokkan and Derek W. Urwin. London: Sage Publications.

Valdivia, Yadira. 1997a. "Imparable el dominio del inglés en Educación." *El Nuevo Día,* San Juan, P.R. (April 23): 10.

———. 1997b. "Boicott a la soberanía del inglés en Educación." *El Nuevo Día,* San Juan, P.R. (April 26): 16.

———. 1997c. "Revolución integral." *El Nuevo Día,* San Juan, P.R. (April 28): 6.

Varela, Luis R. 1986a. "Jarabo se opone a la eliminación del inglés." *El Nuevo Día,* San Juan, P.R. (January 12): 11.

———. 1986b. "Alarma con la reforma educativa." *El Nuevo Día,* San Juan, P.R. (January 16): 5.

———. 1986c. "Populares difieren por el inglés." *El Nuevo Día,* San Juan, P.R. (January 19): 10.

———. 1988. "Constituyente para ampliar el ELA." *El Nuevo Día,* San Juan, P.R. (October 23): 6.

———. 1990. "Para la próxima sesión el proyecto sobre el idioma." *El Mundo,* San Juan, P.R. (September 20): 11.

———. 1993. "Defiende RHC su gestión puertorriqueñista." *El Nuevo Día,* San Juan, P.R. (January 3): 12.

———. 1997a. "Segura la plaza magisterial." *El Nuevo Día,* San Juan, P.R. (May 12): 20.

———. 1997b. "A laborar en la Isla profesores de EE.UU." *El Nuevo Día,* San Juan, P.R. (September 19): 14.

Vélez, Diana L. 1986. "Aspects of the Debate on Language in Puerto Rico." *Bilingual Review* 13, no. 3: 3–12.

Vélez, Jorge A., and C. W. Schweers. 1993. "The Decision to Make Spanish the Official Language of Puerto Rico." *Language Problems and Language Planning* 17, no. 2: 117–39.

Viseras, Carlos. 1988. "'Resuelto' el status." *El Nuevo Día,* San Juan, P.R. (October 24): 8.

Vogt, W. P. 1993. *Dictionary of Statistics and Methodology: A Nontechnical Guide to the Social Sciences.* Newbury Park, Calif.: Sage Publications.

Von Neumman, John, and Oskar Morgenstern. 1953 [1944]. *Theory of Games and Economic Behavior.* 3d ed. Princeton: Princeton University Press.

Weber, Eugen. 1976. *Peasants into Frenchmen: The Modernization of Rural France, 1870–1914.* Stanford: Stanford University Press.

Weinstein, Brian. 1983. *The Civic Tongue: Political Consequences of Language Choices.* New York: Longman.

Weisskoff, Richard. 1985. *Factories and Food Stamps: The Puerto Rican Model of Development.* Baltimore: Johns Hopkins University Press.

Wells, Henry. 1979. *La modernización de Puerto Rico: Un análisis político de valores e instituciones en proceso de cambio* (The modernization of Puerto Rico: A political analysis of values and institutions under change), trans. Pedro G. Salazar. Río Piedras, P.R.: Editorial Universitaria.

Wittman, Donald. 1983. "Candidate Motivation: A Synthesis of Alternative Theories." *American Political Science Review* 77, no. 1 (March): 142–57.

———. 1990. Spatial Strategies when Candidates Have Policy Preferences. In *Advances in the Spatial Theory of Voting*, ed. James M. Enelow and Melvin J. Hinich. Cambridge: Cambridge University Press.

Zagare, Frank C. 1984. *Game Theory: Concepts and Applications.* Sage University Paper Series on Quantitative Applications in the Social Sciences, series no. 07-041. Beverly Hills, Calif.: Sage Publications.

Zentella, Ana C. 1990. "Return Migration, Language, and Identity: Puerto Rican Bilinguals in Dos Worlds/Two Mundos." *International Journal of the Sociology of Language* 84: 81–100.

Index

Amílcar Antonio Barreto is professor of Cultures, Societies, and Global Studies at Northeastern University. He is the author of several books, including *Nationalism and Its Logical Foundations*, and is coeditor of *American Identity in the Age of Obama*.

www.ingramcontent.com/pod-product-compliance
Lightning Source LLC
Chambersburg PA
CBHW021357090426
42742CB00009B/896